Early Native American Writing is a collection of critical essays discussing the works of American Indian authors who wrote between 1630 and 1940 and produced some of the earliest literature in North America. The first collection of critical essays that concentrates on this body of writing, this book highlights the writings of the American Indian authors considered, many of whom have only recently been rediscovered, as important contributions to American letters.

American Indians writing in English offer a permanent record of the dramatic and often tragic confrontation between native culture and the communities of settlers arriving in the New World over four centuries. As white settlers arrived in North America, bringing with them disease, technology, and Christianity, they also brought writing – a tool that Native Americans, accustomed to an oral tradition, would adopt. As the essays in this volume suggest, writing in English became a way to convey protest and legitimacy for American Indians – a way to argue with missionaries, to record the ravages of smallpox, to mythologize contemporary heroes, to expose the depredations of the doctrine of manifest destiny. Serving in their own time as a means of addressing a heedless oppressor, Native American writings have since become a vital record of an experience whose history, as written by mainstream writers, is incomplete. The essays collected here seek to recover that history while bringing new attention to the texts themselves.

CAMBRIDGE STUDIES IN AMERICAN LITERATURE AND CULTURE

Early Native American Writing: New Critical Essays

Continued on pages following p. 238

EARLY NATIVE AMERICAN WRITING:
NEW CRITICAL ESSAYS

Edited by

Helen Jaskoski
California State University,
Fullerton

Published by the Press Syndicate of the University of Cambridge
The Pitt Building, Trumpington Street, Cambridge CB2 1RP
40 West 20th Street, New York, NY 10011-4211, USA
10 Stamford Road, Oakleigh, Melbourne 3166, Australia

First published 1996

Printed in the United States of America

Library of Congress Cataloging-in-Publication Data
Early Native American writing : new critical essays / edited by Helen
Jaskoski.
        p.   cm.—(Cambridge studies in American literature and
culture ; [102])
Includes index.
ISBN 0-521-55509-4. – ISBN 0-521-55527-2 (pbk.)
1. American literature – Indian authors – History and criticism.
2. Indians of North America – Intellectual life.   3. Indians in
literature.   I. Jaskoski, Helen.   II. Series.
            PS153.I52E27   1996
820.9'897 – dc20   95-26723
                                                          CIP

A catalog record for this book is available from the British Library.

ISBN 0-521-55509-4 hardback
ISBN 0-521-55527-2 paperback

CONTENTS

―――――

FOREWORD

A. LAVONNE BROWN RUOFF

Early Native American Writing: New Critical Essays is the first volume devoted to this significant but neglected area of American Indian written literature. Whereas most scholarly books on Native American literature concentrate on traditional oral or contemporary written literature, *Early Native American Writing* breaks new ground by focusing on how Native American written literature evolved from its beginnings to become a highly imaginative, polished, and vibrant literature that has won its authors international acclaim.

Early Native American writers faced the dilemma of how to survive as Indians while coping with the dominant society's demand that they abandon their tribal cultures, world views, and oral traditions in order to assimilate to a Western European, Christian culture that revered written texts. George Copway (Ojibwe) dramatically describes this dilemma in *Life, Letters and Speeches*: "I loved the woods, and the chase. I had the nature for it, and gloried in nothing else. The mind for letters was in me, but was asleep, till the dawn of Christianity arose, and awoke the slumbers of the soul into energy and action" (11). Like the Native American authors discussed in this volume, Copway acted as a bridge between native people and the dominant society. To persuade his white audiences that native peoples were rational human beings, Copway emphasizes the innate ability of Indians to learn and to adapt. By appealing to his white readers as fellow Christians, he subtly underscores the equality of Indians with whites – an equality non-Indians too often ignored.

Copway's statement introduces a crucial issue that several scholars discuss in *Early Native American Writing*: How did individual authors adapt their sense of Indian self and their writing to the expectations of their white teachers and audiences? In " 'Honoratissimi Benefactores': Native American Students and Two Seventeenth-Century Texts in the University Tradition" Wolfgang Hochbruck and Beatrix

Dudensing-Reichel discuss the authorship, form, backgrounds, and connection to contemporary colonial discourse of two texts by seventeenth-century students at Harvard's Indian College: "Honoratissimi Benefactores" by Caleb Cheeshateaumauk (Natick), dated 1663, and Eleazar's "In Obitum Viri vere Reverendi D. Thomae Thacheri" (1679). Written in Latin and Greek, these tributes demonstrate the Indian students' efforts to master European genres emphasized by their Harvard teachers. Such mastery was often used as a yardstick to measure whether Native Americans were capable of being educated.

The complicated relations between Indian student and white teacher is the subject of Laura Murray's " 'Pray Sir, consider a little': Rituals of Subordination and Strategies of Resistance in the Letters of Hezekiah Calvin and David Fowler to Eleazar Wheelock." As their corespondence reveals, Wheelock, by emphasizing the father–child metaphor for their relationship, enmeshed his Indian students in powerful bonds of duty and debt, which he manipulated to make it difficult for them to escape. In " '(I speak like a fool but I am constrained)': Samson Occom's *Short Narrative* and Economies of the Racial Self," Dana Nelson uses the artist/creator metaphor to demonstrate the impact of Wheelock's educational system on Samson Occom and other Indian students. Nelson stresses that Occom's growing consciousness of the systematic robbery of his Indian selfhood is the underlying organizational principle of his narrative.

Whereas these earliest examples of written literature were university exercises, correspondence, or personal history not intended for publication, Indian authors soon used the written word to fight for Indian rights or to define their culture to non-Indians. In " 'Where, then, shall we place the hero of the wilderness?' William Apess's *Eulogy on King Philip* and Doctrines of Racial Destiny," Anne Marie Dannenberg reveals how the author defies the myth of the disappearance of the doomed Indian warrior by making strong statements of cultural nationalism for American Indians and indicting whites for their treatment of his people.

As Daniel F. Littlefield demonstratres in " 'They ought to enjoy the home of their fathers': The Treaty of 1838, Seneca Intellectuals, and Literary Genesis," Maris Bryant Pierce and Nathaniel Thayer Strong used their mastery of English to take strong stands on tribal treaties. Especially significant is Pierce's *Address on the Present Condition and Prospects of the Aboriginal Inhabitants of North America, with Particular Reference to the Seneca Nation* (1838), which urges the Senecas to resist removal while arguing that they can and must assimilate.

In " 'This voluminous unwritten book of ours': Early Native Amer-

ican Writers and Oral Tradition," William M. Clements stresses that
Native American authors of the nineteenth and early twentieth centuries incorporated traditional storytelling into their writing. Helen
Jaskoski also emphasizes the importance of oral tradition in " 'A
terrible sickness among them': Smallpox and Stories of the Frontier." She uses the smallpox stories by Francis Parkman, Andrew J.
Blackbird, and William Warren to exemplify how scholars need to
consult Indian as well as non-Indian accounts to understand the history of Indian–white relations.

Women, too, addressed issues of Native American cultural nationalism, as Carol Batker makes clear in " 'Overcoming all obstacles':
The Assimilation Debate in Native American Women's Journalism
of the Dawes Era." According to Batker, Indian women journalists
demonstrated a complex negotiation between Native and non-Native
practices that emphasizes cultural dynamism rather than cultural loss
as a paradigm for assimilation.

Many of the essays in *Early Native American Writing* examine the
literary techniques that Native American authors used in their autobiographies and fiction. The genre in which native Americans have
written most from the late nineteenth through the mid-twentieth
centuries is autobiography. In " 'An Indian . . . an American': Ethnicity, Assimilation, and Balance in Charles Eastman's *From the Deep
Woods to Civilization*," Erik Peterson describes Eastman's second autobiography as a spiritual journey and an intricate "balancing act"
of negotiation between two worlds in which the author juxtaposes
contradictions and opposing forces to demonstrate a structure of
inclusion. Robert Sayre, in " 'A desirable citizen, a practical business
man': G. W. Grayson – Creek Mixed Blood, Nationalist, and Auto-
biographer," suggests that the fact that Grayson consciously wrote
autobiography was a sign of his acculturation. Unlike such earlier
autobiographers as Apess, Copway, or Eastman, Grayson does not
use either the religious conversion or the spiritual journey as an
organizing principle.

By the mid-nineteenth century, American Indian authors were beginning to publish fiction. In " 'I am Joaquin!': Space and Freedom
in Yellow Bird's *The Life and Adventures of Joaquin Murieta, the Celebrated
California Bandit*," John Lowe argues that John Rollin Ridge's 1854
romance utilizes the realization that the American dream has always
depended on the appropriation of space for a concept of identity,
and he demonstrates how the politics of displaced and relocated
peoples can give rise to heroic and sometimes mythical folk literature.

Martha L. Viehmann's " 'My people . . . my kind': Mourning

Dove's *Cogewea, the Half-Blood* as a Narrative of Mixed Descent'' examines Mourning Dove's use of the themes of biological mixed descent and legends of cultural contact, as well as the differences
between Lucullus McWhorter and Mourning Dove in their appeals
to white readers. Birgit Hans's " 'Because I understand the storytelling art': The Evolution of D'Arcy McNickle's *The Surrounded*" contrasts one manuscript version of this novel with the final published
text, showing how a conventional romance became transformed into
a powerful naturalistic novel.

The essays in this volume make it clear that early Native American
writers soon learned that written English was a powerful medium for
educating white audiences about the intellectual and creative abilities of Indian people, the value of their tribal cultures, and white
injustice to Native peoples. The works of these Indian authors demonstrate both their mastery of a variety of non-Indian literary genres
and their skill in using the written word as a sharp weapon in the
cultural word wars. As Gerald Vizenor (Ojibwe) reminds us in *Manifest Manners*, ''Tribal imagination, experience, and remembrance
are the real landscapes in the literature of this nation; discoveries
and dominance are silence'' (10).

Works Cited

Copway, George. *The Life, Letters and Speeches of Kah-ge-ga-gah-bowh, or G. Cop-
way, ...* New York: Benedict, 1850.
Vizenor, Gerald. *Manifest Manners: Postindian Warriors of Survivance.* Hanover,
NH: University Press of New England, 1994.

PREFACE

━━━

I may surprise you yet, James LaGrinder! even if I am a "squaw" as
you call me . . . I may use the pen!

Mourning Dove, *Cogewea*

This declaration by the protagonist early in *Cogewea* follows on her
resolve to record "the woof of her people's philosophy," the traditional wisdom that she sees passing away with the loss of elders like
her grandmother. Such in fact was the work that Cogewea's creator,
Mourning Dove, herself undertook, later publishing a collection of
traditional Okanogan stories. Cogewea might be a fictional model
as well for many of the writers whose works are examined in this
volume, as they also frequently expressed the intention of preserving
a wisdom that they saw as dying away. The passage also reflects the
adversity under which so many of these writers labored. Addressing
an audience at best insensitive and all too often hostile, they undertook a labor that enjoyed little support from any source and was
generally unrewarded. Against such odds, these authors made a
unique contribution to American culture.

There is a theory that considers American Indian literature to be
only those texts (oral and written) produced by Native people and
addressed primarily to a Native audience; it is a comparative theory,
and it offers a rewarding basis for studying those texts that it can-
onizes. Such a formulation, however, excludes the authors considered in this volume, for all of them wrote in European languages,
and most of them directed their words to an audience of non-Native
people. The works examined in the essays collected here must be
seen, rather, as always involved in a dynamic negotiation across many
boundaries, barriers, gaps, and silences characterizing the discourse

of the emergent nation. Their undertaking speaks to a profound faith in the possiblity of language to overcome ignorance and hostility, as well as a remarkable trust – which in the light of history may seem to have been misplaced – in the capacity of their audiences to be persuaded by rational argument and humane principles. This volume seeks to continue a process, recently begun, of recovering these authors and their works from marginalization and neglect and restoring them to the significant place they merit in American literature.

Support for this volume has been generous and welcome. My warmest thanks go to Eric Sundquist, series editor for Cambridge University Press's Studies in American Literature and Culture, whose encouragement and help with this project is only one of the manifestations of his professional generosity. Susan Chang made early and astute suggestions, and Camilla Palmer was supportive through upheavals and personnel changes while the book was in production. The Faculty Research office at California State University, Fullerton, provided a grant toward editing the manuscript of the collection.

Several of the pieces gathered here are reprinted from earlier publications. This project originally grew out of a special issue of *SAIL – Studies in American Indian Literatures*, numbers 2/3 of the 1992 volume. Versions of the following articles appeared in the *SAIL* issue: "Honoratissimi benefactores" by Wolfgang Hochbruck and Beatrix Dudensing; "Pray sir, consider a little" by Laura Murray; "I am Joaquin!" by John Lowe, which appeared as "Space and Freedom in the Golden Republic"; "An Indian . . . An American" by Eric Peterson; "Because I understand the storytelling art" by Birgit Hans, originally entitled "Re-Visions." Robert Sayre's "A desirable citizen, a practical business man," originally titled "G. W. Grayson," is reprinted from *A/B:Auto/Biography* by permission of the author.

Finally, it is my pleasure to express my gratitude to three other groups of people without whom this book could not exist. The contributors have been unfailingly patient, waiting out wearying periods of review and cheerfully revising and reformatting documentation; I am grateful. Most constant has been my husband, Dan Brown, to whom I owe not only loving support and good humor but corrections of Latin translations. My son, Andrew Brown Jaskoski, has been a faithful typist and incisive critic. Finally, and most of all, we are all in the debt of the authors whose works are examined in these essays. It is my hope that this volume will contribute to the work of communication and education that they undertook in their writings.

Helen Jaskoski

CONTRIBUTORS

CAROL BATKER teaches ethnic and women's studies at Florida State University, Tallahassee. She is currently working on a book that examines the relationship between ethnic women's literature and political journalism in the United States at the turn of the twentieth century.

WILLIAM M. CLEMENTS teaches at Arkansas State University. His publications in Native American studies include *Native American Folklore, 1879–1979: An Annotated Bibliography* (with Frances M. Malpezzi) and *Native American Folklore in Nineteenth-Century Periodicals.*

ANNE MARIE DANNENBERG is of Anglo-Cherokee descent. She teaches at the University of California, Davis. Her current work, on William Apess, Sarah Winnemucca Hopkins, Charles A. Eastman, and Zitkala-Ša, treats discourses of "Indianness" in early Native American autobiography.

BEATRIX DUDENSING-REICHEL was born in Rheinfelden, Germany. She studied Latin, history, and American literature at the Albert-Ludwigs-Universität in Freiburg and at the University of Iowa. Her doctoral thesis is on James Fenimore Cooper, and she now works as a subject specialist at the University Library in Göttingen.

BIRGIT HANS is Associate Professor in the American Indian Studies program at the University of North Dakota. She is editor of *The Hawk Is Hungry and Other Stories,* a collection of the short fiction of D'Arcy McNickle.

WOLFGANG HOCHBRUCK is Assistant Professor of American and Canadian Studies at the University of Stuttgart. He has published on

American and Canadian literatures and is currently writing a book on *Re-Written War: Literature and the Memory of Armed Conflicts.*

HELEN JASKOSKI edited *SAIL – Studies in American Indian Literatures,* second series, 1989–92. She has published fiction and poetry, as well as articles on multiethnic literature and poetry therapy.

DANIEL F. LITTLEFIELD, JR., Cherokee, is Professor of English and Director of the American Native Press Archives at the University of Arkansas at Little Rock. He is author of *Alex Posey: Creek Poet, Journalist, and Humorist* and editor of the collected Fus Fixico letters of Alexander Posey.

JOHN LOWE is author of *Jump at the Sun: Zora Neale Hurston's Cosmic Comedy* and has published articles in *American Quarterly, Appalachian Journal, The Journal of the Short Story in English,* and other periodicals.

LAURA J. MURRAY is Assistant Professor of English at the University of Toronto, where she teaches writing, American literature, Native North American literature, and postcolonial theory. Her edition of the writings of Joseph Johnson, *To Do Good to My Indian Brethren,* is forthcoming from the University of Massachusetts Press.

DANA D. NELSON is Associate Professor of English at the University of Kentucky. She is currently at work on a book-length study of civic identity, scientific authority, masculinity, and race in the early United States.

ERIK PETERSON's dissertation in American Studies at the University of Minnesota, Twin Cities, examines how many Americans have drawn on the language of psychotherapy to describe and define a democratic society in the late-twentieth-century United States.

A. LAVONNE BROWN RUOFF is author of *American Indian Literatures: An Introduction, Bibliographic Review and Bibliography* and coeditor with Jerry Ward of *Redefining American Literary History.* Her essays on Native American literature have been published in numerous collections and periodicals. She is general editor of the American Indian Lives series from University of Nebraska Press.

ROBERT F. SAYRE is author of *The Examined Self,* a recently republished study of American autobiography. He is also the author of *Thoreau and the American Indians* and is editing an anthology of American autobiographies.

MARTHA L. VIEHMANN received her Ph.D. in American Studies from Yale University. She is adjunct professor of English at the University of Denver and is completing a monograph on *Writing Across the Cultural Divide.*

1

"HONORATISSIMI BENEFACTORES"

NATIVE AMERICAN STUDENTS AND TWO SEVENTEENTH-CENTURY TEXTS IN THE UNIVERSITY TRADITION

WOLFGANG HOCHBRUCK AND
BEATRIX DUDENSING-REICHEL

Some of the earliest literary texts written in European languages by Native American authors were written in the seventeenth century by students at Harvard's Indian College. The fact that they were written in Latin and Greek, the languages of university education, as well as their limited accessibility,[1] probably explains why these pieces have so far received next to no critical attention.[2] Two texts by Harvard Indian students have survived. The main purpose of this essay is to reprint them together with approximate translations as well as observations on the form, structure, and grammaticality of the texts and their background in literary tradition. In addition, the problem of their authorship will be discussed. Finally, an attempt will be made to position them historically and ideologically within the context of seventeenth-century colonial discourse.

In 1656, some twenty years after its foundation, Harvard College incorporated the first institution of higher education for the aboriginal population in the English colonies. The aim of the "Indian College" (*Vom Puritanismus* 98) was the education of Indian youths who appeared to be promising proselytes and who could later propagate the gospel as well as European civilization among their tribes. In this the Puritans were following the example of the Spanish colonizers, whose attempts to train Native Americans as teachers and preachers, however, proved more successful. The comparable success of the Spanish (and, to a lesser degree, the French Jesuits) can be attributed to their relative flexibility in regard to their students' needs and wants. They shaped their training accordingly, whereas the Puritans, utterly convinced of the singular rightness of their ways and methods, made their Indian students adhere to the same rigid code to which they subjected themselves (see Axtell, *The European and the Indian* 66). What awaited the student at Harvard becomes apparent from the 1665 code of College Laws:

In the first yeare after admission for four dayes of the weeke all Students shall be exercised in the Study of the Greeke and Hebrew Tongues, onely beginning Logicke in the Morning towardes the latter end of the yeare unlesse the Tutor shall see Cause by reason of their ripenesse in the Languages to read Logicke sooner. Also they shall spend the second yeare in Logicke with the exercise of the former Languages, and the third yeare in the principles of Ethickes and the fourth in metaphisicks and Mathematicks still carrying on their former studies of the weeke for Rhetoricke, Oratory and Divinity.[3]

Descriptions of the College and the number of its students given in the primary and secondary sources vary.[4] Apparently only a small number of Indian students attended regularly, and few of those lived to tell the tale. The unfamiliar system of education, as well as the living conditions and the diet, appear to have taken a deadly toll. Of those who did not fall victim to disease, at least two were murdered,[5] and "only one Indian, Caleb Cheeshateaumuck, class of 1665, completed the four year program."[6]

Caleb Cheeshateaumauk: "Honoratissimi Benefactores" (1663)

Walter Meserve, probably following Drake's *Biography and History of the Indians of North America* (1834), spells the name of this Indian College graduate "Chaesahteaumuk." Meserve believed that the piece of writing in the archive of the Royal Society, London, was the Indian's "graduation address to his 'most honored benefactors,' written and delivered in Latin" (264). The single paragraph on Caleb Cheeshateaumauk[7] in Meserve's article has served as an unquestioned basis for information for scholars up to the present. To quote just one example, Andrew Wiget writes: "Caleb Chaesahteamuk [sic], a Natick and the first Native American college graduate, was fluent in English, Hebrew, Greek, and Latin when he gave his 1665 Harvard commencement address in the latter tongue" (48–9).

Unfortunately, most of this is assumption. In fact, John Winthrop the Younger sent Cheeshateaumauk's "Honoratissimi Benefactores" to Robert Boyle, "together with a similar piece by another American Indian whose Christian name was Joel."[8]

To Robert Boyle, whose purview embraced both the Royal Society and the Propagation of the Gospel, he forwarded two papers in Latin, warranted the work of two young aboriginals, who had been Hebraically redesignated Joel and Caleb and enrolled at Harvard. Winthrop had been so impressed (as he seldom was by Indians) that he wondered if the Royal Society might not be interested also. (Black 307–8)

The date and contents of the letter provide two important pieces of information that suggest that "Honoratissimi Benefactores" was not written or even intended as a graduation address. The "Joel" to whom Winthrop refers must have been Joel Hiacoomes or "Iacoomis as he signs himself on a fly-leaf of a Comenius *Janua Linguarum*" (Morison 354). He and Caleb were in the same class, but Joel was killed before his graduation.[9] More conclusive is the date on the letter. According to the Harvard records, Caleb graduated in 1665, whereas Winthrop's letter is dated November 3, 1663. Not many students write their graduation address two years in advance, and it becomes obvious that in conjunction with Winthrop's letter the text was meant to be an address expressing appreciation and gratitude toward persons like Boyle, who raised and donated funds for the education of the Indian students and were in a financial sense "Honoratissimi Benefactores."

The manuscript[10] attributed to Cheeshateaumauk reads as follows:

Honoratissimi Benefactores
Referunt historici de Orpheo musico et insigni Poeta quod ab Appolline Lyram acceperit eaque tantum valuerit, ut illius Cantu sylvas saxumque moverit et Arbores ingentes post se traxerit, ferasque ferocissimas mitiores rediderit imo, quod accepta Lyrâ ad inferos descenderit et Plutonem et Proserpinam suo carmine demulserit, et Eurydicen uxorem ab inferis ad superos evexerit: Hoc symbolum esse statuunt Philosophi Antiquissimi, ut ostendant quod tanta et vis et virtus doctrinae et politioris literaturae ad mutandum Barborum Ingenium: qui sunt tanquam arbores, saxa, et bruta animantia: et eorum quasi matephorisin efficiendam, eosque tanquam Tigres Cicurandos et post se trahendos.
    Deus vos delegit esse patronos nostros, et cum omni sapientiâ intimâque Commiseratione vos ornavit, ut nobis paganis salutiferam opem feratis, qui vitam progeniemque a majoribus nostris ducebamus, tam animo quam corporeque nudi fuimus, et ab omni humanitate alieni fuimus, in deserto huc et illuc variisque erroribus ducti fuim[us].
    O terque quaterque ornatissimi, amantissimique viri, quas quantasque quam maximas, immensasque gratias vobis tribuamus: eo quod omnium rerum Copiam nobis suppetitaveritis

propter educationem nostram, et ad sustentationem corporum nostrorum: immensas maximasque expensas effudistis.

Et praecipuè quas quantasque, Gratias Deo Opt. [imo] M[a]x. [imo] dabimus qui sanctas scripturas nobis revelavit, Dominumque Jesum Christum nobis demonstravit, qui est via veritatis et vitae. Praeter haec omnia, per viscera miserecordiae divinae, aliqua spes relicta sit, ut instrumenta fiamus, ad declarandum et propogandum evangelium Cognatis nostris Conterraneisque: ut illi etiam Deum Cognoscant: et Christum.

Quamvis non posumus par pari redere vobis, reliquisque Benefactoribus nostris, veruntamen speramus. nos non defuturos apud Deum supplicationibus importunis exorare pro illis pijs misericordibus viris, qui supersunt in vetere Angliâ, qui pro nobis tantam vim auri, argentique effuderunt ad salutem animarum nostrarum procurandam et pro vobis etiam, qui instrumenta, et quasi aquae ductus fuistis omnia ista beneficentia nobis Conferendi.

Vestre Dignitati devotissimus: Caleb Cheeshateaumauk

The Latin text contains several minor grammatical mistakes. Some are spelling errors (e.g., "posumus," "redere," "miserecordibus," "propogandum," "veruntamen," and, repeatedly, "tanquam" instead of *possumus, reddere, misericordibus, propagandum, verumtamen,* and *tamquam*). In "Barborum" the second syllable of *Barbarorum* was omitted. A problematic spelling is "Tigres Cicurandos" (obviously not *Citurandos* as Morison has it), for *cicurare* is a Latin word rarely used. The only source that Cheeshateaumauk could have known is Varro, *De Lingua Latina*, 7, 91. The meaning, however, is the same as in *securare,* so "Cicurandos," if not from Varro, could be a misspelling (substitution of "c" for "s" can occasionally be found in Puritan texts) or the word was mis*heard* – which would imply that the text was dictated. This could also account for the other spelling mistakes in the text.

The most puzzling phrase in the manuscript is "quasi matephorisin efficiendam" near the end of the first paragraph. Along with Latin, Greek was part of the curriculum at Harvard, and the author of the text obviously meant to include here a word borrowed from the Greek, probably *metamorphosis* – which would make sense. Winthrop told Boyle that he "had questioned the Indians in Latin and received good answers in the same language, and heard them both express several sentences in Greek also" (Wright 117; see also Morison 354). If one of the two Indian students actually spoke Greek, it certainly was not Cheeshateaumauk. In order to mistake *metamorpho-*

sis so as to spell something like "matephorisin," the author cannot have been too familiar with Greek. To use a word and not be able to spell it at all would again indicate that the text may have been dictated rather than composed in written form. This possibility will be considered again later on.

In English, the text reads approximately as follows:

Most honored benefactors,

Historians tell of Orpheus, the musician and outstanding poet, that he received a lyre from Apollo, and that he was so excellent with it that he moved the forests and rocks by his song. He made huge trees follow behind him, and indeed rendered tamer the most ferocious beasts. After he took up the lyre he descended into the nether world, lulled Pluto and Proserpina with his song, and led Eurydice, his wife, out of the underworld into the upper. The ancient philosophers say that this serves as a symbol to show how powerful are the force and virtue of education and refined literature in the transformation of the nature of barbarians. They are like trees, rocks, and brute beasts, and a substantive change (metamorphosis) must be effected in them. They have to be secured like tigers and must be induced to follow.

God delegated you to be our patrons, and He endowed you with all wisdom and intimate compassion, so that you might perform the work of bringing blessings to us pagans, who derive our life and origin from our forebears. We used to be naked in soul and body, alien from all humanity, led around in the desert by all sorts of errors.

Oh threefold and fourfold most illustrious and most loving men, what kind of thanks, if not the greatest and most immense, should we give you, for you have supported us with an abundance of all things for our education and for the sustenance of our bodies. You have poured forth immense – the greatest – resources.

And we will especially give great thanks to God the most excellent and highest, who has revealed the sacred scriptures to us, and who has shown to us the Lord Jesus Christ, who is the way of truth and of life. Besides all this, another hope is left us through the depths of divine mercy: that we may become instruments to spread and propagate the gospel among our kin and neighbors, so that they also may know God, and Christ.

Even though we cannot commensurately reciprocate your kindness and that of our other benefactors, we do hope, however. We are not left alone praying before God with importunate supplications for those pious and merciful men who are still in old England, who disbursed so much gold and silver for us to obtain the salvation of our souls, and for you as well, who were instruments like aqueducts in bestowing all these benefits on us.

Most devoted to your dignity: Caleb Cheeshateaumauk

The five paragraphs of the letter can be roughly divided into two parts. The first part compares certain aspects of the Orpheus myth to the present situation of the students; the second part, following up this demonstration of learnedness, is an expression of gratitude to the benefactors combined with a tribute of thanks to the Lord and Christ.

The use of the Orpheus myth is of particular interest, both for its function as a documentation of scholastic achievements and for the way in which a classical myth was coopted to the needs of the author. During the Middle Ages and the Renaissance, Orpheus had been interpreted as the unhappy lover and as a bringer of humanism, respectively. The Orpheus figure in this text accesses an older tradition; the figure combines the classical theme in which Orpheus acts as a bringer of civilization with the typical early Christian topos in which Orpheus plays the similar role of priest and harbinger of Christianity.[11] Logically enough, this Christian interpretation specifically omits the loss of Eurydice and the final failure of Orpheus's rescue attempt, and concentrates on the poet's ability to transform the spirits of nature and its inhabitants. The analogies the author draws are obvious: Teachers and, for the purpose of this letter, financial donors like Boyle are likened to Orpheus; their efforts and missionary work to the lyre; and, lastly, the wildness of the stones, forests, and animals to the savageness of nature's human inhabitants, among which were the Indian students themselves.

This analogy between Indian students and "bruta animantia" is not, as it may initially appear, a Puritan device comparable to Cotton Mather's dictum about an Indian who warned his tribesmen against attacking the colony: "Thus was the tongue of a dog made useful to a feeble and sickly Lazarus" (quoted by Zolla 35). Within the text of "Honoratissimi Benefactores," "Philosophi Antiquissimi" are given as a source of this interpretation. More probably the author drew from the so-called Fathers, notably Clement of Alexandria and Eusebius: Clement was the first who dared to typify Christ through the Orpheus figure of Greek mythology, and Eusebius considered Christian man an instrument like Orpheus's lyre to pacify the fierce, angry passions of the barbarians (Irwin 51). The curriculum at Harvard explicitly contained the study of "theology . . . from the sources: the Bible, the Fathers, and the great commentators" (Morison 276), so Cheeshateaumauk would have been exposed to Clement and Eusebius.

Other passages and formulas in the text can also be traced to classical and biblical sources: *terque quaterque*, with or without the "O," is used by Vergil on four occasions in the *Aeneid*, and *via veritatis et vitae* is obviously biblical (John 14:6). All of these references serve the same purpose as the text itself: They exhibit the capacities and achievements of the Indian student and demonstrate to financiers like Boyle that their donations were productively invested.

Eleazar: "In obitum Viri verè Reverendi D. Thomae Thacheri" (1679)

The other surviving text by a Native American Harvard student is a reverence to his late teacher, Reverend Thomas Thacher, who had come to Boston in 1635. It is written in a classical form: an elegy in Latin distichs with four closing lines in Greek. Cotton Mather used this poem as an epitaph for Thacher in the third book of his *Magnalia Christi Americana*, which contains biographical essays on a number of New England priests and preachers. Introducing the poem, Mather writes:

> An epitaph must now be sought for this Worthy Man. And because the Nation and the Quality of the *Author*, will make the Composure to become a Curiosity, I will here, for an *Epitaph* insert an Elegy, which was composed upon this Occasion, by an *Indian Youth*, who was then Student of Harvard Colledge. (His name was, Eleazar.)

In obitum Viri verè Reverendi
D. Thomae Thacheri
Qui Ad
Dom. ex hâc Vitâ migravit, 18.8.1678

Tentabo Illustrem, tristi memorare dolore
  Quem Lacrymis repetunt Tempora, nostra, Virum.
Memnona sic Mater, Mater ploravit Achillem,
  Justis cum Lacrymis, cumque Dolore gravi
Mens stupet, ora silent, justum nunc palmo recusat
  Officium: Quid? Opem Tristis Apollo negat?
Ast Thachere Tuus conabor dicere laudes

Laudes Virtutis, quae super Astra volat.
Consultis Rerum Dominis, Gentique togatae
    Nota fuit virtus, ac tua Sancta Fides.
Vivis post Funus; Faelix post Fata; *Jaces Tu?*
    Sed *Stellas* inter *Gloria* nempe *Jaces*
Mens Tua jam caelos repetit; Victoria parta est:
    Iam Tuus est Christus, quod meruitque tuum.
Hic Finis Crucis; magnorum haec meta malorum;
    Ulterius non quo progrediatur erit.
Crux jam cassa manes; requiescunt ossa Sepulchro;
    Mors moritur; Vitae Vita Beata redit
Quum tuba per Densas sonitum dabit ultima Nubes,
    Cum Domino Rediens Ferrea Sceptra geres.
Caeles tum scandes, ubi Patria Vero piorum
    Praevius hanc patriam nunc tibi *Jesus* adit.
Illic vera Quies; illic sine fine voluptas;
    Gaudia & Humanis non referenda sonis
Σῶμ'ἔχει ἡ κονὶν, ἐπὶ γῆς τ' ὄνομ'οὔποτ' ὀλεῖται,
    Κλεινὸν ἐν ἡμετέροις κ' ἐσομενοῖσι χρόνοις
ψυχὴ δ'ἐκ ῥεθέων πταμένη, βῆ οὐρανον αἰπὺν,
    Μιχθεῖσ' ἀθάνατος πνεύμασιν ἀθανάτοις. (153)

Training in the Greek classics appears to have improved between
1663 and 1679. A mistake like Cheeshateaumauk's ominous "matephorisin" is not repeated. The form "κονὶν" should read "κονὶς,"
but "κονὶν" as a poetic subform can be found in Homer's *Iliad* 18:
23 and in Theocritus 24:93. The orthographical mistakes ("palmo"
and "vero" instead of *palma* and *vera*) in a text revised by Cotton
Mather are surprising but could be attributed to the printer.
Translation:[12]

On the death of that truly venerable man
D. Thomas Thacher
who went to the Lord from this life, 18:8.1678

I seek to commemorate this illustrious man with sad grief,
    Whom our times reclaim with tears, this man.
Thus Memnon's mother; thus his mother wept for Achilles
    With justified tears; and with grieving pain
The mind is stunned, mouths are silent. Now the hand
        refuses its proper
    Service: What? Grieving Apollo refuses his help?

Nonetheless, Thacher, I, one of yours,[13] will try to speak
    praise,
    Praise of virtue, which ascends higher than the stars.
To men of high learning and to people of standing[14]
    Your virtue was known, as also your Holy Faith.
You live on after the funeral, happy following [the fulfillment
    of] your fate; do you lie [dead]?
    But among the stars you lie indeed as in glory;
Your spirit already returns to the heavens; victory has been
    achieved:
    Yours already is Christ, yours what He merited.
Here is the end of the cross [of life's sorrow]; here the end
    of great evil;
    Further than that there is nowhere whence He could
    proceed.
You, cross, already stand empty; the bones rest in the grave;
    Death dies; Blessed Life returns to life
When the last trumpet shall sound through dense clouds.
    Returning with the Lord, you carry iron sceptres.
Then you will ascend into the heavens,[15] home of the truly
    pious;
    Jesus precedes you now on the way to this homeland.
There is true rest, there is delight without end,
    Joys human voices cannot describe.

Dust receives your corpse, but your name, famous in our own
and in future times, will never perish on earth; the spirit, flying
from your limbs, climbs up to steep heaven, immortal, mingling with immortal spirits.

The name of the author is given as "Eleazar *Judus* Senior So-
phista."[16] Although the text is far from being a masterpiece, the
form and meter are rather regular. As in "Honoratissimi Benefactores," some passages evoke classical models. In this poem, these
allusions serve the same purpose as in Cheeshateaumauk's letter, to
demonstrate learnedness. The results are sometimes puzzling. For
example, the third line is a direct quotation from Ovid, *Amores* IX,
1. The *Amores* seem an unlikely text for a Puritan school, and they
certainly are not exactly appropriate for use in an obituary elegy.
Also, Cheeshateaumauk's use of Orpheus as mythological intertext
seems more fitting than Eleazar's use of the warriors Memnon and
Achilles of Homeric tradition in a eulogy on a man of the cloth. An
interesting parallel emerges, though, in that both texts follow a similar model. Eleazar, like Caleb, begins his text with an allusion to

Greek mythology and then switches to biblical motifs, concentrating on aspects of salvation.

Indian Students and the Question of Authorship

Eleazar's poem was edited for reprint. This raises the question of authorship again: Could both texts discussed in this essay possibly have been designed, dictated, or even written by somebody other than the signed authors? The answer is yes, *possibly*, but the problem cannot be solved easily, if at all. As was said before, "Honoratissimi Benefactores" bears some traces indicating that the text may have been dictated. In his letter to Boyle, John Winthrop, Junior, claimed that Caleb Cheeshateaumauk and Joel Hiacoomes wrote "with their owne hands" (Morison 354), which does not necessarily imply that the texts were their own idea, even though this may be pushing the argument too far.

On the whole, it would not come as a surprise if the texts by Cheeshateaumauk and Hiacoomes (the latter of which was lost) were falsifications. Both texts were expressions of gratitude for received funding, and when it came to fund-raising campaigns, the Puritans showed remarkably little hesitation in making the end justify the means. The seal of the colony, depicting an Indian saying "Come Over and Help Us," was adopted for the sole purpose of stimulating additional funding (Axtell, *Invasion Within* 134). If fund-raising was the purpose of Winthrop's letter, the effort was successful, for Boyle not only supported missions among the Indians during his lifetime but also willed the substantial amount of £5400 to pious and charitable uses – money that went into "a school for Indians at Virginia's new college" (Axtell, *Invasion Within* 190).

There is more reason to be skeptical. Some Puritan officials apparently took a rather selective position when it came to preserving documents relating to Indian affairs:

> one can say with confidence that the interpretations provided in Winthrop's *History* are unlikely to be accurate representations of the vanished texts. . . . Winthrop probably rewrote the substance of the Indian treaties to meet the Puritans' political and ideological needs, and then he or a devoted descendant destroyed the originals. (Jennings, *Invasion of America* 182)

Even though Jennings concedes that "the case cannot be proved because the essential evidence is gone," he presents a strong argument that John Winthrop *Senior* falsified records. Jennings records another occasion when John Eliot, the famous missionary, tried to

conceal that he had attempted to take the credit for missionary efforts that were not his and made some changes in an application for
funds, writing that " 'his earlier statement had a great (I) redundant
which maketh the sence untrue,' brightly adding that everything
would read quite accurately if only the name of the Indian Hiacoomes
was substituted for the first person singular pronoun that Eliot has
used as the subject of his credit-grabbing sentence." Jennings goes on
to remark that "this must be the only time that the term *redundant*
has been used to mean 'substituted.' " The aim was to gain money:
"Winslow used Eliot's letters, including the 'I-Hiacoomes' one, to
win Parliament's authorization for a nationwide collection of missionary funds, and the New England Company was established to
transmit the funds to Eliot's mission" ("Goals and Functions of Puritan Missions" 208, 209). All this may serve to illustrate why the
authorship of Cheeshateaumauk and Hiacoomes must be seen as
doubtful. If a "substitution" like the one described by Eliot happened once, why not twice? This is, after all, obviously the same Joel
Hiacoomes whose letter went via Winthrop to Boyle.

On the other hand, none of this can conclusively prove that
Cheeshateaumauk and Eleazar were not the authors of the respective
texts attributed to them. To discount their authorship on the basis
of the ideological content of the texts is not possible. In fact, missionary zealots like Eliot and Winthrop would not have needed to
dictate or falsify their students' literary efforts. These young Indians
were educated under a system designed to erase their tribal identities. If the system was effective, the results were texts like "Honoratissimi Benefactores" – self-deprecating and abounding in exuberant
praise for the "benefactors."

From the perspective of those of their contemporaries who ad-
hered to traditional beliefs and values, the Indian students had
forsaken their cultural identity.[17] "The Indian who embraced Christianity was compelled, in effect, to commit cultural suicide. He was
required to renounce not only his own personal past, but that of his
forefathers as well, forsaking – and despising – all traditional beliefs"
(Ronda 38). The position held by the Indian students was, at best,
one between the cultures. As authors, however, Joel, Caleb, and Eleazar even became contributors to the Puritan colonial master narrative and could be used as part of the colonial discourse.[18] To try to
ascribe undercurrents of traditional Indian cultures to these works
does not make sense.

Within the context of an incipient literature written by Native
Americans, the Harvard Indian college for several reasons turned
out to be a dead-end road. One reason is, of course, that the most

promising students died prematurely. Joel Hiacoomes, as stated before, was murdered; Eleazar died shortly before his graduation; and
Caleb survived his graduation to live just one more year. The school
itself was abandoned after King Philip's war. A second reason is that
Latin and Greek were rapidly going out of use as the standard languages of education. Assimilationist sentiments, however, remained
the rule rather than the exception with early Native American texts
well into the nineteenth century.[19]

Notes

1. After most of the research for this essay had been completed, the authors obtained a copy of Samuel Morison's *Harvard College in the Seventeenth Century,* which prints "Honoratissimi Benefactores" (Morison
   355). The manuscript, a single sheet beginning "Honoratissimi Benefactores" and signed "Caleb Cheeshateaumauk," is in the Boyle correspondence (BL 2.12) in the archive of the Royal Society, London.
2. Meserve focuses on texts written in English.
3. Charles Chauncey, quoted in Morison 144f.
4. See Jennings *Invasion,* 247f, and Salisbury 46f; the most extensive and
   probably the most reliable account is in Morison 342ff.
5. For more detailed accounts see Morison 352ff; Axtell, *The Invasion Within*
   182ff; Vaughan 282ff.
6. Vaughan 284. Szasz and Ryan have claimed that "two (Joel Hiacoomes
   and Caleb Cheeshahteaumuck) completed their education" (286), but
   all sources available to the authors indicate that in fact only the latter
   graduated.
7. This is the spelling of the name on the manuscript and the spelling used
   in this essay.
8. Alan J. Clark, Deputy Librarian, The Royal Society, London: letter to W.
   Hochbruck 16 May 1989. The letter by Joel (Hiacoomes) has not survived (letter to W. Hochbruck, March 7, 1991). We are grateful to Mr.
   Clark, who not only provided a copy of the manuscript but also added
   information both helpful and enlightening to our task.
9. He survived a shipwreck off the coast of Massachusetts only to be murdered by local Indians (Morison 356; Meserve 274).
10. This is a transcript of the original manuscript. The version printed in
    Morison contains several mistakes corrected here.
11. See the article on "Orpheus" in Frenzel 573–79; also see Robbins.
12. An early English rendition of this poem by a "Philo Muses" in the
    American Magazine & Historical Chronicle not only changes the meter into
    (rather badly rhyming) heroic couplets but also deletes the Greek part.
    Instead of the original twenty-eight lines, the poem is almost doubled in
    size (fifty lines). For example, the first two lines turn into "While weep-
    ing Friends around thy Funeral mourn / And pay their last sad Honours

to thine Urn / The Muse officious to attend the Hearse / Offers her
Tribute in Elegiac Verse" ("Philo Muses" 166).

13. The original possibly had *tuas* to read "your praise."
14. The phrase *consultus iuris*, "knowledgeable in matters of law," is common; *rerum* sounds a bit awkward. *Gentique togatae* could also mean "or-
dained people."
15. Probably *caelos*.
16. Not *Indus*, as Morison writes (196).
17. The voices of some traditionalists and dissenters are also preserved, for
example, in John Eliot's *Indian Dialogues,* in Roger Williams's *Key into the
Language of America,* and in the *Jesuit Relations.* Eliot and Williams present
typical dialogues with obstinate Indians in order to equip fellow missionaries and teachers with material for use in answering possible questions from their students and congregations, and the Jesuits document
many cases of Indians defending their traditions with skill and cunning.
For more detail, see Ronda.
18. The first Native American author who successfully used English for his
own purposes (and personal advantage) rather than for the aims pursued by his instructors was also the only Harvard student to survive
longer; one "John Wompow-ess" or "Wampus" (also Wompas and
Wampas), who changed professions several times during his life and,
after King Philip's War, was in jail for debt. In this situation he used his
freshman English to write a " 'humble Peticion . . . to the King's most
excellent Majesty,' . . . praying his gracious Sovereign to issue a royal
command to 'Sir John Leveritt Knight Governor of Massij Chussit Bay'
that he be released forthwith" (Morison 356–7).
19. The authors are grateful to Prof. Dr. Paul G. Schmidt, specialist in
medieval Latin at Freiburg University, for his help with the texts discussed in this essay, as well as to E. Stein and especially to Beth Satre
for her comments and the revision of the manuscript. The editor also
thanks Daniel A. Brown, Professor of Latin and Religious Studies at
California State University, Fullerton, for assistance with idiomatic English translations. The authors take responsibility for any remaining mistakes.

Works Cited

Axtell, James. *The European and the Indian. Essays in the Ethnohistory of Colonial
North America.* New York: Oxford University Press, 1981.
The Invasion Within: The Contest of Cultures in Colonial North America. New
York: Oxford University Press, 1985.
Black, Robert C., III. *The Younger John Winthrop.* New York: Columbia Uni-
versity Press, 1966.
Frenzel, Elizabeth. *Stoffe der Weltliteratur.* Stuttgart: Kröner, 1983.
Irwin, Eleanor. "The New Song of Orpheus and the New Song of Christ."
Warden 51–62.

Jennings, Francis. "Goals and Functions of Puritan Missions to the Indians."
    Ethnohistory 18 (1971): 197–212.
    The Invasion of America: Indians, Colonialism, and the Cant of Conquest. Chapel
    Hill: University of North Carolina Press, 1975.
Mather, Cotton. *Magnalia Christi Americana, or the Ecclesiastical History of New-
    England.* Vol. 3. London: Parkhurst, 1702.
Meserve, Walter T. "English Works of Seventeenth-Century Indians." *Amer-
    ican Quarterly* 8 (1956): 264–76.
Morison, Samuel E. *Harvard College in the Seventeenth Century.* Vol. 1. Cam-
    bridge, MA: Harvard University Press, 1936.
"Philo Muses." "Poetical Essays." *American Magazine & Historical Chronicle* 1
    (1743–4): 166–70.
Robbins, Emmet. "Famous Orpheus." Warden 3–23.
Ronda, James P. " 'We Are Well As We Are': An Indian Critique of Seven-
    teenth-Century Christian Missions." *William and Mary Quarterly* 34
    (1977): 66–82.
Salisbury, Neal. "Red Puritans: The 'Praying Indians' of Massachusetts Bay
    and John Eliot." *William and Mary Quarterly* 31 (1974): 27–54.
Szasz, Margaret C., and Carmelita Ryan. "American Indian Education." *His-
    tory of Indian–White Relations,* ed. Wilcomb Washburn. Vol. 4 of *Handbook
    of the American Indian,* ed. William Sturtevant. Washington, DC: Smith-
    sonian Institution, 1988. 284–300.
Vaughan, Alden T. *New England Frontier: Puritans and Indians 1620–1675.*
    Boston: Little, Brown, 1965.
Vom Puritanismus bis zum Bürgerkrieg. Vol. 1 of *Geschichte der nordamerikanischen
    Kultur,* ed. Gert Raeithel. Weinheim and Berlin: Quadriga, 1987.
Warden, John, ed. *Orpheus: A Metamorphosis of a Myth.* Toronto: University of
    Toronto Press, 1982.
Wiget, Andrew. *Native American Literature.* Boston: Twayne, 1985.
Wright, Louis B. *The Cultural Life of the American Colonies, 1607–1763.* New
    York: Harper, 1957.
Zolla, Elemire. *The Writer and the Shaman,* trans. Raymond Rosenthal. New
    York: Harcourt Brace Jovanovich, 1973.

2

"PRAY SIR, CONSIDER A LITTLE"

RITUALS OF SUBORDINATION AND STRATEGIES OF RESISTANCE IN THE LETTERS OF HEZEKIAH CALVIN AND DAVID FOWLER TO ELEAZAR WHEELOCK

LAURA J. MURRAY

The most wise, righteous, and gracious God doth oftentimes leave for a season his own children to manifold temptations, and the corruptions of their own hearts, to chastise them for their former sins, or to discover unto them the hidden strength of corruption, and deceitfulness of their hearts, that they may be humbled; and to raise them to a more close and constant dependence for their support upon himself, and to make them more watchful against all future occasions of sin, and for sundry other just and holy ends.

Church of Scotland, *The Confession of Faith*, 1756

... the best way in which the master can serve his own interests is to work away, day in, day out, with constant care and attention, weaving the ethical and affective, as well as economic, bonds which durably tie his *khammes* to him. ... [I]f the master wants to persuade the *khammes* to devote himself over a long period to the pursuit of the master's interests, he has to associate him completely with those interests, masking the dyssymetry of the relationship by symbolically denying it in his behaviour. The *khammes* is the man to whom one entrusts one's goods, one's house, and one's honour. ... And just as [the *khammes*] never feels entirely freed from his obligations towards his former master, so, after what he calls a 'change of heart' he may accuse his master of 'treachery' in abandoning someone he had 'adopted.'

Pierre Bourdieu, *Outline of a Theory of Practice*, 1977

I

In 1754, Eleazar Wheelock opened his Indian Charity-School in Lebanon, Connecticut, with the goal of educating Indians to be missionaries and schoolteachers among their own people. He began

15

with an endowment of land and a couple of buildings, two small Delaware boys for students, and unbounded optimism. Not only did he expect Indians from various tribes and of various ages to be amenable to religious, linguistic, and cultural conversion, but, as he explains in his *Plain and Faithful Narrative of the Indian Charity-School,* he expected that training these Indians in obedience and humility would both fulfill his duty to God and the king and reduce Indian violence against English settlers.[1] In the same narrative, the first of several accounts of the school written for fund-raising purposes, Wheelock also justifies his idea of training Indian rather than white missionaries: Indians do not trust the English, he reminds his patrons, but they will trust other Indians. Furthermore, he claims that Indian missionaries cost less, will be more culturally compatible, will not "scorn to be advised or reproved" by their superiors, and do not need interpreters (15–23). Like other white educators of Native peoples before him and since, Wheelock believed that he had to remove Indian students from their families in order to "cure them of such savage and sordid Practices, as they have been inured to from their Mother's Womb" (25), and he set about "curing" them with great fervor and rigor. As the years went by, however, almost all of Wheelock's assumptions at this early stage of his project in Indian education turned out to be false, and he turned most of his attention to educating white boys when he founded Dartmouth College in 1769.

Among the documents of Wheelock's work in Indian education are the letters and confessions written to him by nineteen of his Indian students, which were collected and published, along with related letters and speeches, as part of the Dartmouth College Manuscript Series in 1932.[2] In this essay, I discuss the letters of two of Wheelock's students, Hezekiah Calvin and David Fowler. Their letters are more numerous than those of most of Wheelock's Indian students, and because they span several years (two and a half years in Calvin's case, and four in Fowler's), they provide particular insight into the nature of Wheelock's relationships with his students and the ongoing role of writing within those relationships.[3]

Calvin and Fowler wrote letters for various purposes and on various occasions. At the school, Wheelock required students to write or sign obsessively detailed confessions of sins. Calvin and Fowler also used writing to ask permission and register complaints even when they were in Lebanon with Wheelock; perhaps they did so because Wheelock required it, or perhaps writing allowed them to broach subjects they did not feel they could discuss with Wheelock face to face. When they were posted to teach away from Wheelock, both Calvin and Fowler wrote to him about many matters, both spiritual and material. However, they were not often rewarded with replies. Wheelock may have written more letters to his Indian students than have been preserved, but among the thousands of letters Wheelock copied out for his records, only a small number are addressed to his Indian students, and as we shall see, the letters of Calvin and Fowler (and other students) contain many complaints about Wheelock's lack of response: It appears that it was common for Wheelock to leave the students' letters unanswered. While the students were trying to encourage or maintain a correspondence with him, Wheelock was directing more of his correspondence to British benefactors and missionary colleagues, sometimes enclosing some of his students' letters as proof of his success in producing literate Indians. Thus Calvin's and Fowler's letters had a dual audience rather than a single correspondent. Wheelock's silence intensified Calvin's and Fowler's dependence on him – in the same way that the *Confession of Faith* of the Scottish church understands the effect of God's silence on the faithful – but his silence also increased their resistance to his authority.

James Scott, in his important study of the subtle manifestations of resistance in conditions of domination, writes that "each and every inference about the attitude behind an act of deference must . . . be based on evidence external to the act itself" (24). Neither the deference nor the defiance in the letters of Calvin and Fowler can be interpreted without considering the context of their silent dual audience, as well as the intensity and complexity of the relationships between the Indian students and Wheelock. For although the students went to Wheelock's school voluntarily or were sent by their parents, they soon found themselves enmeshed in powerful bonds of duty and debt that were difficult for them to escape. Hezekiah Calvin captures this situation in the following letter to Wheelock:

> Your goodness binds me to you in all thankfulness, but how shall I, or in what Language or words shall I express the sense of Gratitude due to your care & tenderness who have all along laid so many obligations on me, so many & in so high degree, that I may as well Number them, which is as impossible as to declare their greatness and worth. . . . (52–3)[4]

The ever-multiplying obligations were not only affective. For example, when James Simon wanted to leave the school, Wheelock wrote the student's mother an angry letter:

> I received your James not to please myself but at your earnest
> Desire by your Daughter Sarah, who told me you had given
> him to me to bring up and despose of as my own Son, and
> only upon such Considerations I took him. . . . & when he is fit
> for it I designd to put him into good Business as I would a
> Child of my own . . . but if I have not understood you right . . .
> I insist upon it that you let me know it now, before I spend
> any more Money to be thrown away upon him, there are hun-
> dreds who would be glad to come into his Room and be at my
> dispose as much my own Children are – (225–6)

Financial factors clearly enter into this part of the letter – "Money
to be thrown away upon him" is a rather strong phrase – but Wheelock does not spell things out until the postscript, where he directly
threatens that Sarah the elder, James's mother, will have to pay back
the full cost of her son's education if he leaves the school.[5] Before
and between these bluntly stated financial concerns, the letter bears
a tone of injured generosity and insulted fatherly love. The language
of emotion and the business dimension of the relationship would
not have been contradictory to Wheelock; legally and customarily,
English children in the eighteenth century were considered to be
the property of their parents or guardians, with the attendant duties
and constraints. Thus, when Wheelock claims that his students are
like his own children, their likeness is based on the fact that, like
Wheelock's children, they are "at [his] dispose," or, as he puts it
elsewhere, available for "special Usefulness" (*Narrative* 26). The students' parents, on the other hand, cast a different light on the ways
in which their children have become Wheelock's children. They expect Wheelock to treat their children as his own, "according to
which they are wont to treat *their* Captives" (*Narrative* 41; my emphasis). There is a certain nice irony in this assertion, as the parents
accuse Wheelock of capturing their children, and use that accusation
to ensure his good treatment of them.[6] But as James Axtell points
out, "what the Indians . . . soon discovered . . . was that English children were treated much differently from children in the longhouse"
(209), and they learned, furthermore, that Wheelock's fatherly affection for his Indian students was distorted by racist expectations
of failure and backsliding.

The father–child metaphor used by all parties in describing the
relationship between Wheelock and his students was a conception
that harmonized with both Christian doctrine and Indian expectations; although defined variously, it was mutually agreed on. The
collective definition of this relationship is in many ways similar to

Pierre Bourdieu's formulation of the master–*khammes* relationship in rural Algeria, sketched out in an epigraph to this essay, in which "there is neither deceiver nor deceived" (196). Bourdieu puts forth a general thesis about the intimate and ever-labor-intensive ways in which a hierarchy is maintained in societies lacking mechanisms to guarantee and objectify it:[7]

> the system contains only two ways (and they prove in the end to be just one way) of getting and keeping a lasting hold over someone: gifts or debts, the overtly economic obligations of debt, or the 'moral,' 'affective' obligations created and maintained by exchange, in short, overt (physical or economic) violence, or symbolic violence – *censored, euphemized,* i.e. unrecognizable, socially recognized violence. There is an intelligible relation – not a contradiction – between these two forms of violence, which coexist in the same social formation and sometimes in the same relationship: when domination can only be exercised in its *elementary form,* i.e. directly, between one person and another, it cannot take place overtly and must be disguised under the veil of enchanted relationships, the official model of which is presented by relations between kinsmen; in order to be socially recognized it must get itself misrecognized. (191)

Like the Algerian masters studied by Bourdieu, Wheelock manipulated two sorts of obligations, gifts and debts, invoking debt obligations only in extreme situations (such as James Simon's crisis of confidence in him), because "overt violence," as Bourdieu would call it (in this case, demanding payment) threatened the stability of his "affective" authority over his students. "Symbolic violence" – "the gentle, invisible form of violence, which is never recognized as such, and is not so much undergone as chosen, the violence of credit, confidence, obligation, personal loyalty, hospitality, gifts, gratitude, piety" (Bourdieu 192) – was more effective for Wheelock than direct economic violence. But the affective relation of father and son was also preferred, if differently defined, by the students and their families: Those Indians who willingly sent their children to Wheelock's school understood that Wheelock would act in loco parentis. And the students, once ensconced in this affective relationship with Wheelock, worked strenuously *within* it to gain concessions from Wheelock before they considered ending the relationship.[8]

Eventually, however, every one of Wheelock's Indian students who lived long enough or studied long enough to take up a post in the field did break with Wheelock. The applicability of Bourdieu's model to missionary–Christian Indian relations in colonial America is thus limited. Colonial New England, however, was part of extensive networks of culture, capital, and communication that rendered more things thinkable than Bourdieu's model would indicate. The Indian students of Wheelock, even while enmeshed in relationships with him, still maintained circles in which they could speak and act outside of his knowledge or control. These circles, "sequestered social sites at which . . . resistance can be nurtured and given meaning" (Scott 20), permitted the development of what James Scott terms "hidden transcripts," discourses of resistance that operate in all but the most atomizing conditions of domination.[9]

Another set of "transcripts" was also operating alongside the discourse of Wheelock and his students: Wheelock, despite his authority over his Indian students, was a participant in an economy of gifts and debts with his patrons in Britain. When he dedicated his *Narrative* to the Marquis of Lothian, Wheelock had to abase himself rhetorically almost as much as his students were required to do for him: He was indebted to British benefactors for their charity as his students were to him. Wheelock's participation in dual economies of debts and gifts allowed his students to understand the limits of his authority over them, and their relations with their people gave them the exteriority to dare to "recognize" their relationship with Wheelock and refuse its "enchantment."[10]

II

Hezekiah Calvin, a Delaware, came to Wheelock's school as a small boy in 1757, arriving on the horse that had carried one of the school's first two students home to die. To Wheelock this replacement of one student lost with one gained, arriving on the very same horse, was a sign of divine favor (*Narrative* 30). But Calvin did not turn out to be the miraculous purveyor of Christianity his arrival may have augured for Wheelock. The twelve letters Calvin wrote to Wheelock between February 1766 and the fall of 1768, as well as several letters about him from others, tell of his loneliness, doubts, drinking, and general cultural dislocation. Posted in 1766 as a schoolteacher to Fort Hunter, New York, Calvin found himself burdened with complicated community demands, persistent discipline problems in his school, and chronic headaches (51). He did not speak the language – later he described himself among the Mohawks as a "dumb stump that has no tonnge to use" (58) – and he felt isolated both from his family and from Wheelock.

One bright spot in Calvin's life around this time was his courtship of Mary Secutor, another Indian student at Wheelock's school, but

his hope for marriage was soon quashed when her father wrote to
Wheelock asking that he prevent the match (for unspecified reasons), which Wheelock did. Devastated by this decision, Calvin's reaction was to lay out in a letter to Wheelock several ideas about
what he might do now: go to sea, return to the Mohawks even
though he doubts he would "be likely of doing them any good"
(58), farm, or go home "that I might learn somwhat of my own Native Language" (58).[11] As for Mary Secutor, Calvin had his conditions: "I can leave her if you will let me go home & never to return
again" (58), he wrote. But in the very next sentence he is all acquiescence: "I leave the affair wholly with you to conclude; for thou
canst advise as a father, &c" (58). The "&c" here indicates that
Calvin is rehearsing a ritual well known to both him and Wheelock
(it is tempting to read it also as a hint that Calvin had in mind some
labels for Wheelock other than "father"); the entire letter is full of
such switches between complex emotion or negotiation and formulaic obedience. However, the rhetorical balancing act is impossible
to sustain for long: "My Mind is full. I cant express myself," Calvin
concludes. "And thus I End Subscribing myself to be your Dutiful
Pupil" (58).

All of Calvin's letters, hardly ever pausing for periods, have a
breathless quality that echoes what he calls his "uneasiness." He uses
the word "uneasy" with great frequency, and it evokes not only a
mood but also a cultural contradiction: Nothing was easy for Calvin,
not even leaving the school that made him miserable.[12] Calvin kept
returning to Lebanon even after he was finished at the school, and
in October 1767 he wrote to Wheelock from there:

> *I am uneasy,* & it seems to me if D[r] Wheelock does not give me
> leave to go, I must go without leave but I had rather go with a
> Dismission, not without Liberty, but *I am uneasy* enough to do
> either of them. . . . *I am uneasy,* Sir I shal turn out as Jacob
> Wolley did if I tarry much longer, so I should rather go before
> the Doc[r] sees that time so I end Your
> Undutiful Pupil Hezekiah Calvin (59; my emphasis)

Calvin may have made such a request in writing because writing
allowed him to control the balance of complaints and gratitude better than he could in person. In writing, he may have had more
courage to stand up to Wheelock. However, writing was also an in-
trinsic part of the "symbolic violence" that constituted the relationship between Wheelock and Calvin, a relationship consisting largely
of distance, discomfort, and discipline both represented by and guar-
anteed by writing. Bourdieu defines "symbolic violence" as "that

form of domination which, transcending the opposition usually drawn between sense relations and power relations, communication and domination, is only exerted *through* the communication in which it is disguised" (237). That is, the written details of a hierarchical relation are not only representations or signs of that relation, but are also constitutive of it. Thus, paradoxical as it is, Calvin's own letters announcing his dissatisfaction could be tools in maintaining the relationship that disciplined him. His writing both disguised and ensured Wheelock's authority.

One of the things that disempowered Calvin was the absence of any reply from Wheelock to his letters, even when they resonated relentlessly with the word "home" and begged for response:

> There is somthing that makes me want to go home, what, I cant tell, Home is in my Mind all the time I want to go Home soon & see my Relations, & it seems to me to Tarry home a while or all the Time, & let me see if that I am able to support myself. I have tarryed upon Charity long enough. . . . (63)

In July 1767 Wheelock suggested in a letter to the missionary John Brainerd that Calvin go to work with him at his mission, saying, "Hezekiah must do or I have done with him" (56); there exists, however, no communication with Calvin himself on this or any other subject. Perhaps Wheelock met with Calvin or sent messages refusing Calvin's demands for freedom. In any case, by May 1768 Calvin's rhetoric has escalated to a degree that strongly indicates that his previous letters had not drawn responses:

> My mind is full of such bad thoughts, so that I cant relate all my bad thoughts, & when my thoughts are off this my Mind is Home continually laying out work for me to do. . . . But I beleive I should soon be tired of Home & yet my Mind is all the while Cleaving to go home, & somtimes it excite a motion in my Breast to go without leting the Doctor know of my Intentions, when I am alone I am almost crazy I will catch my hair & pull & Cry, for to go Home . . . hopeing the Docter will give me Leave to go home I subscribe myself. . . . (64)

Whether or not Calvin went home, we do know that he visited the Narragansetts in Rhode Island, and here, as we move to documentary evidence beyond Calvin's own letters, we see Calvin's independence from Wheelock assert itself more fully. A letter written to Wheelock in June 1768 by Edward Deake, a white schoolmaster at Charleston, Rhode Island, reports a whole string of accusations Calvin had leveled against Wheelock, including charges of stealing from students, stealing from the commissioners, mistreating pupils, and failing to provide adequate education; the list ends with the statement that "ye Indians are ready to conclude, that their Fellow-Indians will never receive any great Benefit of ye Large sums of Money contributed by good People, to promote so good a Caise" (65). Calvin's charges are so numerous, and the written list of them such a convincing document, that Deake, having written them out but taken aback by their force, added as an afterthought: "P.S. The above has not enter'd my Heart as Truth. I write in hast, Hope you'll excuse me" (65). Deake's indirect report of Calvin's clear and un-abashed criticism reminds us, limited as we are by scanty documen-tation of Calvin's opinions, to refrain from assuming that Calvin's letters to Wheelock reflect his broader thoughts and statements. Writing may have helped Calvin to express what he was afraid to say directly to Wheelock, whereas Calvin did feel comfortable speaking directly to his Narragansett friends and acquaintances. Such oral communication usually went unrecorded; Deake's letter provides us with only one window into the "hidden transcripts" of resistance to power, a window into an alternate narrative to set beside Wheelock's *Narratives* of the Indian Charity-School that claim a "Plain and Faith-ful" evenhandedness.[13]

The last document of Hezekiah Calvin's life is a brief report from Wheelock that Calvin had been arrested for "forging a pass for a Negro" (47). Calvin did, then, put his literacy to use in his larger network of relations by appropriating the tool that Wheelock – his master and a slave master too – had given him. Calvin's aid to an escaped slave is also perhaps evidence of how he conceptualized his own relationship with Wheelock, a relationship Calvin did not feel he could terminate unilaterally: At least six times in writing he had sought a formal guarantee of his freedom from Wheelock, without which he felt he could only remain an "undutiful servant." Not only did Calvin seek to be freed from symbolic obligations "so many & in so high degree" (52) that he had deemed them too numerous to be counted, but he also no doubt wanted to be released from financial debt to Wheelock as well. Calvin sought, in effect, "free papers" to affirm the cancellation of all debts, just as a slave needed written confirmation of manumission.

If such a comparison seems extreme, we can consider that with his slaves Wheelock was known to be affectionate; he was even "on occasion ready to give a slave his freedom if the slave proved com-petent and law-abiding" (McCallum, *Eleazar Wheelock* 68). Whee-lock's Indian students, however, were granted freedom only if Wheelock deemed them selfish ingrates or incompetent drunkards

and apostates, and even then they had to run away to escape hu-
miliation and financial debts. Not one of Wheelock's Indian students
left Wheelock's service by mutual agreement. For example, when
Samson Occom, Wheelock's star student, broke off relations with
Wheelock because of Wheelock's misappropriation of funds that Occom had raised for Indian education, Wheelock laid the blame on
Occom. A more common situation was Samuel Ashpo's suspension
from his post for "Quarrellg, Indecent, unChristian behaviour"
(46). Only students who died very young, such as Joseph Wooley, or
those few who managed to negotiate a more independent position
in relation to Wheelock, such as Joseph Johnson and Tobias Shattock, remained in Wheelock's good graces at the end of their lives.

For using his literacy for his own ends Calvin was punished. It is
not known what his sentence was, but there are no further records
of his life. "I hear that poor Hezekiah Calvin has got into Prison at
Littleease . . . & that it is probable he will fare badly. I hope God will
humble him & do him Good by it" (47), Wheelock wrote, with his
usual habit of blaming all of his students' misfortunes on their inherent pride.[14] Pride may seem to be precisely what is in short supply
in Calvin's letters, which sound like the words of a man who has
barely been allowed to retain the minimum level of pride needed to
survive. But the pride Wheelock feared was an independence and
self-esteem that did not derive from or represent itself in letters directed to him. Wheelock encouraged his students to write letters in
order to reveal this thing he called "pride" so that it could be attacked and refuted point by point, but since he was not the only
source of his students' self-esteem and critical thought, and since the
letters were not their only avenue of communication, such contain-
ment was not possible. Paradoxically, only through mobilizing his
education in a way that suited him *and* got him thrown in prison
did Calvin free himself from Wheelock once and for all. Once Calvin's letters cease, we can read the silence they leave behind as Calvin's statement of independence from Wheelock.

III

In contrast to Hezekiah Calvin, David Fowler, a Montauk from Long
Island, was rather a teacher's pet at Wheelock's school. Whereas Calvin tended to sign his letters "your unworthy servant," sometimes
adding "undutiful and ungrateful" for good measure, Fowler's standard concluding phrase was "your affectionate though unworthy
pupil," which within the standard self-abasements of eighteenth-
century style is noticeably more confident. Fowler wrote to Wheelock

about a young woman he was courting, Amy, saying, "I believe I may venter to write my secrets to you as I wont to do. since I have so often seen and felt your tender Cares and Affections" (102). And when Fowler says of the Oneidas that "they are lazy and inhuman pack of Creatures as I ever saw in the World" (98), he is strategically invoking rhetoric that he might have heard used against himself in order to make himself seem more like Wheelock. "I wish I had some of Mrs. Wheelock's Bread & Milk, little sweet Cake and good boild Meat" (94), he complains. Fowler was also very adept at the necessary skills of flattery, as one of his outbursts of thankfulness – which shows not only abjection but also the pride of being distinguished from other Indians – demonstrates: "O that my Heart would melt with Gratitude both to God and Man for his wonderful goodness to me," he wrote to Wheelock, "for he has distinguishd me from many of my poor Brethren, in seting me up to be their Instructor" (106). In a deft detail or fortuitous slip of grammar, the conflation of God and "Man" through the pronoun "his" effectively conflates Wheelock and God.[15]

The earliest letter we have from Fowler, despite his favored status, is a confession. Several such confessions exist from several students, so Fowler's is only one example of Wheelock's undisguised use of his students' writing (or ventriloquisms of it) to enforce discipline and to establish his own credibility in the eyes of his superiors. Wheelock was certain that he and his students were always being watched from above, and he was as concerned about earthly benefactors as he was about Godly omniscience. In his *Narratives* he often reports the tactics of various enemies of the school, such as "letters sent abroad to be concealed from the injured party" (*Continuation*, 1771, 41), and he links political with spiritual troublemaking by tending to consider all interference as "the work of the great enemy indeed" (*Continuation*, 1765, 15). Thus, for reputation's sake as well as in support of religious rigor, Wheelock insisted that students' misdemeanors be fully and publicly reported and reprimanded. Discipline of other students was also an issue. Fowler's misstep was to leave the school without Wheelock's permission, an act of independence that could have sparked imitation in other students if it were not abjectly confessed, as the wording of the confession makes clear:

> I David Fowler acknowledge, that while M[r]. Wheelock was abroad on a Journey, I being in a bad State of Health and not able to pursue my Studies, and understanding that my aged Father was much in Debt and reduced to great Difficulty thereby which moved my Compassion towards him, and made

me earnestly Desire to contribue to his Releif which I supposed
I was able to do tho' my Indisposition was such as would not
allow me to prosecute my Studies. I went away without M^r
Wheelocks Leave, and continued absent till yesterday. In doing
which I acknowledge I acted Disorderly, and gave a bad Example to others which if they Should follow must Terminate
in the Disgrace and ruin of this School, and restrain charitably
Disposed Persons from further Expressions of their Charity towards it, or Endeavours to promote it.

I did not doubt but my Reasons were Such as Mr Wheelock
would have thought Sufficient if I had Submitted them to his
Judgment and Determination. and I acknowledge that in my
neglecting to do it as I did I have treated Mr Wheelock unwor-
thily. I ask his Forgiveness. . . . and promise by divine grace I
will walk orderly, and Shew proper Respect to the Authority of
the School for Time to come. And I earnestly Desire that my
late conduct may not encourage Others to do the like. . . . (87)

This is a dramatization of hierarchy, an unequivocal statement that
even if an Indian thinks through a problem and comes up with the
same conclusion as a white person, this response is not correct until
"submitted . . . to [the] Judgment and Determination" of the white
person. Wheelock and Fowler do not disagree here about Fowler's
action: This is not a confession of drunkenness or blasphemy or
fornication, but purely a matter of insubordination. It shows the
white teacher/Indian student relationship in its pure "disen-
chanted" form, to use Bourdieu's term.

Fowler's confession is in Wheelock's hand, which means either
that Wheelock wrote it or that he copied it. If Wheelock wrote the
confession, he went to great lengths to show both the validity and
humanity of Fowler's actions, as well as their inadmissibility: The
combination is strikingly sadistic, but it clarifies for us the fact that
insubordination was considered dangerous only if it occurred publicly. Because other students might have known of Fowler's initiative
in leaving the school, he had to make a public apology – to pay his
"symbolic taxes" through presentation of a "simulacrum of sincere
obedience" (58), as Scott puts it. If Fowler wrote the confession, we
might see the juxtaposition of justification of private motivations versus disavowal of public actions as recalcitrance: He was going along
with the required ritual of subordination, but not without justifying
his actions first. In either case, the writing down of Fowler's actions
was itself a punishment, reminding the confessor of the inferiority
of his judgment and causing him to relive the embarrassment of

misconduct reproved.[16] Most of the letters of Fowler and his classmates contain an element of confession or apology. Even when full
of good news they shared the performance element of the confession. Letters detailing conscientious work and Christian spirit were
the positive counterpart of the confessions, because when Wheelock
sent them or reports of them to Britain, the credit went to him or
to God, not to the students' own hard work and devotion. Thus these
letters also insisted on the students' inferior and dependent status.

The first serious break between Fowler and Wheelock took place
when Fowler bought wedding clothes for a price Wheelock thought
unreasonable. In August 1766, Fowler wrote from Lebanon – perhaps he wrote this statement down in order to give it more weight
or to give himself courage to be clear – revising his assessment of
their relationship:

> I think it very hard that I must be blam'd so much as I have
> been since my Return from home, and all for taking up those
> things at Mr Breeds, when I have Orders from Mr Wheelock to
> get them, for which I am now accounted a Devil or Proude as
> the Devil. . . . You know, Sir, I have always been governd and
> advis'd by you with all ease imaginable.
>
> This brings into my mind what Treatment I met since I came
> here. yea it is shameful, when I have been so faithful to you as
> if I was your Negro, yea I have almost kill'd myself in Labour-
> ing. . . . I am greiv'd that I have troubled you so much as I have.
> I am sorry those things were not denied me at first and then
> it would been allwell and easy before now – But asure you, Sir,
> you shall receive Payment from me yearly till every Farthing be
> paid, it shall not be said all that Money and Pains which was
> spent for David Fowler on Indian was for nought. I can get
> Payment as well as white Man. O Dear me! I cant say no more,
> I am
> your unworthy Servant David Fowler. (103)

Fowler had thought himself to be a son, as is evident in his earlier
letters ("I . . . ask a favour as a Child from kind Father or Benefactor" [102], he had written just three months earlier), but he found
out rather abruptly, as he was cheerily planning for his wedding,
that this was not at all the case. Of course, Fowler knew that he was
not in any irrevocable sense a son of Wheelock's; what he really
discovered was that Wheelock was unwilling to maintain the mutually
agreed-on *fiction* of the father–son relationship. Thus, it was Wheelock, not Fowler, who broke the "enchantment" of the relationship,
to use Bourdieu's term, by denying trust and breaking promises to

Fowler. But it was Fowler who then dared to "recognize" his relationship to Wheelock for what it was. Bourdieu writes that "if the system [of exchange of gifts and debts] is to work, the agents must not be entirely unaware of the truth of their exchanges . . . while at the same time they must refuse to know and above all to recognize it" (6). Fowler broke the compact in this letter when, like Hezekiah Calvin, he likened himself to a slave and then proceeded to bring the financial dimensions of the relationship into the open. Furthermore, by calling himself "David Fowler on Indian" and insisting that he could "get Payment as well as white Man," Fowler revealed his hitherto unspeakable knowledge of Wheelock's racist expectations that Indians could not and would not pay back debts.

For his part, Wheelock could not allow Fowler to reduce their relationship to financial terms. As James Scott explains, "any particular refusal to comply is not merely a tiny breach in a symbolic wall; it necessarily calls into question all the other acts that this form of subordination entails" (205). Not only did Wheelock need to make sure that his patrons always "misrecognized" his enterprise, which he preferred to present exclusively in terms of Christian love, but he also was caught up in the symbolic enchantment and too accustomed to thinking in terms of kinship and emotion to give up that discourse easily. Thus, his reply to Fowler, one of the few extant replies to his Indian students, masterfully attempts to restore the veneer to their relationship and vividly demonstrates what David Murray describes as "the way decorum, and all the arsenal of a Christian gentleman, can be used as a way of keeping social inferiors off balance and aware of their inferiority" (55). "Now David cons^r a little," Wheelock writes with a condescending weariness, "Is this Just comely and reasonable Treatment of me" (104); he goes on to reiterate, oozing sympathy and patience, his version of events, the fact that both of them have to be careful because "ye Eyes of all Europe & America w^{re} Upon y^o and me too," and his faith that if Fowler goes his own way, he will not "feal very Easie" (105) until he returns to the fold.

Although he continued to work for Wheelock for a short time after this dispute, Fowler was no longer more "Easie" within the relationship than Wheelock thought he would be without it. Like Calvin and other Indian students of Wheelock, Fowler received replies to his letters much less frequently than he expected. As schoolteacher to the Oneidas, while working and sharing a house with Samuel Kirkland – a non-Indian missionary who had also been a student of Wheelock's – Fowler was frustrated that Kirkland got more attention from Wheelock. He complained to Wheelock about it:

I take it very hard that I have not receiv'd one Line when others have received Folio's after Folio's. – But since I am forsaken – I now beg the Favour of you to bury my Name entirely and never mention it no more to any one abroad but bury into oblivion though you may hear of my good Behaviour my Managments and my Prospects and what soever you may hear from me that is worthy to be reported let it never go out off your Doors, – But I shall always remember my obligations to you till the Day my of Death – My Scholars learn very fast some of them have got to the twenty fourth Chapter of Matthew. (108)

We know that Wheelock required his students to report back to him from their posts; here we learn from Fowler that the students also required Wheelock to write to them. Fowler clearly regards Wheelock's silence as a breach of obligation ("But *I* shall always remember my obligations to *you* till the Day of my Death," he writes).[17]

Fowler knew that Wheelock needed model students to people the narratives he sent overseas to solicit funding; one of Fowler's letters written the previous spring apparently replies to Wheelock's request for a letter to be used for fund-raising, saying, "I am very sorry I cain't write you a Letter, which can be seen abroad. because Mr Kirtland is so much hurrid to get down: but he can give you a proper Idea of my School and my own Affairs" (102). By refusing Wheelock the right to write *about* him because he would not write *to* him, Fowler exposed the falsity of any ideal of dialogue that we might associate with letter writing. As we saw in Calvin's case, when Wheelock heard from a student, his reaction was often not to write back to that student, but rather to write to Britain or to non-Indian colleagues about that student. Thus, whereas Fowler needed letters from Wheelock for emotional and material reasons, Wheelock too not only gained gratitude and information from students' letters but also used them to raise his status as well as money – "symbolic capital" as well as "economic capital," in Bourdieu's terms – in Boston and on the other side of the Atlantic.

Hezekiah Calvin's repeated pleas for a written dismissal from Wheelock demonstrated that students needed to establish dialogue with Wheelock before they could reestablish unconstrained dialogue with their families. Likewise, the students' letters, particularly polite and correct letters such as David Fowler's, gave Wheelock grounds on which to establish a dialogue with England and Scotland. Fowler understood the dynamics of these interconnected dialogues. The *pièce de resistance* in the letter in which Fowler refuses Wheelock the privilege of displaying his successes is his offhand comment that "My Scholars learn very fast some of them have got to the twenty fourth

Chapter of Matthew," a remark that flaunts with devastating bravado Wheelock's dependence on such information.

Fowler soon felt the need to apologize for this brazen, and quite unenforceable, disciplining of Wheelock. The letter that follows on the heels of the challenge is an intense and abject apology. It does, however, register some sort of excuse through a complaint about Kirkland's authoritarianism – "As I am an Instructor I am able to act for myself, without having a master over me" – and an odd solution to the problem of his receiving no letters from Wheelock: Fowler asks Wheelock to ask Kirkland not to "mention one Syllable" about any letter he receives from Wheelock (109).

Forsaking Wheelock's design for Christianizing the Iroquois sometime in 1767, Fowler returned to Long Island to teach. In his last letter to Wheelock, written from Long Island, Fowler claims that Wheelock has not dealt with him justly in granting to Samuel Kirkland certain tools that were rightly Fowler's. He recalls that Wheelock had given the tools to him, quotes Wheelock's saying that "to give Gifts is like casting them into the Sea" (113), and then, having set up his argument, asks Wheelock how he could grant to Kirkland things he had previously given to another. Furthermore, Fowler says, he considers these things not to be gifts, but rather payment for "Hunger, Cold, Heat, and Weariness." He refuses to admit himself indebted to Wheelock and thus attacks a source of Wheelock's power over him. Fowler continues:

> Pray Sir, consider a little what I have done for Mr Kirtland. I helpd to build his House and cleared two Fields, all this work I give him freely, as you would give a meal of Victuals to a perishing man. (113)

A diligent schoolboy, Fowler has learned to imitate his schoolmaster, but now he has turned that mimicry to his own ends, imitating the condescending phrasing he had heard from Wheelock: "Now David consider a little" (104), he was told when he compared himself to Wheelock's slave and threatened to leave Wheelock, and "Pray Sir, consider a little," he writes back.

As Homi Bhabha points out, mimicry encouraged by the colonizer has its price. When the colonizer indulges a "desire for a reformed, recognizable Other, as *a subject of a difference that is almost the same, but not quite*" (126; Bhabha's emphasis), he allows for an "area between mimicry and mockery, where the reforming, civilizing mission is threatened by the displacing gaze of its disciplinary double" (127). Not only does Fowler appropriate Wheelock's rhetoric, he also mobilizes the dynamics of debts and gifts – usually controlled by Wheelock – to put himself in the superior position with respect to

Kirkland. The "perishing man" is now reduced to the pitiful place usually occupied by the "poor Indian," and the Indian is now in the place of a charitable benefactor. Wheelock could have considered Fowler's gifts of labor to Kirkland to be not outright gifts but payment of already incurred debts – a lowly Indian could not give gifts because he was infinitely indebted – and thus Fowler's equation of his own gift of labor with Wheelock's gift of tools would be an aggressive refusal of Wheelock's understanding of the symbolic economy between master and student. Fowler demands the right to "give . . . freely" and to assume the corresponding status and allegiance in symbolic exchange. "Now I call for my own property" (113), he writes.

At this point in the letter, Fowler abruptly switches style: The tone of the last two paragraphs is strikingly blunt and rushed compared to the measured cadences of the first two. "Dont fail of getting Money and send it down to Sister Occom. if you dont allow me but three Pound I shall be glad of it because I shall be troubled if I dont get the Money," he writes; "I write in utmost hast for my company are waiting." (113). We can read this sudden switch two ways: Either it was a conscious strategy of Fowler's to lay his requests out with absolute clarity and urgency after drawing Wheelock in with rhetorical mimicry and elegant argument, or else the switch was indeed the product of a moment of haste and desperation. If the latter is the case, the letter illuminates the material differential between Wheelock and Fowler: It contrasts the rhetoric of which Fowler was capable with the language afforded by his conditions as a poor and hungry man who had to get the letter out at the first opportunity because he desperately needed the money. However, the shift in style could also represent a shift in strategy on Fowler's part. By switching to a blunt and apparently careless style, Fowler "ruined" his letter so that Wheelock could not display it to benefactors as a fine example of his student's linguistic facility. Fowler flies in the face of "appropriate" rhetorical form and formal etiquette, which according to Bourdieu is the crux of the mutual misrecognition of the exchanges that constitute hierarchical relationships:

What distinguishes the gift from mere 'fair exchange' is the labour devoted to *form*: the presentation, the manner of giving, must be such, that the outward forms of the act present a practical denial of the content of the act, symbolically transmuting an interested exchange or a simple power relation into a relationship set up in due form for form's sake, i.e. inspired by pure respect for the customs and conventions recognized by the group. (194)

In the second half of his last letter to Wheelock, David Fowler refuses to follow the form of prior relations with Wheelock: He departs from decorum, and he abandons the obsequiousness usually attendant on requests for money. He has thus reduced Wheelock's generosity to self-interest and has reduced a father–son relationship to an undisguised power relationship.

No later letters from Fowler to Wheelock are extant, but Fowler continued his selective appropriation of tools and strategies taught him by Wheelock. He used his literacy to exchange fond family news and favors with his brother-in-law, Samson Occom, and he became a leading citizen of Brotherton, a Christian Indian settlement among the Oneidas in upstate New York. As it was conceived by Fowler and others, Brotherton was an attempt to use Christianity and European-style agriculture and town government to ensure the physical, cultural, and political survival of Indian people. Brotherton was a tricky almost-paradox in its strategy of establishing independence through imitation. But from their years with Wheelock, Indians such as Fowler were well practiced at the day-to-day maintenance of this strategy.[18]

IV

The letters of both David Fowler and Hezekiah Calvin demonstrate an elaborate combination of deference and defiance that is determined by the specific and immediate conditions of their writing as well as by the overall lines of their relationship with Wheelock. On first reading, Calvin's letters in particular may seem to present a picture of a pitiful Indian groveling at the feet of a white master. However, even moments of apparently transparent acquiescence in the letters may not be what they claim to be, since members of subordinate groups often learn "in situations short of those rare all-or-nothing struggles, to clothe their resistance and defiance in ritualisms of subordination that serve both to disguise their purpose and to provide them with a real route of retreat that may soften the consequences of a possible failure" (Scott 96). This is not to say that all obsequiousness in the letters is simply a disguise for real feelings hidden beneath the surface; the different levels of discourse all infuse and complicate each other so that, above all, the letters are characterized by ambivalence and ambidexterity between discourses. If we did not know that both Calvin and Fowler ultimately broke away from Wheelock's authority, we might not be able to read resistance in so much of their writing. Nor am I arguing that there was no option other than subtle resistance for Indians in the Northeast in the 1760s; on the contrary, of course, violence, retreat, legal action, and diplomacy were all options exercised by many tribes, at least through the American Revolution. The number of Indians "adopted" by Wheelock and his missionary colleagues was exceedingly small. Rather, I would suggest that it was the immediate availability of those other paths of action more dangerous to the colonizers that infused the textual resistance of Calvin and Fowler with real possibility, to Wheelock's great uneasiness and to their own advantage. They were thus in a position to negotiate within and without Wheelock's strictures in order to retain or regain some degree of autonomy from his authority.[19]

In closing, I should like to sketch out a more recent context for the reading of these letters – that is, the Dartmouth College Manuscript Series in 1932 – that sets my own reading in relief and leads to comparison between these letters and later texts produced by American Indians in collaboration with white Americans. James Dow McCallum edited the *Letters of Eleazar Wheelock's Indians* – the possessive here speaks volumes about McCallum's approach – as part of a series of books devoted to illuminating Dartmouth's early history. The first few sentences of his introduction show with breathtaking clarity the kind of response he expected the letters to evoke:

> In this volume the Indian scholars who attended Moor's Charity School during the lifetime of Eleazar Wheelock have been allowed to speak for themselves. At times the editor has been obliged to prompt them by means of footnotes, but his ambition has been to gather these contemporaries of Pontiac around a council fire (which to them would have been quite novel), that they might by themselves confess their sins, carry on their courtships, and express their religious convictions. Many of the letters are quaint; some are humorous; a few are of importance historically – all are misspelled. The reader who is not accustomed to such material will be amused at first as though he were watching some captive animal performing his tricks. . . . (11)

This passage epitomizes white attitudes toward Indian writing over the whole span of time between the writing of the letters – which are among the earliest preserved texts actually written down by Indians themselves – and the era of their republication, another period of intense interest in Indian writing. The condescending magnanimity of McCallum's first statement that "Eleazar Wheelock's Indians" have "been allowed to speak for themselves" comes up again and again in white authors' or editors' or amanuenses' commentary on Indian texts. In fact, there was very little charity involved in letting Hezekiah Calvin, David Fowler, and their classmates speak for themselves through their letters: Arnold Krupat, David Murray, and other scholars of Native American writing have noted that as the Indians began to "vanish" by massacre, disease, displacement, or ideological erasure, there arose a great demand for their reappearance on paper, and a special premium was placed on having them address a white audience directly. As Krupat explains it, white guilt demanded statements of forgiveness and justification from representatives of Indians who had already been made to "vanish," and "the production of an Indian's own statement of his inevitable disappearance required that the Indian be represented as speaking in his own voice" (35).

Although Krupat is speaking of nineteenth-century Indian autobiographies, the need of white Americans to hear American Indians themselves say that their demise was inevitable is also manifested in autobiographies as late as those written in the 1930s, such as John Neihardt's rendition of Black Elk's autobiography; these texts played a supporting role within the dominant ideology even while representing resistance to and subversion of that ideology.[20] In a move ideologically analogous to Neihardt's transformation of Black Elk's narrative into an elegy for a lost race, McCallum attempts to contain any critical or disruptive content in the letters of Wheelock's students by reducing the letters to a token of his own generosity. As Wheelock sought to subject his Indian students through the gift of Christianity and the corresponding debt they would incur to him, McCallum offers permission to speak and invokes the debt of gratitude in order to permit him (or his ideal readers) to discount as ungrateful any defiance the letters may bear.

McCallum's offer of freedom of speech to the Indian letter writers, carefully circumscribed as it is, is immediately utterly undermined by his perversely cute notion of being "obliged to prompt them" from some hundred and fifty years' distance and by his metaphor (inappropriate, as he acknowledges) of having them sit around a council fire and chat with each other. In trying to locate the source of McCallum's burdensome obligation, we can rule out David Fowler, certainly, as well as the other students who asked that their writing not be made public. For example, Joseph Johnson explicitly requested confidentiality: "please sir to overlook my hast, and the many Blunders which I suppose are in this paper. I have no time to write it over or correct it. dont Expose it. so I remain your Humble Servant" (133). McCallum's sense of obligation comes, rather, from his own desire to enhance the importance of his editorial role and from the Dartmouth College Manuscript Series' inclination to uphold a rosy view of Dartmouth's history in Indian education.[21] Furthermore, we might say that McCallum is ideologically obliged to confirm that, as he puts it, "the Indian . . . is a dullard, often a drunkard, an unwilling pupil . . . a consumptive, simple, and simple-minded" (11), even when educated and Christianized. Thus, like Wheelock, McCallum implies that his primary obligation is to the Indians, when in fact he is invoking this obligation in order to fulfill other obligations to various networks of institutional, racial, and personal politics.

In later texts produced by whites and Indians in collaboration, similar distortion of the agency and obligations involved in the production of the work often takes place. A white person in charge of publication or dissemination can make an Indian text into something very much like a confession by remaining silent about his or her involvement in the material, when in fact the Indian who spoke or wrote it meant it to be an argument, a meditation, part of a dialogue, or a protest. I suggest that at least for the purposes of comparison we may take the letters between Wheelock and his students, as a whole, to be a collaborative text. From these letters through autobiographies of Black Hawk, Black Elk, Sam Blowsnake, Don Talayesva,²² and so on, white participants have effaced their own presence while exercising considerable influence over the material by asking questions, editing, writing responses, or inventing. Like Wheelock, who used his students' writing to raise his own status in the eyes of benefactors and peers, the journalists, poets, and anthropologists who have "collected" so many Indian autobiographies are being disingenuous if they claim that their only obligation is to their Indian collaborator.

Many contemporary cross-cultural collaborative projects are much more self-conscious about the interplay of differing or conflicting obligations and intentions, and much work is currently attempting to restore the context of production to early Indian writing produced with white mediation or collaboration. David Murray writes that

> only in this way, paradoxically, does the subject have a chance of not becoming totally object, since what we then become aware of is the interplay of two or more voices. If the white voice which is asking the questions and eliciting and guiding the story by means of them is suppressed in the final text, the effect is not, as often claimed, to allow the speaking subject to appear in his own right, but to give a false, because incomplete, account of the production of the text. (67)

The letters of Hezekiah Calvin, David Fowler, and other Indians to Eleazar Wheelock will not let us forget the imbalanced dialogue of which they are a part, and thus they are a valuable companion piece for later collaborative texts that may be less obviously askew. Even when Wheelock absents himself from dialogue with the students, we are constantly aware, through their demands or mimicry or argument, of his presence. Calvin's and Fowler's letters simultaneously demonstrate the tangible reality of constraints on the conditions of production and a determination to resist those constraints. And they require readings in which "resistance" and "subordination" are understood not as diagnostic absolutes, but as relational elements of cultural change only obliquely represented in the written record.[23]

Notes

1. Wheelock educated girls as well as boys at his school, but he trained the girls to be not schoolteachers or missionaries themselves but helpmates to the male graduates. For a discussion of these female students, few of whose writings survive, see Szasz, chapter 9. Wheelock also educated non-Indian boys; many of their writings can be found in the Wheelock Papers at Dartmouth College.

2. McCallum lists 89 names of Indians who attended the Charity-School during Wheelock's lifetime but notes that Macclure, Wheelock's first biographer and a student at the school, puts the number at 150 (298). Of the total, many students left the school for personal, medical, or political reasons after only a short stay, and many died extremely young.

3. Most students are represented by only one or two letters or confessions; Joseph Johnson and Samson Occom are the only profuse letter writers besides Hezekiah Calvin and David Fowler. Johnson's letters span over ten years and are especially rich in their manipulation of the idea of the "poor Indian" and in their depiction of Johnson's development from wayward student to important Indian leader. Samson Occom was Wheelock's first and best-documented Indian student; for biographical information and selected letters, see the works of Blodgett, Love, and Richardson.

4. All quotations from the letters of Wheelock and his Indian students are from McCallum's edition of the *Letters;* I give only page numbers. I have not changed the spelling or punctuation.

5. The mother, Sarah Simon (the elder), must have heard Hezekiah Calvin's claim that her daughter and another female student had "been kept as close to work, as if they were your Slaves. . . . Jeams Simon is to be Bound to a Farmer" (65), and she probably also heard her other son's complaint that "if we poor Indians Shall work as much as to pay for our learning, we Can go Some other pace as good as here for learning" (221).

6. Contrary to the settler mythology, Indians treated captive children well, formally adopting them in the place of those who died from disease or warfare. Indians were even known to adopt missionaries: Samuel Kirkland, a white student of Wheelock's, remembered Sir William Johnson

telling him, when he arrived to establish a mission among the Senecas in 1764, that "if I was cordially received by the Seneka's, I should in a week or two be *adopted* in some one of the principal families and that I must pay particular attention to my new relations. It would give me the liberty of applying to them for any thing I wanted" (*Journals* 4). Kirkland had to obey his adoptive Indian father's counsel in return for protection from hostile factions in the community. Thus, the Indian parents' comparison of residential education and captivity did not necessarily carry the same violent valence for them as it would have for Wheelock. On the other hand, Indians were indeed sometimes captured – literally rather than metaphorically – to be educated: Students at the College of William and Mary in the early eighteenth century were forcibly held in order to ensure the peaceful behavior of their kin (Axtell 191). Much later in the history of Indian education, the first Indian students to be admitted to Hampton School in the late nineteenth century were prisoners of war.

7. Bourdieu is speaking here of precapitalist formations, such as rural Algeria; he is also speaking of authority structures within one society, whereas I am discussing the interaction between two societies. I would argue, however, that the early colonial situation in America can be illuminated by his paradigm since white settlers clearly desired authority over Indians but were not at all secure, and continually had to reinforce their position by a combined strategy of economic violence (land grabs), physical violence, and symbolic violence (encouragement of dependency relationships through religious conversion).

8. In his article about the diaries of the Virginia planter Colonel Landon Carter (written between 1752 and 1778), Rhys Isaac analyzes the ways in which slaves took advantage of Carter's inconsistent deployment of two models of authority – the patriarchy of governance versus a more sentimental paternalism – to gain concessions from their master. Isaac argues that "the plantation organization was a framework . . . within which a struggle for advantage was relentlessly pursued" (287) and thus finds even in slavery a space for power for the slave; his study serves as a companion piece for my analysis of similar dynamics between Wheelock and his students.

9. Wheelock's Indian students have a few pages of fame in Louise Erdrich and Michael Dorris's novel, *The Crown of Columbus*, when the narrator, Vivian, a professor at Dartmouth College, comes across their letters and declares the students "totally brainwashed" (137). As should be evident, I do not concur with this reading. However, academic studies of Indian education have presented such a judgment of educated Indians. In his survey of the colonizing function of American Indian education from the early 1600s to the 1980s, Jorge Noriega writes that "Indian students targeted for training in the early stages of U.S. colonialist education were used essentially as a virus, a medium through which to hurry along a calculated process of sociocultural decay 'from within' " (379). Although this description may be apt when applied to the coercive and widespread Indian education of the nineteenth century and later, one

38   LAURA J. MURRAY

might give the objects of colonizing education more credit for independent motives. The classmates of Fowler and Calvin who became prominent diplomats or leaders – Tobias Shattock, Joseph Johnson, Joseph
Brant, and Samson Occom, for example – came to Wheelock as agents
seeking tools (literacy and knowledge of the colonizer's culture) to use
to their own ends; I would like to avoid the lack of agency that the
metaphor "virus" may suggest.

10. Not unlike his students, Wheelock often wrote because he had to: His
Narratives and many of his letters were written to fulfill obligations to
the commissioners and their funding sources. Samuel Kirkland, a white
missionary who had studied with Wheelock, kept a journal because he
was required to by his employers. He recalled in later years that "reviewing, correcting, and transcribing these documents . . . is certainly an
irksome & disagreeable task, as it affords very little intellectual improvement of the understanding or pleasure to the heart. . . . Yet I am conscious it is a part of my *duty*" (*Journals* 43). All in all, then, the writing
of the white missionaries was part of a larger economy of obligation.

11. Wheelock taught his students Latin, Greek, Hebrew, and English, but
Calvin learned soon enough that the neglect of his own language and
other languages that he would need among the Iroquois left him unable
to communicate with people at home and in his work. Calvin's thoughts
of "home," expressed so passionately in his letters, must have been intensified by this sense of loss.

12. The word "uneasy" comes up in other students' writing as well. Sarah
Simon (the younger), for example, writes, "my being So unwell it make
me unesa" (228), and her letter dramatizes this uneasiness in its many
"buts" and its convoluted syntax as she tries to get Wheelock to permit
her to leave the school.

13. James Scott would make an even larger claim for Calvin's criticism of
Wheelock: "as long as the elite treat such assaults on their dignity as
tantamount to open rebellion," he writes, "symbolic defiance and rebellion do amount to the same thing" (196). I would not equate these
acts, but considering that Edward Deake clearly did consider Calvin's
intercourse with the Narragansetts to be threatening, the importance of
spheres of communication among the Indians that allowed Calvin to
think beyond the strictures of his relationship with Wheelock is clear.

14. Axtell points out that "When Jacob Wooley, a twenty-year-old Delaware,
got drunk, threw a clench-fisted tantrum, cursed God, and tried to throw
his bed out the window, Wheelock judged him not culturally disoriented
or personally frustrated but simply guilty of 'Pride of Heart' " (211).
Confessions of misdemeanors of all sorts, often written by Wheelock and
signed by the student in question, always include abject apologies for
"Pride." On the other hand, Wheelock allowed himself considerably
more pride than he allowed his students; in his *Narratives* he alternates
between giving all the credit for the successes of the school to God and
taking some of it himself.

15. Wheelock's students compare, conflate, or juxtapose God with Whee-

lock in their letters, but Wheelock's dependence on British benefactors and colleagues makes this association seem ironic as well as inappropriate. Whereas God, according to the *Confession of the Faith,* "is alone and unto himself all sufficient, nor standing in need of any creatures that he hath made" (31), Wheelock did stand in need of the "creatures" he had made. Not only reputation was at stake; Samson Occom, Wheelock's first Indian student, raised the money on which Dartmouth College was built, and Axtell claims (204) that Wheelock was prompted to open the Charity-School by a need to supplement his minister's salary.

16. The confessions merit more attention. For example, Jacob Wooley's confession is an obsessively vivid reenactment of Wooley's violent display of temper. Wheelock forced Wooley to describe his own actions from the point of view of a judge: The disgust Wooley was forced to display toward himself is excruciating when compared with the disgust and anger that he must have already felt in order to behave so violently in the first place (254; see also note 14). Further study of these confessions might reveal whether they can be considered, in Scott's terms, "rituals of subordination" or whether they had more profound effects on the subjectivities of the students.

17. Other students' letters indicate similar expectations: Joseph Johnson wrote to Wheelock that "it is not only your Order, but my Indispensable Duty to write to you at every opportunity" (127). Sometimes, however, Johnson emphasized *his* duty in order to allude to Wheelock's neglect of his reciprocal duty, as did Jacob Wooley in his correspondence with Samuel Kirkland (*Journals* 17).

18. Fowler's letters to Occom are at the Connecticut Historical Society. The most complete account of the Brotherton settlement is in Love; see also Kirkland.

19. Although by the late eighteenth century the New England tribes were no longer a serious military threat, they still pursued land claims that, if won, would have caused major dislocation and expense to the colonies (see Baker, chapter II). And the Iroquois were still a formidable adversary. In their considerable efforts to maintain Iroquois neutrality or alliance during the American Revolution, colonial governments called on several occasions on Wheelock's students David Fowler, Jacob Fowler, and Joseph Johnson (see Love). Joseph Brant, another of Wheelock's students, became a leader of the British-allied Mohawks.

20. Michael Staub puts Black Elk's autobiography and other Native American texts of the 1930s in the context of the politically progressive documentary trend of this period.

21. In his Foreword to the *Letters,* Dartmouth College Manuscript Series's general editor, Leon B. Richardson, claims that "The history of Dartmouth College, during its period of inception and during the earlier years of its existence, differs markedly from that of its contemporary institutions" since Dartmouth was "founded primarily to promote the christianizing of the Indians." This is a myth, since in fact the founding of Dartmouth marked the waning of Wheelock's interest in educating

Indians. Despite the image of an Indian man bearing a book on its crest, Dartmouth's commitment to Native American education is equivocal: Money raised by Samson Occom for the education of Indians was absorbed by the Dartmouth budget, but Dartmouth graduated only three Indians in the eighteenth century and eight in the nineteenth (Axtell 215).

22. Black Hawk originally dictated his autobiography to Antoine Le Clair, who translated it and passed it on to John B. Patterson for editing and rewriting. *Black Elk Speaks* was substantially changed by its editor, John G. Neihardt (see DeMallie). Paul Radin published *Crashing Thunder: The Autobiography of an American Indian* as an autobiography of Sam Blowsnake, but it is in fact a compilation of writings and oral testimony given by both Sam and his brother Jasper (Krupat 95–106). Like Blowsnake, Don Talayesva wrote down many of his reminiscences (some 8,000 pages of diary, in fact); what is presented to the reader of *Sun Chief* is a highly edited selection of this writing (Brumble 106). Talayesva is particularly interesting in comparison with Fowler and Calvin because of the way his writing was solicited and directed by the anthropologist Leo Simmons. See Krupat and Brumble for discussion of further examples of collaborations misrepresented by white editors.

23. I would like to thank my writing group at Cornell, as well as Annette Jaimes and Katheryn Rios, for incisive and wide-ranging comments on earlier drafts of this essay.

Works Cited

Axtell, James. *The Invasion Within: The Contest of Cultures in Colonial North America*. New York: Oxford University Press, 1985.

Baker, Henry A. *History of Montville, Connecticut*. Hartford, 1896.

Bhabha, Homi. "Of Mimicry and Man: The Ambivalence of Colonial Discourse." *October* 28 (1984): 125–33.

Blodgett, Harold. *Samson Occom*. Hanover, NH: Dartmouth College Publications, 1935.

Bourdieu, Pierre. *Outline of a Theory of Practice*, trans. Richard Nice. Cambridge: Cambridge University Press, 1977.

Brumble, H. David, III. *American Indian Autobiography*. Berkeley: University of California Press, 1988.

Church of Scotland. *The Confession of Faith, the Larger and Shorter Catechisms, with the Scripture-Proofs at Large . . . of Public Authority in the Church of Scotland*. Edinburgh: 1756.

DeMallie, Raymond J. *The Sixth Grandfather: Black Elk's Teachings Given to John G. Neihardt*. Lincoln: University of Nebraska Press, 1984.

Erdrich, Louise, and Michael Dorris. *The Crown of Columbus*. New York: HarperCollins, 1991.

Isaac, Rhys. "Communication and Control: Authority, Metaphors and Power Contests on Colonel Landon Carter's Virginia Plantation, 1752–1778."

Rites of Power: Symbolism, Ritual, and Politics Since the Middle Ages, ed. Sean Wilentz. Philadelphia: University of Pennsylvania Press, 1985.

Jackson, Donald, ed. *Ma-Ka-Tai-Me-She-Kia-Kiak: Black Hawk, An Autobiography.* 1833. Rpt. Urbana: University of Illinois Press, 1955.

Krupat, Arnold. *For Those Who Come After: A Study of Native American Autobiography.* Berkeley: University of California Press, 1985.

Love, William DeLoss. *Samson Occom and the Christian Indians of New England.* Chicago, 1899.

McCallum, James Dow, ed. *The Letters of Eleazar Wheelock's Indians.* Hanover, NH: Dartmouth College Publications, 1932.

Eleazar Wheelock, Founder of Dartmouth College. Hanover, NH: Dartmouth College Publications, 1939.

Murray, David. *Forked Tongues: Speech, Writing, and Representation in North American Indian Texts.* Bloomington: Indiana University Press, 1991.

Neihardt, John G., ed. *Black Elk Speaks.* 1932. Rpt. Lincoln: University of Nebraska Press, 1979.

Noriega, Jorge. "American Indian Education in the U.S.: Indoctrination for Subordination to Colonialism." *State of Native America,* ed. Annette Jaimes. Boston: Southend Press, 1992: 371–402.

Pilkington, Walter, ed. *The Journals of Samuel Kirkland.* Clinton, NY: Hamilton College, 1980.

Radin, Paul. *Crashing Thunder.* 1926. Lincoln: University of Nebraska Press, 1983.

Richardson, L. B. *An Indian Preacher in England.* Hanover, NH: Dartmouth College Publications, 1933.

Scott, James C. *Domination and the Arts of Resistance: Hidden Transcripts.* New Haven, CT: Yale University Press, 1990.

Simmons, Leo, ed. *Sun Chief: The Autobiography of a Hopi Indian.* 1942. Rpt. New Haven, CT: Yale University Press, 1974.

Staub, Michael. "(Re)Collecting the Past: Writing Native American Speech." *American Quarterly* 43.3 (1991): 425–56.

Szasz, Margaret Connell. *Indian Education in the American Colonies, 1607–1783.* Albuquerque: University of New Mexico Press, 1988.

Wheelock, Eleazar. *A plain and faithful Narrative of the Original Design, Rise, Progress and present State of the Indian Charity-School at Lebanon, in Connecticut.* Boston: Richard and Samuel Draper, 1763.

A Continuation of the Narrative . . . From the Year 1768 to the Incorporation of it with Dartmouth-College, and Removal and Settlement of it in Hanover, in the Province of New Hampshire. 1771.

A Continuation of the Narrative . . . With a Dedication to the Honorable Trust in London . . . Hartford: Ebenezer Watson, 1775.

3

"(I SPEAK LIKE A FOOL BUT I AM CONSTRAINED)"

SAMSON OCCOM'S SHORT NARRATIVE AND ECONOMIES OF THE RACIAL SELF

DANA D. NELSON

Samson Occom, Mohegan, Methodist convert, Indian missionary, and founder of Brothertown, is perhaps best remembered for his role in raising the funds that made Dartmouth College's charter possible. His most famous work, "Sermon on the Execution of Moses Paul," has been paid sporadic attention by scholars of American and American Indian literature. Two Dartmouth biographers have made use of his diaries, though lamenting the sparsity of Occom's entries (e.g., Blodgett 32; see also Love). His hymns have been paid less notice and his autobiographical narratives virtually none. Before the publication of the *Heath Anthology of American Literature,* few students of American literature had occasion to become familiar with any works by Occom, whose 1768 autobiographical narrative and 1771 sermon on the execution of Moses Paul are reprinted there.[1]

Occom's *Short Narrative of My Life* consists of some ten manuscript pages from the Dartmouth archives. On its own, but even more particularly in contrast to other early American autobiographical narratives, it suggests the arbitrariness and even violence entailed in early American constructions of subjectivity/self. His text allows us to see how, as Henry Louis Gates, Jr., puts it, "colonialism inscribes itself on the colonized" (469). At the same time, it can help us to question the depoliticized logic of the proprietal self figured positively (even mythically) in figures like Franklin. It traces the unacknowledged connections between the individual, property, colonialism, and "race" in early America's Protestant culture, thus also suggesting avenues for inquiry into how colonialism inscribes itself on the *colonizer.*

In his *Short Narrative,* Occom essays to counter essentialist and hierarchical notions of difference with his own abilities as translator. He counters, in other words, repressive and oppressive mono-logic with his own expertise in and plea for dialogue/dialogic, replacing a model of deficiency/sufficiency with one of equivalence. Reading his *Short Narrative* on its own terms offers a way to read it as a text that is literally *about* finding a multiculturalist vision of America.

One of the implications of the multiculturalist vision – both for Occom and for us now – is that we should not read any text as though it can be self-sustaining. For that reason, I want to contextualize carefully my reading of Occom's work. In what follows, I first analyze the biographical events that surround Occom's composition of his *Short Narrative*. I trace out what Occom stood for to Wheelock and the Christian colonial mission to reveal one of the primary challenges facing Occom in his autobiographical project. Last, I analyze the strong critique of the colonial missionary system suggested in Occom's narrative. The fact that this critique is not fully evident at first reading is a product of both the reader's incomplete understanding of the cultural complexities of Occom's positioning and the liminal consciousness that those complexities evoked for Occom. As Jean and John Comaroff argue:

> Between the conscious and the unconscious lies the most critical domain of all . . . for the analysis of colonialism and resistance. It is the realm of partial recognition, of inchoate awareness, of ambiguous perception, and sometimes, of creative tension. (I: 29)

The confusion manifest in Occom's 1768 narrative, I argue, is a creative confusion, gesturing toward a self-affirming articulation of identity that would later be evidenced more explicitly in Occom's actions toward Wheelock and the Christian missionary project.

I

Samson Occom was born in 1723 in the town of Mohegan, Connecticut. This village was the primary residence of the Mohegan people, the population of which had been reduced by disease and colonial military attack to a number that is estimated at between 350 (Peyer, "Samson Occom" 209) and 750 (DeForest 324; cf. McCallum 39) at the time of Occom's birth. Occom was descended on his mother's side from the renowned Mohegan leader Uncas. His mother, Sarah, was a Christian convert; it was she who made arrangements with Eleazar Wheelock to obtain an English education for her son. But throughout Occom's childhood, she and her husband, Joshua, led a traditional "commuting"[2] Mohegan lifestyle, combining hunting, fishing, and gathering with regular returns to the central village.

As the Great Awakening of the 1740s swept the northeast, the Mohegans were visited by revivalist missionaries. Occom responded to the call: At the age of seventeen he made, as he puts it, "a Discovery of the way of Salvation through Jesus Christ" that gave him "Serenity and Pleasure of Soul" (*Narrative* 731). At this time, Occom felt impelled to learn how to read so that he might instruct his "poor Kindred" in the ways of his newly discovered religion (731).

Occom's religious awakening did not divert him from attending to the political issues that concerned the Mohegan community. He was appointed, along with his father, as a councillor for the Mohegan on July 1, 1742, at the age of nineteen (Szasz 196). At the same time, then, that he was seeking a Christian and English education, he assumed a position of leadership among the Mohegans. As he became deeply involved in the study of Christian religion, he maintained a steady involvement in Mohegan political issues, especially in what is known as the "Mason Controversy."

The Mason Controversy had divided the Mohegan people since 1640, when the Mohegan sachem Uncas somewhat ambiguously conveyed to the British all his rights "to land that doth belong, or ought of right to belong, to me, by what name soever it be called, whether Mohegan, Yomtake, Aquapankuks, Porkstannocks, Wippawocks, Massapeake or any other," save for the land that he cultivated for his own use, in exchange for "five and a half yards Trucking Cloth, with Stockings, and other things, as a gratuity" (Blodgett 74–5; Caulkins 266–70).[3] In 1659 Uncas transacted a new deed for his lands with Major John Mason,[4] which formed the basis for a dispute that arose in 1705 between a number of the Mohegan people siding with the Mason heirs and an opposing group of Mohegans who sided with the Connecticut colony. The former contended that Uncas had conveyed the lands to Mason in trust as a preemptive move that would disallow seizure by Connecticut settlers. Connecticut, on the other hand, argued that Mason had received the lands in a deed of sale in his capacity as an agent for the colony (Blodgett 74–7; Love 119–29).

Occom's involvement on behalf of the Mason heirs surfaced repeatedly throughout his missionary career. In 1743, a year after being appointed councillor by Ben Uncas, he cosigned a formal letter to the colony of Connecticut regarding Mohegan interests in the case. In 1765, the Connecticut Board of Correspondents would require Occom to apologize formally for his involvement with the affair, threatening him with the revocation of his ministerial licenses. Further, Occom's missionary supporters in America compelled him to promise not to testify on behalf of the Mason interest during his

London trip – a promise he apparently did not keep (Blodgett 79–80, 102–4; Richardson, 28–9).

When in the late 1760s the case was decided in favor of the colony, Occom would describe the defeat as one significant to the political future of the Mohegans:

> I am afraid the poor Indians will never stand a good chance with the English in their land controversies, because they are very poor, they have no money. Money is almighty now-a-days, and the Indians have no learning, no wit, no cunning: the English have all. (quoted in Blodgett 77)[5]

If Occom's evangelical interest in the spiritual condition of Native peoples was a continuous thread of his life, so too was his concern for their economic and political security.[6]

Occom's British benefactors considered his steady interest in the Mason Controversy as a nuisance to, perhaps even in conflict with, his work on behalf of the Christian mission. Although Occom's involvement is typically treated as being tangential to his conversion and his role in raising funds for Wheelock's charity school, it seems entirely plausible that they were connected in Occom's mind, as each related to the future of the Mohegans and other Indian peoples. I am not suggesting that his conversion was not a true one; there is no reason to doubt Occom's sincere embrace of Christianity.[7] But we should not overlook how the spiritual and political converge in his actions. His Christian conversion could have been as much a politically strategic choice as a private decision (our common assumption about religious conversion), made as part of a complex and calculated response to dwindling Mohegan populations, political power, and land entitlements.

Occom has not left much specific commentary on his motives for conversion. We know that he began studying with the Rev. Eleazar Wheelock in 1743, a year after his appointment as a Mohegan councillor. Within four years, though impeded by bad health and poor vision, he had proved a very successful student – so much so, in fact, that Wheelock decided to found an Indian charity school based on the promise of Occom's performance. While Occom labored for the next fifteen years as a missionary to the Oneidas and as a teacher in the Long Island village of Montauk, Wheelock founded and gradually expanded his ambitions for Moor's Indian Charity School.

Wheelock's central scheme was to educate Indians to serve as missionaries to Indian peoples, as Occom currently was doing. Not only was this project more efficient, it would be less expensive. As Wheelock argued in 1763, Indian missionaries would be "at least four

times as serviceable" among their own people and "may be supported with less than half the Expense, that will be necessary to
support an *Englishman*" (quoted in Szasz 235; Wheelock's emphasis). Wheelock had attempted since the mid-1750s to secure a patent
for the charity school, which would guarantee him the funds that he
needed for both the project and his own livelihood. He was rebuffed
first by England and then by Connecticut.[8]

Thus, in 1764 Wheelock began planning to send Occom to England and Scotland to raise the money for his project. Occom had just
concluded a successful mission to the Oneidas, disrupted by the outbreak of the Pontiac war. Following a suggestion from George Whitefield, the famous revivalist Methodist minister, Wheelock decided that
Occom was the best means for making his own case overseas. Opposition to these plans surfaced, however, from the Boston Commission
of the London Society, which had for several years provided some financial support for Occom's work. Annoyed that Wheelock was apparently taking sole credit for Occom's successes, they concluded that
he was preempting credit more generally for Indian mission work.
Their response was a campaign to defame *Occom*, spreading rumors
that he was not an authentic convert or even a Mohegan Indian (Blodgett 84–7).[9] Despite their opposition, Wheelock went forward with his
plans, and Occom set sail with Nathaniel Whitaker for what would be
a two-and-a-half-year trip on December 23, 1765.

Notably, both ends of Occom's London trip are marked by the
production of an autobiographical narrative, the first one page long,
the second ten.[10] Both documents were framed to quell doubts
about his authenticity as an Indian and a Christian convert, the two
roles he was sent to England to represent. As part of his fund-raising,
Occom preached widely throughout England, Scotland, and Ireland.
He met church dignitaries and was even approached by the Epis-
copalians, who offered to ordain him (he refused). He created
enough of a sensation to be lampooned in London theaters, an
event that ironically highlighted the theatricality of his own role in
the fund-raising mission. He was made into – as Occom puts it – a
"gazing stocke, yea even a Laughing Stocke" (1771 letter to Wheelock; quoted in Blodgett 123).

We can only guess from fragments of his writing how Occom felt
about his experiences in England. He was without doubt made to
juggle impossible demands. In addition to combatting suspicions
about his Indian "nature" and Christian "character" from Wheelock's enemies and having constantly to present those culturally opposing entities to his audiences, he was further besieged by his
ostensible allies. Whitaker and Wheelock dosed him with steady

warnings against developing "that Indian distemper, *Pride,*" as he associated with the British (quoted in Blodgett 95; Wheelock's emphasis). Little wonder that Occom writes with what sounds like exhausted resignation halfway through the trip:

> if I was not fully Persuaded and Asure'd that this work was of god, and I had an undoubted Call of god to Come over into this Country, I wou'd not have come over, like a fool as I did, without any Countenance from our Board, but I am Will Still to be a fool for Christ Sake – this Eleviats my Heart amidst all my Burdens, and Balances all my Sorrows at Times, or enables me to bear my Trials, that I am in the way of my Duty, and the Lord uses me in any Shape to promote his kingdom in the World. (quoted in Richardson 222)

This passage suggests Occom's pain at his objectification ("the Lord uses me in any Shape") and his implicitly contrasting desire to be regarded not as a "fool" but rather, as he was apparently by John Thornton, a human and an equal (cf. Blodgett 113–37). It seems quite possible that by the time of his second autobiographical narration, written September 17, 1768 (Peyer, 1982b, 12), garnering such respect more widely might have been one of Occom's primary aims.

By the accounts of his contemporaries and his biographers, Occom did in fact return from his British tour a changed man.[11] After years of serving at Wheelock's beck and call, he refused to answer Wheelock's almost immediate demands that he resume missionary work among the Iroquois, choosing instead to attend to his ill wife and his family's impoverished condition. He also refused to answer Wheelock's charges that he had misappropriated funds.[12] This new pattern of defiance is most clearly evidenced, though, in his angry letters charging that *Wheelock* was misappropriating the funds Occom had worked so hard to raise by virtually abandoning the Indian charity project and focusing his energies on the newly chartered Dartmouth College instead:

> I am very jealous that instead of your Semenary Becoming alma Mater, she will be too alba mater to Suckle the Tawnees, for She is already aDorned up too much like the Popish Virgin Mary. She'll be Naturally ashamed to Suckle the Tawnees for she is already equal in Power, Honor and Authority to any College in Europe, I think your College has too much Worked by Grandeur for the Poor Indians . . . your having so many White Scholars and so few or no Indian Scholars gives me great Discouragement – I verily thought once that your Institution was

Intended Purely for the poor Indian. (July 24, 1771; quoted in Blodgett 122–3)

Occom frames these charges against Wheelock three years after the 1768 autobiographical narrative. By reading that narrative in the context of his evolving relationship with Wheelock and more generally with the Christian colonial mission, we can see how Occom begins to articulate a position of greater authority that eventually enables him not only to assert himself against Wheelock but also to divert his energies away from the British-managed mission, directing them instead to his own goals for Brothertown. As Jean and John Comaroff observe in their study of the African colonial mission:

> Just as technologies of control run the gamut from overt coercion to implicit persuasion, so modes of resistance may extend across a similarly wide spectrum. At one end is the organized protest, explicit moments and movements of dissent that are easily recognizable as 'political' by western lights. At the other are gestures of tacit refusal and iconoclasm, gestures that sullenly and silently contest the forms of an existing hegemony. For the most part, however, the ripostes of the colonized hover in the space between the tacit and the articulate, the direct and the indirect. And far from being a mere reflection – or a reflex expression – of historical consciousness, these acts are a practical means of *producing* it. (I: 39)

It is in this light – as an instance of productive critical articulation – that I will read Occom's narrative in Section III.

Wheelock, for his part, seems to have dissociated himself from obligations to Indian education largely by discrediting Occom's own character. Availing himself of anecdotes about Occom's occasional drunkenness, Wheelock made it known that Occom's behavior demonstrated the uselessness of Indian education.[13] From this time on, Wheelock turned his attention to Dartmouth College. Though he concluded finally that his Indian students reflected badly on his efforts, these men and women have passed down through history as "Wheelock's Indians." In the following section, I analyze what the experience and designation of "Wheelock's Indian" may mean for Occom and for our reading of his *Short Narrative.*

II

In a 1761 letter to George Whitefield, Wheelock describes the difficulties of Indian education:

None know, nor can any, without Experience, well conceive of, the Difficulty of Education an Indian. They would soon kill themselves with Eating and Sloth, if constant care were not exercised for them at least the first Year – they are used to set upon the Ground, and it is as Natural for them as a seat to our Children – they are not wont to have any Cloaths but what they wear, nor will without much Pains be brot to take Care of any. – They are used to a Sordid Manner of Dress and love it as well as our Children to be clean. – They are not used to any Regular Government, the sad Consequences of which you may little guess at. . . . Our Language when they seem to have got is not their Mother Tongue and they cannot receive nor communicate in that as in their Own. – It is a long time before they will learn the proper Place & use of the Particles. *a, an the,* & c. And they are as unpolished & uncultivated within as without. however Experience has taught us that it may be done. (Quoted in McCallum 17; Wheelock's emphasis)

Wheelock's response to his perception of disorder was a disciplinary one, like that of most of his contemporary educators. As Margaret Connell Szasz summarizes in her study of colonial Indian education, a typical day at Wheelock's school began before sunrise and was filled with work, study, meetings, and prayer until bedtime seven days a week (Szasz 223; see also Axtell, *European and the Indian,* 99–101). Wheelock's steadiest work seemed to consist of battling the misbehavior of his students, who fought and drank and ran away. His records are full of "confessions" from disobedient students, often in Wheelock's own handwriting.

David Murray observes that Wheelock's ongoing use of the confession in fact demonstrates "the connection he clearly made between institutional control and writing" (49). As Murray argues, Wheelock's use of written confession grounds the subjectivity of the Indian student in *subjection* to a superior authority – ultimately God but more immediately Wheelock (Murray 49–52). Wheelock's assumptions about disciplinary hierarchy permeated his relationship with his students, as we see demonstrated in the way he taught his students to sign their letters. The strings of self-abasements – "your dutiful tho unworthy servant," "thy unworthy and ungrateful servant," "your affectionate though unworthy servant," "your humble and obedient pupil" – sound, Murray notes, as ritualistically hollow as the confessions themselves.

It could be argued that Wheelock's intention was to teach his converts Christian humility. But *subordinative* humility is not recip-

rocated by Wheelock's signatures, where he signs as "your sincere
well-wisher," or "your friend."[14] The social interplay of signatures
here provides a concise example of how the colonial project maps its
own desires onto the native: Wheelock himself seems to insist on
equality in his signatures ("your friend") while teaching his students
to beg for a hierarchical relationship in theirs ("your unworthy servant"). The paternalistic and race-marked language with which
Wheelock often addressed and referred to his students, as "amiable
little black savage Christian[s]" or "black son[s]" (Szasz 224; Love
92), reinforces that hierarchical relationship.[15] Wheelock's educational system effectively worked to undermine his Indian students'
sense of cultural and personal authority in order to subject it to his
own. His methods reflect attitudes about religious education common
throughout colonial New England. As Ivy Schweitzer states, the Cal-
vinist conversion process "affirmed the existence of a new kind of
interiority, of a private, unique, inner space – the space of self-
consciousness, of subjectivity – only to demand its sacrifice, renunci-
ation and occupation by Another. . . . Conversion required the willing
abdication of will" (22). Ideally, the convert's actions would evidence
Christ himself, although, as Schweitzer observes, the doctrine of *exemplum fidei* worked effectively as a "check upon subjectivism, for individual experience had to conform to the group's – and by
implication, the minister's – notion of saving faith" (9). If the cultural
ideal was that the convert should substitute Christ's will for the fallen
personal will, the practical effect was determined by how well he or
she manifested the will of fathers and ministers. It is this practical effect that I want to highlight for our reading of Occom's *Short Narrative.*

In a striking letter by John Smith, one of Wheelock's patrons, we
can find a telling instance of how the theological ideal of *exemplum
fidei* translates into a secular utility. Smith first relates going miles
out of his way to see "Mr. Wheelock's Indian School," with which
he was greatly impressed. He describes how Wheelock leads the lessons and prayers, which the Indian students follow with a "charming
. . . Obedience to God" and "a fillial [sic] Love & Reverence to Mr.
Wheelock" (McCallum 74). Describing a young and recently converted Indian woman whom Wheelock brings to his notice, Smith
remarks on the "exquisite . . . pleasure" of seeing "the Savageness
of an Indian moulded into the Sweetness of the follower of the
Lamb" (75).

Smith's comment suggests that the "mould" is not Christ "the
Lamb" but rather Wheelock, "the follower of the lamb." It may
seem like splitting hairs to insist on that distinction, but it does help
us make better sense of the remarkable passage that follows:

In passing some Days after this through the Mohegan Country
I saw an Indian Man on Horseback whom I challenged as Mr.
Occum & found it to be so. There was something in his mein
and Department both amiable & venerable & though I had
never before seen him I must have been sure it was he. – He
certainly does Honour to Mr. Wheelock's indefatigable, judicious, pious Intentions to send the Gospel among the Indians.
I heard Mr Ashpo was among them but at a Distance & I being
hurried & tired Lost the opportunity of seing [sic] Mr Wheelock in him & more especially of seeing Christs Image in this
Tawney Man. (quoted in McCallum 75)

Here we see the productive slippage between the ideal of *exemplum
fidei* and its practical effect: In the figure of the Indian convert, Smith
expects to see the example not simply of Christ but also of *Wheelock*.
"This Tawney Man," in other words, is viewed not as a member of
the Christian brotherhood but as an object who reflects the agency
of (white) Christians back at themselves for their own admiring approval.

In his essay "Myth Today," Roland Barthes analyzes an image that
correlates strikingly with the one Smith offers. There Barthes considers a photograph of a black man in French uniform saluting (presumably) a French flag on the cover of a *Paris-Match*. In that photo he
traces the operations of cultural mythology, how the saluting man
stands in the gaze of the viewer, not for himself or even for the particular history of his people. Instead, the man shows "that France is a
great Empire, that all her sons, without any color discrimination,
faithfully serve under her flag, and that there is no better answer to
the detractors of an alleged colonialism than the zeal shown by this
so-called Negro in serving his so-called oppressors" (116). As Susanne
Kappeler would point out, the viewer of the photo was not intended
to be other colonized black people but a French citizen. Similarly, the
structure of representation that surrounds Occom and Ashpo includes an artist/creator (Wheelock) who has transformed the "tawney" men from the state of nature by "illuminating" them with
Christian grace. Wheelock puts on this performance in the body of
the Indian for the approval and support that his Christian brothers
(viewers) will give to *him*.[16] Occom and Ashpo in this way "stand for"
Wheelock's benevolence, zeal, and Christian fraternity rather than
their own human agency; that is why Smith, in missing the "Wheelock
Indian" Samuel Ashpo, felt that he missed seeing *Wheelock*.

Such (mis)reading of the native is symptomatic of colonial rep-
resentational strategies, as a host of postcolonial scholars including

Barthes, Jan Mohamed, and Said have observed. Most specifically, this "way of seeing" appropriates whatever subjectivity the native might claim and calls it the achievement of the colonizer.[17] In other words, any testimony Occom offers of his own abilities can always be reinscribed by his colonial viewer as evidence not of his own Christian agency but of Wheelock's. Occom's autobiographical narrative thereby becomes a double bind: As he describes his achievements on his own behalf (the typically self-affirmative format of Western autobiography), he makes those very achievements susceptible to colonial appropriation. As I argue later, his growing consciousness of the systematic robbery of Indian selfhood is important to the organizing logic of the *Short Narrative*.

III

Brian Swann and Arnold Krupat observe in their introduction to *I Tell You Now* that

> the form of writing generally known to the West as *autobiography* had no equivalent among the oral cultures of the indigenous inhabitants of the Americas. Although the tribes . . . kept material as well as mental records of collective and personal experience, the notion of telling the whole of any one individual's life or taking merely personal experience as of particular significance was, in the most literal way, foreign to them, if not also repugnant. (ix)

Yet, as David Brumble has argued in his landmark study of American Indian autobiography, Native American cultures did utilize frameworks that were arguably autobiographical. Brumble terms such frameworks "preliterate autobiographical narratives" (21–3).[18] Of the six frameworks Brumble locates, "self-vindication" – a narrative form structured by charge, self-vindication, and countercharge (32–9) – provides the most helpful beginning for making sense of what appears as fragmentation of purpose at the end of Occom's narrative.

Let me briefly summarize the content and structure of Occom's *Short Narrative*. Occom himself labeled three subdivisions: "From my Birth till I received the Christian Religion," "From the Time of our Reformation till I left Mr. Wheelock's," and "From the Time I left Mr. Wheelock till I went to Europe." The first section describes the orientation (or lack thereof) of the Mohegans toward British schooling and religion before the impact of the Great Awakening. The second section focuses on Occom's discovery of his own religious conviction and then describes his studies with Wheelock. The third section focuses mainly on his teaching in Montauk, his marriage and his manner of subsisting there, and then, indirectly, his missionary work among the Oneidas. Each section is longer than the preceding one.

The last section is the most unaccountable one by the lights of Western autobiographical conventions, because at this point Occom apparently loses his focus. Here he veers from telling a coherent story about his life to complaining about his poverty and underpayment by the missionary societies. At the end of the narrative, he is no longer justifying his life for his viewer/patrons but instead trying to make sense of their behavior toward him:

> So I am *ready* to Say, they have used me thus, because I can't Influence the Indians so well as other missionaries; but I can assure them I have endeavored to teach them as well as I know how; – but I *must Say*, "I believe it is because I am a poor Indian." I Can't help that God has mad me So; I did not make my self so. – (735)

Brumble's formula of "self-vindication" offers us a way to read positively what initially seems like a fragmented autobiography. In Occom's *Short Narrative*, the charge (i.e., you are not a real Indian/not a real convert) implicitly provides the occasion for Occom's account. Vindication is what Occom offers in the first three-quarters of the narrative: "From my Birth till I received the Christian Religion . . . From the Time of our Reformation till I left Mr. Wheelock's . . . From the Time I left Mr. Wheelock till I went to Europe" he was both a "real" Indian and a "real" convert. The last quarter of the *Short Narrative*, where Occom seems to abandon his autobiographical project, is structured by the logic of countercharge.

That countercharge is articulated most directly toward the end of the longest paragraph in the text. Occom recounts learning that despite his poverty, the Boston Commission had reported displeasure at his "extravaga[nce]" and for that reason refused his request for a raise on his fifteen-pound annual salary. "I Can't Conceive," complains Occom, "how these gentlemen would have me Live" (734). Though he would be willing to attribute their stinginess to an ignorance of the expenses related to his work, he is unable to do that in light of the fact that "it can be proved to the world that these Same Gentlemen gave a young Missionary a Single man, *one Hundred Pounds* for one year" (735). Occom's countercharge thus seems to be that even though he has converted and is working on behalf of what are now common Christian interests, he is still treated as though there is no distinction between himself and those he "converted" from or, even more to the point, as though there *is* a significant difference between himself and those whose mission he shares. "Now you See what difference they made between me and other missionaries," he says, in direct appeal to his audience, and then turns to a story about an indentured Indian boy who was beaten by his master "because [he] was a poor Indian" (735). Occom thus concludes by supplying this answer to his countercharge that his fellow Christians are not treating him fairly: "I believe it is because I am a poor Indian."

Yet to the extent that Occom relocates the difficulty he attributes to his "enemies" to himself, he apparently deflects his countercharge. And there are other difficulties that we cannot resolve positively simply by applying Brumble's framework – for instance, the odd fact that in a document produced ostensibly to justify his status as a Christian convert-missionary, the Rev. Samson Occom does not even *mention* his ordination. If we are to comprehend Occom's argument, we need to attend more carefully to the terms he chooses to vindicate himself – terms that clarify his changing relationship to the colonial project and that plausibly explain his subsequent refusal to cooperate with it according to Wheelock's dictates.

Since, as Patricia Meyer Spacks has argued, eighteenth-century Western autobiographies generally tended to rely on a defensive "rhetoric of explanation, shading even toward self-justification," we could argue that Occom's narrative is exemplary even by European standards (313). But autobiography, as Spacks observes at the outset of her study, is structurally affirmative, too: It works to "present to the reader some real version of a human being" (1). As I suggested in Section II, we can see how the affirmation of Occom's humanity becomes not simply an elocutionary move but also an ideological and even epistemological challenge for him. The reason his narrative was produced was, baldly put, to validate his worth as a product: a real Indian really converted, a stabilized and recognizable "marker" for colonial strategies of conversion. To this extent, his representation of himself, as well as his physical presence in England for fund-raising, was to be commodified and used as a resource to benefit not him but the process that produced him. In his text Occom, as an Indian convert, is made generic and thereby fully exchangeable for others just like him.

We should not fail to note, then, that Occom's countercharge implicates both his detractors and his mentors, implying that neither group grants him individual recognition or even human status (or the pay necessary for it) equivalent to what they grant themselves. Occom's self-vindication aims at self-affirmation by making a claim

within the framework of his identity as a Christian for the entitlement of human status (or Subject status) within the mission. The
mission's recognition will be given, according to Occom's argument,
when he receives equal pay for equal work. He hereby disrupts the
terms of his commodification with a demand that he be recognized
as an agent rather than a token within that economy.

As part of the logic of his countercharge, Occom's *Short Narrative*
emphasizes the reciprocity that structures his relationship with the
Christian colonial mission. The mission has not just benefitted Occom with its "gifts" of Christianity and civility; he offers advantages
to the Christian missionaries and their project, specifically through
his ability as a translator. Occom embodies three values for that ability: linguistic, pedagogical, and cultural. Whereas the first serves the
monologic drive of British colonialism, the latter two assert Occom's
dialogic – what we would now think of as multiculturalist – agenda.

First, Occom highlights his abilities as preacher and teacher, repeatedly asserting his ability to exhort, explain, and elaborate "in my
own tongue." His bilingualism establishes his extra worth by the ad-
ditive logic he discerns in the way the various missionary societies pay
their other workers. He, unlike other missionaries, is a teacher,
preacher, and translator all in one: "In my Service . . . I was," as Occom puts it, "my own Interpreter. I was both a School master and Minister to the Indians, yea I was their Ear, Eye & Hand, as well as Mouth"
(735). His argument, then, is that he *triply* facilitates the conversion of
"Heathenish" or "poor Kindred" into Christians, thereby amply re-
ciprocating the benefits he gained in his own conversion.

In this first capacity, he serves as a medium for British colonial
intent in that he does not complicate or undermine that unilateral
agenda. It is therefore significant when Occom suggests that his
translating abilities offer civilizing improvements not just to his
"poor kindred" but also to the British. One of the ways he does this
is by outlining how he devises pedagogical strategies acceptable to
Montauk culture that succeed where the British ones have failed.
For instance, by devising a game based on alphabet letters made
from wood chips, Occom teaches the Montauks to read where his
predecessor, Azariah Horton, had failed.

Occom's innovations contrast sharply with his own first encounter
with literacy under the British teacher Jonathan Barber:

> when I was about 10 years of age there was a man who went
> about among the Indian Wigwams, and wherever he could find
> the Indian Children, would make them read; but the Children
> Used to take Care to keep out of his way; – and he used to
> Catch me Sometimes and make me Say over my Letters. (731)

Occom suggests, in contrast, that he is able to devise better methods for conversion than the monolingual, monocultural British ones precisely because of his bilingualism and biculturalism. Perhaps equally important, he is able to translate the actual process from one of violence – as he learned it – to one of gentleness as he teaches it. By describing what the missionaries can learn from him, Occom asserts his right to modify the methods of the missionizing/colonizing agenda. He suggests the possibility of mutually informative dialogue and mutually beneficial exchange and emphasizes his own ability to facilitate that project. Another way of putting this would be to say that Occom insists on a mission of conversion that deals more in dialogue than in monologue, one in which "improvement" moves bilaterally rather than unilaterally.

Somewhat less explicitly, Occom suggests his right to challenge the cultural goals of the missionary agenda. The clue to this critique is the odd fact that Occom twice finds it necessary to explain to his reader what a wigwam is – a "sort of tent . . . covered with mats and made of flags" (731, 734). We might read Occom's repeated definition as sloppiness (he forgot the first instance) or humility (he would not expect his audience to bother to remember the trivial details of Indian life). Structurally speaking, though, any time Occom translates an Indian term for his British audience, he is critiquing colonialists who steadfastly refused to learn Native American languages and cultures while expecting the natives unquestioningly to adopt theirs. In this sense, his almost verbatim repetition of the definition of "wigwam" challenges an audience who cannot be depended on to comprehend anything about Indian language – even when they are told twice. But it is possible to read in this repetition an even sharper critique, given the aim of Occom's countercharge. His purchase into Christianity was simultaneously a purchase into the "civilized" lifeways of the British; as we have seen, for Wheelock, the adoption of a "civilized" lifestyle was a precondition for Indian conversion. When he first defines "wigwam," he is describing the ways of his life before his conversion, studies, ordination, and hiring as a missionary. But the second definition comes in describing his living conditions among the Montauks as a minister and missionizing agent.

Careful reading of other sections of the narrative seems to confirm that Occom intended a more pointed critique. In his description of the lifeways of his people before his conversion, for instance, his wording seems too careful to overlook: "they strictly maintained and followed their Heathenish Ways, customs and Religion," strategically complicating the derogatory "Heathenish" with the positive connotations of "Religion" – a religion "strictly maintained" at that

(730). And later, Occom interpolates into his account of his Montauk years the comment that "as our custom is, we freely entertain all visitors" (732). In this short account, we are drawn to contrast Occom's assertion of native hospitality with the oppressive miserliness that the New England Company and Scotch Society demonstrate toward Occom personally. The logic linking these two passages supports the context of his second translation of the term "wigwam," emphasizing the poverty he must endure because of his terrible pay – a poverty that forces him to live *like* the "poor" Indian he has supposedly been converted *from*. If we accept that Occom meant this charge, then we must consider the boldness of his claim, which does not so much challenge isolated missionary practices as their underlying bad faith.

This, of course, would be a strong charge from one whose livelihood depended on that very mission. So we could attribute Occom's circumlocution on the topic to a fear of the backlash that might further penalize his finances if he were to be any more explicit. But we should also consider that Occom's failure to make his charge unambiguous could result from his own reluctance to confront what that accusation means for his own efforts on behalf of the colony. I am suggesting that the structural and psychological ambivalence of Occom's position within the colonial project infiltrates and compromises his sense of purpose.

Albert Memmi's summary of the power dynamics embedded in colonial language exchange helps contextualize two distinct aspects of psychic self-division that are relevant to understanding the tone, structure, and argument of Occom's narrative:

> Colonial bilingualism cannot be compared to just any linguistic dualism. Possession of two languages is not merely a matter of having two tools, but actually means participation in two psychical and cultural realms. Here the two worlds symbolized and conveyed by the two tongues are in conflict; they are those of the colonizer and the colonized.
>
> Furthermore, the colonized's mother tongue, that which is sustained by his feelings, emotions and dreams . . . is precisely the one which is the least valued. (107)

Despite the positive value of Occom's arguments about his ability to translate languages, pedagogies, and cultures, his ability works against him in the dominant culture. Although Occom refuses to hide his language, as Memmi puts it, from the sight of strangers, he cannot escape knowing that his Indian language, like his Indian appearance, confirms his inferiority within the logic of the dominant

community. Despite his offer of bilateral translation, he is unilaterally translated by the dominant culture's concept of "Indian-ness"
in ways that seem virtually nonnegotiable.

We can trace what I am arguing is Occom's own sense of self-
division in his plaintive (or angry) parenthetical appeal near the end
of the *Short Narrative*. This passage makes clear a pained awareness
of the contradictions that finally may have no resolution within the
(mono)logic of colonialism. As he pleads for higher pay by pointing
out that he does as much work as three British agents, Occom literally interrupts himself: "In my Service (I speak like a fool but I
am Constrained) I was my own interpreter" (735).

In the parenthetical "I speak like a fool" we can read the structural hegemony of colonialism that undercuts Occom's attempt to
argue his own worth. The complaint condenses colonialist mythology: Occom feels that he speaks "like a fool" – like one deficient in
reason or intelligence – exactly at the moment that he compares
himself to a white missionary. Just as he asserts a fuller worth *because*
of his ability to speak his native tongue, he finds himself compelled
to apologize for his lack of eloquence in English. Thus he becomes
trapped in what Eric Cheyfitz calls the "poetics of imperialism":
What constitutes his sense of importance within the colony is precisely his inadequacy as it is judged within that economy. This structural disparity between how Occom experiences himself and what
the mission can recognize in him is the first important aspect of
Occom's self-division.

That ruptured sentence, both in structure and in content, illustrates Occom's own purchase in the (il)logic of colonial rhetoric,
how English literacy at once empowers him and alienates him from
the very sense of agency he seeks. His assertion that "I was my own
interpreter" ironically traces how his own adoption of Christianity
and English ways interrupts and divides his sense of self. He must
translate his humanity into English for his English audience's com-
prehension and acknowledgment. But this particular project of
translation, perhaps more than any other, requires him to confront
the fact that the people whose language he has learned in order to
gain entrance into the Christian brotherhood ultimately refuse to
comprehend his humanity, and thus in that language he will always
"speak like a fool." It was, as I have suggested in my analysis of
Wheelock's relation to his Indian students, an almost impossible
game for Occom to win.

We cannot, of course, know precisely what Occom meant in the
phrase "but I am constrained." It is possible that, by one contemporary usage, he meant that his autobiographical defense was a dif-

ficult exertion. Or he might have been referring to his obligation to defend himself to his British and colonial patrons. In yet another contemporary usage of the word, he could have been alluding to an oppressed condition, a force compelling him in some way toward an undesired end – speaking "like a fool." This last sense is closest to that in which he would use the word a few years later to castigate Wheelock about Dartmouth: "Modesty woud forbid me, but I am Constraine'd So to write" (quoted in Blodgett 124). From this vantage point, we could read Occom's complaint as a flag for the failure of dialogue in British culture and how that failure is projected onto Occom himself ("I speak like a fool"). He resists that inscription by indicating that what appears as his foolishness (or deficiency) is actually the result of force ("but I am Constrained"). As Cheyfitz states of colonial "translation": "The failure of dialogue, figured as a genetic inability in the other, rather than as a problem of cultural difference, is the imperial alibi for domination" (16).

If Occom's use of the word "constrained" denotes arbitrary force, then it is certainly relevant that the idea of domination becomes the most insistent point of the remainder of Occom's narrative. Occom offers a powerful example in his parable of the "poor Indian." Questioning why other missionaries were paid as much as twelve times more per year, Occom concludes:

> I can't think of any thing, but this as a Poor Indian Boy Said, Who was Bound out to an English Family, and he used to Drive Plow for a young man, and he whipt and Beat him allmost every Day, and the young man found fault with him and Complained of him to his master and the poor Boy was Called to answer for himself before his master, and he was asked, what it was he did, that he was So Complained of and beat almost every Day. He Said, he did not know, but he Supposed it was because he could not drive any better; but says he, I Drive as well as I know how; and at other Times he Beats me, because he is of a mind to beat me; but says he believes he Beats me for most of the Time "because I am an Indian." (735)

By extension, Occom sees himself as that beaten Indian boy, carrying out his mission of Christianizing and civilizing for the benefit of the colony as well, he says, "as I know how." He has emphasized earlier that his own methods are better – both more effective and more humane – than those of his British colleagues. By associating himself with the "poor Indian," Occom links this parable to his first encounter with literacy, of being chased down and forced to recite the alphabet. Opening and closing with these examples of forceful and finally violent imposition, Occom's narrative emphasizes the dominative rather than fraternal logic that undergirds colonial Christian ideology. His anecdotal frame work suggests that the Indian who becomes literate in the language of the colonizer is a beaten Indian no less than the brutalized Indian of Occom's parable. It reveals how, in Cheyfitz's phrase, the colonial mission "civilizes the other in order to savage" him (21).

Memmi argues that because of the self-alienating politics of colonial language acquisition, the colonized subject can "almost never succeed in corresponding with himself" (140). The narrative's fragmented closing passage may testify to a second aspect of Occom's sense of entrapment and division as a colonized *colonizer*. This reading is suggested both by the narrative's fragmented ending, "I can't help it that God has made me so; I did not make myself so," and by the pronominal confusion in the parable, where "he" alternately designates the "poor Indian" and his violent master. Occom, as both "poor Indian" and missionary, must identify with both referents.

I would argue that in the course of composing his narrative, though, Occom is increasingly able to understand his experience of self-division in a different way, as the betrayal of the promises of conversion. What he gets, in other words, is not what he feels he was promised. This important critique surfaces in the narrative's almost obsessive focus on Indian poverty. He provides what the Comaroffs might describe as an "inchoate" analysis of colonial dispossession. When in the early sections of the narrative Occom describes Indian brethren as "poor," the adjective seems to imply a deficiency of knowledge at least, and in the context of Occom's account of his spiritual conversion, perhaps a religious poverty as well. But increasingly, as Occom complains about his own difficulties, the word "poor" begins specifically to denote financial impoverishment. As this semantic shift occurs toward the end of his narrative, Occom suggests a revealing analysis of the Christian mission: Indians are not "poor" because they are lacking in spiritual knowledge, but rather because the British systematically appropriate from them everything that affirms value, specifically property, labor, and selfhood.

C. B. MacPherson details the ideological linkages between developing a logic of possessive individualism and Puritan ideas about selfhood. Increasingly throughout the eighteenth century, a person's political entitlement and economic rights were described in metaphors of possession and were linked to the actual possession of material goods, particularly land. Puritan social structures in fact amplified secular versions of possessive individualism by adding, as MacPherson observes, "moral obloquy to the political disregard in which the poor had always been held" (226–7). The countercharge of Occom's account unmasks the implied correlation between wealth and humanity in possessive individualism and its converse affiliation of poverty and immorality. Thus we should read Occom's repeated use of the adjective "poor" not simply as a figure of speech or a rhetoric of humility, although it may in part be both of these. Within the structure of Occom's narrative, which is all about money and unfairness, his repetition of "poor Indian" points insistently toward another reading. The closing section of his narrative, by linking his own treatment with that of the "poor Indian boy," powerfully draws our attention to how the colonizer, relying alternately on the promises of conversion and on out-and-out force, refuses to share land, pay, and finally human dignity with the Indians. The fact that Wheelock gets credit for "his" Indians' achievements is a correlative theft, one that hinders Occom's presentation of himself as anything other than the "poor Indian" he bitterly, perhaps sarcastically, claims himself to be at the close of his narrative.

The critique that I am suggesting Occom's *Short Narrative* poses would be perfectly in keeping with his analysis of the Mohegan land case. "I am afraid the poor Indians will never stand a good chance with the English in their land controversies, because they are very poor, they have no money" (quoted in Blodgett 77). Indian poverty, as Occom's account describes, is not natural or essential to Indians: It is beaten into them by the Christian agent of the British colony. Thus Occom's countercharge suggests that, as Abdul Jan Mohamed puts it, "the perception of racial difference is, in the first place, influenced by economic motives" (80).[19] In his defamiliarizing repetition of "poor Indian," Occom suggests a reorientation of human valuation and racial categorization. By asking his readers to see the "poor Indian" as the *result* of the colonial missionary project, he reveals the symbiotic relationship between the spiritual mission and the colonial economic structure, both needing "poor" Indians for their own furtherance. In that assertion Samson Occom reaches, it seems, toward a different understanding of his own agency outside the race-essentializing symbolic economy that enables him to deal more effectively with the colonial political economy that he must live in, as we see in his subsequent turn away from Wheelock and to the Brothertown project.

Occom's narrative should undoubtedly occupy an important position in American literature. It offers a powerful claim to personhood within the context of a strong critique of British colonial politics. It highlights the psychological complexities that arise out of oppressive economic and social practices. By learning to read works like Occom's, we can understand more about the diversity and divergences of experience in the colonial period. Such study can also teach us how "marginal" experiences like Occom's are in fact *central* to the constitution of life for those in the "center." The *Short Narrative* represents the social fabric that is literarily repressed, and literally oppressed, by Franklin's celebratory individualism. By reading Occom's narrative, we can see how it is only at the psychic, economic, and social expense of people like Occom that the bourgeois class structure could rise and proclaim its universalizing and "self"-sustaining logic of possessive individualism.[20]

Notes

1. As far as I know, the only other place Occom's 1768 narrative has been printed is in Peyer, *The Elders Wrote.*
2. The term is Jennings's.
3. The lands at stake covered the area of Colchester, Windham, Mansfield, Hebron, and portions of other towns (Caulkins 266).
4. This is the same John Mason who commanded the assault on the Pequot village of Mystic in 1638 and who was then serving as deputy governor of the Connecticut colony. Shortly after this new transaction with Uncas, Mason bequeathed power over the lands to the Connecticut colony.
5. Caulkins dates this letter as postrevolutionary, but Occom's signature reproduced in Caulkins is dated 1754.
6. After the resolution of the Mason Controversy and following the American Revolution, Occom would continue in his efforts to secure land interests for Indian peoples in Brothertown, an intertribal Christian settlement on lands granted by the Oneidas, and later in New Stockbridge.
7. James Axtell frames the issue here (sincerity of conversion) more generally in his essay "Were Indian Conversions *Bona Fide?*" in *After Columbus* 100–21. I find his arguments compelling, but I find the arguments of those he criticizes (Salisbury, Blanchard, Jaenen, and Trigger, cf. pp. 102–5) also well worth considering. Mostly, I think blanket generalizations are not worth making; when we have some kind of clear evidence – personal writings, documented lifestyle patterns over a period of time – then perhaps we have room to build an argument, as we clearly do in the case of Occom.
8. Wheelock's first biographers suggest that he was inspired in part to begin the charity school to supplement an inadequate income as pastor of the North Society in Lebanon, Connecticut. See David M'Clure and Elijah Parish, *Memoirs of the Rev. Eleazar Wheelock*, 1811, p. 20, referenced in McCallum 14.
9. For a summary of the funds provided by the London Society to Occom, see Richardson 129, n. 1. It is important here to emphasize that the aspersions cast on his "authenticity" or character by the London Society

quite arguably had nothing to do with Occom himself. Occom was highly regarded by those who knew him for his intelligence and sincerity. For instance, in a letter to a friend dated 1764, John Smith, a Boston merchant, described Occom as "amiable and venerable" (quoted in McCallum 75). Occom created a similar impression in England. John Thornton entertained Occom on several occasions during his stay in London and became a patron of sorts after Occom's return to the colonies. Unlike Wheelock, Thornton treated Occom like an equal and advocated for him even as Wheelock attempted to discredit him after the London trip (for details of Thornton's intercessions on Occom's behalf after his return to the colonies, see Richardson 358–62).

10. See Richardson 70–1 for a reproduction of the prevoyage narrative.

11. See, for example, Blodgett 115.

12. Occom apparently purchased a set of books for the charity school, which he subsequently refused to surrender to Wheelock without a salary advance.

13. Blodgett, who is generally sympathetic to Wheelock, summarizes the clergyman's behavior in this instance in an unflattering way: "it seems unfortunate that [Occom's] friends should have so tactlessly confirmed in their letters and gossip the extravagant story of his fall" (111).

14. Laura Murray observes that Wheelock had similar relations with *his* benefactors: "Wheelock had to abase himself rhetorically almost as much as his students were required to do for him" (53). Yet, as she points out in personal correspondence to the author (February 2, 1993), "Wheelock grovels in one context in order to gain power in another, and it's not so clear what his students gain from *their* grovelling" (emphasis Murray's).

15. Axtell makes this observation on Wheelock's choice of adjective: "As an owner of black slaves for much of his life, Wheelock was perfectly capable of distinguishing the two races; that he did not suggests an unconscious reduction of the people he was consciously trying to elevate and a deep ambivalence about his 'Grand Design' " (*European and the Indian* 105). Alden T. Vaughan reads from a more general and historical perspective the colonists' shift from "red" to "black" when describing the Native Americans during this period.

16. I am relying on Kappeler's discussion of what she analyzes as the *Pornography of Representation*.

17. Of course, "subjectivity" is not a natural or neutral concept but is culturally constructed. Acknowledging that, however, should not mean that we would overlook the various ways in which colonized peoples struggle to appropriate the space of subjectivity for entitlement or resistance within the colonizing culture.

18. For a germinal discussion of preencounter Native American autobiographical forms, see Hertha Wong, *Sending My Heart Back Across the Years,* especially chapter one.

19. In his germinal essay "The Economy of Manichean Allegory: The Function of Racial Difference in Colonial Literature," Jan Mohamed argues

that the trope of race was deployed under a colonial regime only after economic possibilities made human subjugation lucrative. Referencing the work of Dorothy Hammond and Alta Jablow, he argues that "Africans were perceived in a more or less neutral and benign manner before the slave trade developed; however, once the triangular trade became established, Africans were newly characterized as the epitome of evil and barbarity" (80).

20. I want to offer heartfelt thanks to Lora Romero, Jerold M. Martin, John Lowe III, and Nadine Romero, each of whom read lengthy drafts and offered invaluable advice on this essay. I owe thanks to Laura Murray, who pointed me toward the important work of the Comaroffs.

Works Cited

Axtell, James. *After Columbus: Essays In the Ethnohistory of Colonial North America.* New York: Oxford University Press, 1988.

  The European and the Indian: Essays in the Ethnohistory of Colonial North America. New York: Oxford University Press, 1981.

  The School Upon the Hill: Education and Society in Colonial New England. New Haven, CT: Yale University Press, 1974.

Barthes, Roland. *Mythologies,* trans. Annette Lavers. New York: Hill and Wang, 1972.

Blodgett, Harold. *Samson Occom.* Hanover, NH: Dartmouth College Publications, 1935.

Brumble, H. David, III. *American Indian Autobiography.* Berkeley: University of California Press, 1988.

Caulkins, Frances Manwaring. *History of Norwich: From Its Possession by the Indians, to the Year 1866.* 1866. Rpt. Chester, CT: Pequot Press, 1976.

Cheyfitz, Eric. *The Poetics of Imperialism: Translation and Colonization from "The Tempest" to "Tarzan."* New York: Oxford University Press, 1991.

Comaroff, Jean, and John Comaroff. *Of Revelation and Revolution: Christianity, Colonialism and Consciousness in South Africa,* Vol. I. Chicago: University of Chicago Press, 1991.

Couser, G. Thomas. *Altered Egos: Authority in American Autobiography.* New York: Oxford University Press, 1989.

DeForest, John William. *History of the Indians of Connecticut from the earliest known period to 1850.* Hartford: W.J. Hamersley, 1851.

Fanon, Frantz. *Black Skin, White Masks,* trans. Charles Lam Markmann. New York: Grove Press, 1967.

Gates, Henry Louis. "Critical Fanonism," *Critical Inquiry* 17 (Spring 1991): 457–470.

Jan Mohamed, Abdul. "The Economy of Manichean Allegory: The Function of Racial Difference in Colonialist Literature." In *"Race," Writing and Difference,* ed. Henry Louis Gates. Chicago: University of Chicago Press, 1985, 1986: 78–106.

Jennings, Francis. *The Invasion of America: Indians, Colonialism and the Cant of Conquest*. New York: Norton, 1975.

Kappeler, Susanne. *The Pornography of Representation*. Minneapolis: University of Minnesota Press, 1986.

Krupat, Arnold. *For Those Who Come After: A Study of Native American Autobiography*. Berkeley: University of California Press, 1985.

Love, William DeLoss. *Samson Occom and the Christian Indians of New England*. Boston: Pilgrim Press, 1899.

MacPherson, C. B. *The Political Theory of Possessive Individualism, Hobbes to Locke*. Oxford: Clarendon Press, 1962.

McCallum, James Dow, ed. *Letters of Eleazar Wheelock's Indians*. Hanover, NH: Dartmouth College Publications, 1932.

Memmi, Albert. *The Colonizer and the Colonized*. Boston: Beacon Press, 1965.

Murray, David. *Forked Tongues: Speech, Writing and Representation in North American Indian Texts*. Bloomington: Indiana University Press, 1991.

Murray, Laura. " 'Pray Sir, Consider a Little': Rituals of Subordination and Strategies of Resistance in the Letters of Hezekiah Calvin and David Fowler to Eleazar Wheelock, 1764–1768." *Studies in American Indian Literatures* 4.2 (Summer 1992): 48–74.

Occom, Samson. *A Short Narrative of My Life*, in *The Heath Anthology of American Literature*, Vol. I, ed. Paul Lauter. Lexington, MA: D. C. Heath, 1990: 730–5.

Peyer, Bernd. *The Elders Wrote: An Anthology of Early Prose by North American Indians, 1768–1931*. Berlin: Dietrich Reimer Verlag, 1982.

"Samson Occom: Mohegan Missionary and Writer of the 18th Century." *American Indian Quarterly* 6.3–4 (1982): 208–17.

Richardson, Leon Burr. *An Indian Preacher in England*. Hanover, NH: Dartmouth College Publications, 1933.

Schweitzer, Ivy. *The Work of Self-Representation: Lyric Poetry in Colonial New England*. Chapel Hill: University of North Carolina Press, 1991.

Said, Edward W. *Culture and Imperialism*. New York: Knopf, 1993.

Spacks, Patricia Meyer. *Imagining a Self: Autobiography and Novel in Eighteenth-Century England*. Cambridge, MA: Harvard University Press, 1976.

Swann, Brian, and Arnold Krupat. *I Tell You Now: Autobiographical Essays by Native American Writers*. Lincoln: University of Nebraska Press, 1987.

Szasz, Margaret Connell. *Indian Education in the American Colonies, 1607–1783*. Albuquerque: University of New Mexico Press, 1988.

Vaughan, Alden T. "From White Man to Redskin: Changing Anglo-American Perceptions of American Indians." *American History Review* 87 (1982): 917–53.

Wong, Hertha Dawn. *Sending My Heart Back Across the Years: Tradition and Innovation in Native American Autobiography*. New York: Oxford University Press, 1992.

4

"WHERE, THEN, SHALL WE PLACE THE HERO OF THE WILDERNESS?"

WILLIAM APESS'S EULOGY ON KING PHILIP AND DOCTRINES OF RACIAL DESTINY

ANNE MARIE DANNENBERG

Between 1829 and 1836 William Apess was highly visible as an activist, lecturer, and author. A Methodist minister and mixed-blood Pequot, Apess was an outspoken advocate for Indian reform – education, christianization, temperance, and equal treatment under the law. Long a controversial figure in his native New England, Apess also briefly drew the eyes of the nation. Until just recently, however, Apess's writings were scattered in obscure repositories across the country and largely unknown to most contemporary scholars. Now, with the 1992 publication of Barry O'Connell's indispensable *On Our Own Ground: The Complete Writings of William Apess, A Pequot*, Apess's five published texts are widely available and are described as "the most considerable [body of writing produced] by any Native American before the 1840s" (xxxix). Largely due to O'Connell's broad-spectrum recovery of his work, Apess is becoming an important reference point amid efforts to retrieve occulted histories.

But despite the many vital contributions to Apess scholarship, there are still issues that make one worry. Even now, the most well-meaning recovery efforts are at times inflected by an Anglo-American view of history that carries a racial destiny – a version of the national creation story in which whites prevail, blacks are rescued from slavery, and Indians vanish. More specifically, since the early nineteenth century, the historical "fate" of Native Americans has been shaped by "vanishing American" ideology (the complex, pervasive nineteenth-century popular and scientific belief that indigenous Americans were a "dying race").[1] Accordingly, American Indians who resisted empire have been read as variants of the savage hero: noble and valiant but ultimately doomed. This tendency to view Native Americans as destined to vanish has thus far too readily framed our understanding of Apess's trajectory: Because the actual circumstances of his death were unknown until only very recently,

the end of Apess's relatively short-lived prominence has been characterized as a "slide into anonymity" (O'Connell xxxviii), a mysterious disappearance from the textual record in 1838; and because
the abolitionist movement is usually characterized as an antislavery
movement rather than an antiracist movement, Apess's political project is understood to have been eclipsed by the emergence of broad-
based support for abolitionism.[2] Accordingly, both Apess and his
reform efforts meet the Indian's "inevitable" fate; both are doomed
by the natural course of history. Ironically, readings that cast Apess
as a "doomed warrior" reaffirm the very ideologies he himself
sought to fracture.

In his 1836 *Eulogy on King Philip*, Apess essayed his own reclama-
tion project in memory of a colonial-era "villain," Metacomet, a
Wampanoag leader known to the English as "King Philip".
Throughout, Apess's *Eulogy* argues that our reading of the past de-
termines our understanding of the present. Similarly, I argue that
our construction of Apess's project in the *Eulogy* is critical to understanding Apess's place in American textual traditions.

* * * * * *

As its full title (*Eulogy on King Philip, as Pronounced at the Odeon, in
Federal Street, Boston*) indicates, this 1836 text was originally presented
as a lecture.[3] Because it was Apess's last known writing, *Eulogy* is often
presented as a sorrowful reminder of Apess's fate – regrettable, un-
timely, and unjust. O'Connell's preface to the *Eulogy*, for example,
concludes with the elegiac assertion that "the *Eulogy* was [Apess's]
final publication of himself to a society that briefly noticed and then
forgot him" (276). But the *Eulogy* itself – arguably the most rhetorically complex of Apess's texts – challenges all assumptions on which
such interpretation rests. To say that Apess was forgotten by society
ignores the complex ideological machinery at play. Moreover, although Apess was in some ways separate and apart from the society
to which he addressed his pleas for reform, he was in other ways
very much part of it. Both Apess's lived experience and the *Eulogy*'s
discursive intricacies suggest that "author" and "audience" are not
so easily demarcated.

Although Apess presents a decidedly "Indian" self, that racialized
self consistently defies a racial essence. Throughout, multiple discourses both shape his appeal for reform and constitute his textual identity. In *Eulogy*, Apess variously identifies himself as Pequot,
(pan-)Indian, colored, Christian, male, (first) American, and embodiment of the Enlightenment notion of the "universal human";
he declares, "My image is of God; I am not a beast" (278). And like

other overtly political texts advocating radical – perhaps revolutionary – social change (Jefferson's Declaration of Independence and
King's "Letter from Birmingham Jail" may be parallels), Apess's *Eulogy* must confirm existing alliances, construct new ones, and, at the
same time, reinforce the oppositions originally necessitating his plea.
Definitive categories (racial, philosophical, religious, political, personal) disintegrate and coalesce by turns; throughout, they are at
once applicable, useful, and contingent. In *Eulogy*, Apess is undeni-
ably an Indian author addressing a non-Indian audience; he is simultaneously – as an advocate of Christian American Enlightenment
humanism – a man and a Christian urging like-minded others to
retrain their sights on shared goals. Thus, one cannot conclude that
Apess adopted an alien discourse in order to address an alien audience. Although his audience in the Boston lecture hall in January
1836 was probably predominantly Christian and non-Indian, Apess's
broader audience was far more diverse.[4]

We do not know specifically what prompted Apess's presentation
of the *Eulogy* at a Boston lecture hall, and there is no record of its
sponsorship. Newspapers show that he lectured twice (January 8 and
January 26, 1836); notices also promised Apess's "full view of the
mission cause" (O'Connell 275).[5] That he was both an Indian and
a minister no doubt made Apess an authority on missionary efforts
among Indians. Yet the *Eulogy*'s range far exceeds an assessment of
evangelizing efforts. With the *Eulogy*, Apess makes a strong statement
of cultural nationalism for Indian peoples and indicts whites' treatment of Indians both past and present. His message is social reform;
his medium is history.

Introducing his subject, Apess pledges to "reveal the true character of Philip, in relation to those hostilities between himself and
the whites" (278). To emend an Anglo-centered reading of colonial
encounters between the Pilgrims and Native populations, particularly in regard to King Philip's War, Apess marshals "a mass of history and exposition" (289). Though he explicitly affirms an
empirically accessible, objective truth that "wants no polishing what-
soever" (308), his handling of the "facts" suggests the quotidian
business of historians to involve multiple provisional truths. He often
introduces his evidence tentatively: Phrases such as "it was said" or
"it appears that" or "[t]he history of New England writers says" or
"as far as we can learn by the records" (285–90) suggest that any
single historical account is only one of many stories that must be
told. But although Apess's counter-memory relies on the provisional
nature of historical truths, his political goals necessitate firmer
ground. Arguing a solid factual basis for his claim that Anglo ag-

gression had been the ultimate cause of all hostilities from colonial times to his own, Apess proposes "one general law" for all (310) – a law presumably grounded in the truth his emended history reveals.

While the *Eulogy*'s surfaces treat history, its undercurrents address race. Whether he is speaking as revisionist historian, Indian activist, or Christian minister, Apess's aims are always political, and to wage politics in Apess's day was to struggle with racialist ideologies. The years when Apess published, 1829–36, are precisely those delimiting Andrew Jackson's presidency – key years for American expansion, critical years for the fate of indigenous populations. Between 1790 and 1830 the population of the western states (i.e., those west of the thirteen original states) rose from less than 3 percent to 28 percent of the total U.S. population, marking, according to Michael Rogin, "one of the great migrations in world history" (4). Continued expansion according to established patterns meant dispossession of the American Indian. Indicating the centrality of the "Indian question" in this period, Rogin maintains that "Indians had not mattered so much, in the history of Europeans in the English new world, since the colonial settlements. They would never matter so much again" (4). Jackson's 1830 Indian Removal Act requiring Indians' forced resettlement to lands west of the Mississippi River was bolstered by emergent doctrines of racial destiny – virulent discourses Apess knew well and perennially sought to undermine.

In his book on the origins of racial Anglo-Saxonism, Reginald Horsman marks 1815–50 as the period when white American society explicitly rejected American Indians (190). From the eighteenth-century flowering of interest in human origins to Apess's day, the History of the Human Race had gradually metamorphosed into the History of Human Race*s*. The period's intellectuals attacked the Enlightenment belief in a common, inherently perfectable, and inalienably equal humankind, a belief that had explained observable, superficial differences in terms of environmental factors. Increasingly, scientists, social philosophers, historians, and charlatans cited arguments and empirical evidence as proof of innate differences among the "races of man." Anglo-Saxons – or "Anglo-Normans," as they were often designated in the South – were deemed patently superior to all other races. Although there was considerable disagreement among scholars as to just which human groups might claim to be Anglo-Saxons, by Apess's time the term "Anglo-Saxon" was popularly understood to mean white. All dark-skinned or "colored" peoples constituted the other, inferior races. Historical studies lauding the Anglo-Saxons' transcendent achievements throughout time began to be understood as a promise of things to come: Anglo-

Saxons were destined to rule the world; other races must either bow or disappear. In the early nineteenth century, this certifiable racial destiny had begun to be used to rationalize social conditions and justify political policy.

As Horsman points out, emergent racialist thinking and the "eighteenth-century transatlantic view" that the Indian was a "fully improvable being" coexisted well into the nineteenth century, and Indians had "major defenders" among whites. But after 1830, neither the American masses nor their political leaders believed that Indians could ever be "enlightened" sufficiently to assimilate fully into American society (which, of course, presumed that Native peoples would desire assimilation). Horsman writes:

> Before 1830 there was a bitter struggle as those who believed in the Enlightenment view of the Indian as an innately equal, improvable being desperately defended the older ideals, but year by year the ideas of those who felt the Indians were expendable were reinforced by a variety of scientific and intellectual arguments. Indian Removal represented a major victory for ideas which, though long latent in American society, became fully explicit only after 1830. Political power was exercised by those who believed the Indians to be inferior, who did not wish them to be accepted as equals within American society, and who expected them ultimately to disappear. In shaping an Indian policy American politicians reflected the new ruthlessness of racial confidence. (190)

Any address by a Native American in 1836 would implicitly concern this "new ruthlessness." Apess's *Eulogy*, however, is more cynical than most. Apess argues that, except for formalized public discourse, the new ruthlessness differed little from the old. Strategically choosing a pre-Enlightenment period (the late colonial era) as his focus and then repeatedly comparing that period with his own, Apess obliterates any illusion that time has brought progress. His own experience had taught him how naive it would be to assume a direct correlation between Enlightenment rhetoric and enlightened practice. The *Eulogy* repeatedly reminds its audience that despite fluctuations in official policy, day-to-day Indian–white relations had changed little over time. Speaking of contemporaries who might be deluded by rhetoric sympathetic to Indians, Apess writes, "Although in words they deny it, yet in the works they approve of the iniquities of their fathers. And as the seed of iniquity and prejudice was sown in that day, so it still remains. . . . [T]he spirit of the Pilgrims yet remains" (287). Arguably, however, together with Christian princi-

ples, Enlightenment ideals offered the best arsenal against burgeoning anti-Indian thinking – perhaps the only tempering influence
available in mainstream discourse. So, throughout the *Eulogy,* Apess
appeals to American Enlightenment values: inalienable human
rights sustained by a just system of laws, basic equality between human beings, a confidence in human reason tempered by faith in
divine providence.

In 1836 Boston, one of the remaining strongholds of Enlightenment aspirations in the early nineteenth century as well as a site of
early antislavery activism, Apess probably attracted an audience that
favored egalitarianism and explicitly opposed racist practices. His
pervasive sarcasm and ironic barbs suggest that he took much support for granted. He both opens and concludes his address with
references to an Enlightenment – and abolitionist – shibboleth: liberty. "I appeal to the lovers of liberty," he states at the outset (277).
In closing, he asks that his "dear affectionate friends" (308), "every
friend of the Indians[,] . . . seize the mantle of Liberty" and make
war on "those corrupt and degrading principles that robs [sic] one
of all rights, merely because he is ignorant and of a little different
color" (307). By invoking liberty, Apess not only consolidates sympathies for a commonly held value but also repudiates long-standing
arguments for Indian inferiority. According to Horsman, the earliest
forms of Anglo-Saxonist racialism (in the seventeenth and eighteenth centuries) celebrated the superiority of so-called Anglo-Saxon
institutions, but by the time Apess was writing, Anglo-Saxonists
focused not on superior institutions but rather on superior blood.

American revolutionaries, notably Thomas Jefferson, drew on a
mythic construction of English history that framed Anglo-Saxon
tribes as the freedom-loving inventors of political institutions designed to preserve "the natural rights of man" – rights on which all
"men" had equal claims. Separation from Britain could therefore
be cast as a return to the supposed purity of this mythic past (Horsman 9–24). In his study of the colonial era, however, Apess examines
a pre-Enlightenment context in which Indians were generally believed incapable of – or, worse, indifferent to – forming systems of
government, and were considered devoid of any sense of rights and
attendant laws to safeguard them. The *Eulogy* refutes colonial
charges that Indian society was basically anarchic. Citing Roger Williams's writings regarding Indian groups' strict geographical boundaries and disputes over the use of hunting grounds, Apess concludes
that "Indians had rights, and those rights were near and dear to
them" (288).

In other, pervasive references to indigenous political structures and social codes, he implicitly makes a case for cultural relativism, arguing, for example, that the Indians' avenging of the colonists' desecration of Indian graves and defacement of Indian monuments should be read not as an act of hostility but rather, "[a]ccording to the Indian custom," as "a righteous act" (282). With such examples, Apess invites his audience to read Indian "aggression" in Indian terms, as a defense of tradition-based, indigenous notions of rights and freedom. In Apess's reading, history shows that "the whites have always been the aggressors, and the war, cruelties, and bloodshed is a job of their own seeking, and not the Indians" (307). Moreover, he connects colonial hostilities with nineteenth-century frontier warfare, asserting that the wars arise "because the same spirit reigns there that reigned here in New England [in Philip's time]; and at present, there is no law to stop it" (307).

Revisions of the first colonists' view of Indian–white relations were not uncommon in Apess's day; many non-Indians, including both scholars and the public, had become critical of the early colonists' treatment of the "poor Indian." Such revisions, indeed, pervade the immensely popular "Indian plays" and romance novels of the period, all of them drenched in regret for the wronged, noble savage, whose fate was sealed by the purportedly inevitable course of human progress.

All such critiques of relations between savage and civilized, whether popular or scholarly, might be seen as continuing a lengthy tradition dating at least from the sixteenth century. Such treatments routinely catalogued the barbarities of so-called civilized nations and then queried just which human society rightly deserved the designation "savage." With this model in view, even Apess's most caustic inversions – for example, his painstakingly prefaced invocations of "white savages" – would not exactly shock his non-Indian audience. So Apess's innovation lies not primarily in his carefully documented exoneration of the "cursed memory" (284) of Philip, for whom he ultimately claims the distinction of being "the greatest man that ever lived upon the American shores" (290). Far more radically, Apess refuses the normalization of "extinction" by pointing out the ideological nature of American jurisprudence, by contending that institutionalized racism – rather than so-called natural processes – threatened the Indian, and by urging political intervention to alter the supposed destiny of indigenous peoples in America.

Although there were certainly Indian–white wars in the 1830s, most removal was achieved without war. Likewise, in Philip's day, most real estate transactions between immigrant settlers and native peoples, although often grossly inequitable, were entirely within the

legal parameters set down by Euro-Americans. Apess devotes a significant portion of the *Eulogy* to recounting details of Philip's "sales
of lands" (290) and attendant court actions. Adducing evidence that
Philip received unfair treatment in the "Pilgrims' court" (291),
Apess adds, "And, indeed, it would be a strange thing for poor unfortunate Indians to find justice in those courts of the pretended
pious in those days, or even since" (291).

As Apess argued his cause in New England, government agents
were busily assisting frontier Indians in the exercise of their right to
sign on the dotted line. As Michael Rogin has noted, the Jackson
administration cloaked efforts to seize Indian lands in a "fiction of
autonomous state and market processes" (223). Astutely, the *Eulogy*
argues that "Indian rights" must be understood in Indian terms, for
in New England as well as in the rest of the country, prevailing laws
and customs marked a travesty of justice. Elaborating on the parallels
between Philip's treatment under the law and the dynamics of Indian–white relations in his own day, Apess writes:

> Who stood up in those days, and since, to plead Indian rights?
> Was it the friend of the Indian? No, it was his enemies who
> rose – his enemies to judge and pass sentence. And we know
> that such kind of characters as the Pilgrims were, in regard to
> the Indians' rights, who, as they say, had none, must certainly
> always give verdict against them, as, generally speaking, they
> always have. (291)

Throughout, the *Eulogy* attempts to persuade so-called friends of the
Indian that they must avoid the trap of thinking themselves powerless to change the course of "destiny."

Michael Rogin has called attention to the mutually reinforcing
contradictions of Jacksonian rhetoric: While posturing as the benevolent parent and protector of the Indian, the federal government at
the same time declared itself powerless to interfere with white settlers' usurpations – with the "natural course" of westward migration.
But the government assured the people that even though such "natural processes" were afoot, the Great White Father, having his Indian children's best interests at heart, could be counted on to
intervene and protect them. So the story went: Although the government could not eradicate the frontier settlers' greed, it could
further Indians' best interests by convincing them that the only resource was to cede their lands. But in reality, Rogin argues, "Intrud-
ers entered Indian country only with government encouragement,
after the extension of state law" (218–20).

Apess makes explicit reference to Jacksonian removal politics in referencing Jackson as the "president of the United States" who "tells the Indians they cannot live among civilized people" and in characterizing the president as saying, in effect, "we want your lands and must have them and will have them" (307). Burlesquing the paternal "protections" of the Jackson administration, Apess writes:

> You see, my red children, that our fathers carried on this scheme of getting your lands for our use, and we have now become rich and powerful; and we have a right to do with you just as we please; we claim to be your fathers. And we think we shall do you a great favor, my dear sons and daughters, to drive you out, to get you away out of the reach of our civilized people, who are cheating you, for we have no law to reach them, we cannot protect you although you be our children. (307)

Thus, throughout his survey of the colonial encounter, Apess exposes the strange alchemy of the Europeans' Enlightenment claims to improve their inferiors and provide equal rights for equal citizens. He renders the first European colonists and their "rights" in terms of high irony: "those who came to improve our race and correct our errors, . . . those who are in the possession of [Philip's] soil, and only by the right of conquest" (277). Under existing laws, he contends, Indian rights amount to the "right" to relinquish rights and property. Eloquently affirming Philip's dire predictions, Apess writes:

> How deep, then, was the thought of Philip, when he could look from Maine to Georgia, and from the ocean to the lakes, and view with one look all his brethren withering before the more enlightened to come; and how true his prophecy, that the white people would not only cut down their groves but would enslave them. . . . Our groves and hunting grounds are gone, our dead are dug up, our council fires are put out, and a foundation was laid in the first Legislature to enslave our people, by taking from them all rights, which has been strictly adhered to ever since. (306)

Native peoples in his day, Apess concludes, remain "chained under desperate laws," just as they were "for nearly two hundred years" (306). Following precedents set in the colonial period, Apess declares, Philip's "few remaining descendants" (277) have been left to "drag out a miserable life as one chained to the galley" (306).

* * * * * *

As both imagery and explicit references in these passages demonstrate, Apess equates the treatment of native peoples with the more overt degradations of institutionalized slavery. Indeed, throughout, the *Eulogy* insists that there is more than a metaphoric link between these two forms of oppression and thus vehemently lays claim to the period's antislavery discourses.

From 1833 on, Apess's writings mark the kinds of connections between enslavement of African-Americans and the dispossession of American Indians that would be fully articulated by other activists and scholars only much later. Apess anticipates, for example, the analysis of contemporary historian Herbert Aptheker. Characterizing abolitionism as "the second successful revolutionary movement in the United States" (xi) (the American Revolution being the first), Aptheker writes: "The central commitment of the Abolitionist movement – its struggle against racism – was directed not only at enslavement but at all manifestations of the poison" (xiv). Patently, racism was as much a hallmark of European-Americans' relations with indigenous peoples as it was of their relations with Africans. Commenting on the relation between America's enslavement of blacks and its subjugation of Native Americans, Aptheker writes:

> Racism permeated slavery in the United States – characterized it, justified it, and sustained it. In another manifestation, in somewhat altered form, racism rationalized the genocidal policy practiced toward the indigenous population, the Native Americans. . . . To attack slavery, then, was to attack racism. (xiv)[6]

From Apess's perspective, to attack racist policies toward Native Americans was to attack slavery. Congruent with historical analyses that view American abolitionism and the struggle for Indian rights as discrete social movements, it has been suggested that Apess's decline as a public figure resulted from the increasing momentum of an abolitionist movement that ultimately "relegated the plight of the American Indian to a secondary place in reform thinking" (McQuaid 623; see also O'Connell xxxix). But such analyses both reduce abolitionism and reinstantiate the discourses that separated African-Americans and Native Americans into distinct races. Apess did not merely appropriate abolitionist rhetoric for a separate Native American political agenda; rather, Apess *was,* in the truest sense, himself an abolitionist.

From his first publication to his last, racist attitudes toward Native Americans are Apess's focus. Commencing with the 1833 publication of *The Experiences of Five Christian Indians of the Pequot Tribe; or, An Indian's Looking-Glass for the White Man,* however, Apess begins to examine parallels between the situations of Indians and Africans. (Notably, 1833 also marked the founding of the American Anti-Slavery Society.) Employing both Christian and Enlightenment rhetoric, Apess notes the lack of protections "in . . . persons and in property" for people of color "throughout the Union" and denounces those who "take the skin as a pretext to keep us from our unalienable and lawful rights" (156). With the chronicle of his role in the insurrection at Mashpee plantation, the 1835 *Indian Nullification of the Unconstitutional Laws of Massachusetts Relative to the Marshpee Tribe; or, The Pretended Riot Explained*, Apess reiterates the correspondences between economic exploitation of the Mashpees and enslavement of Africans. Presenting both historical and economic justifications to identify the oppression of Native Americans with that of Africans, Apess bitterly concludes: "It is a fine thing to be an Indian. One might almost as well be a slave" (188).

Although Apess clearly drew heavily on formalized abolitionist rhetoric in articulating such parallels, one need not assume that his ideas were borrowed from abolitionists. Apess's awareness of his own mixed biological heritage, his personal experience, and his social context could easily have suggested such equations. Census documents show that both Apess and his wife might themselves have been part African-American (O'Connell xxvii, fn. 17). Moreover, no doubt among his constituency in general, and certainly among the Mashpees with whom he lived and helped to organize an insurrection to demand legal rights, there was a great deal of intermarriage between Africans and Indians.[7]

Additionally, the ongoing Seminole War provided a compelling backdrop for Apess's arguments implicitly advocating a joint black–red resistance. In that war – ultimately the longest and costliest "Indian war" in U.S. history – free blacks, escaped black slaves, and Seminole Indians fought side by side against American forces (Rogin 235ff.). No doubt, this protracted conflict would have revealed the many contradictions inherent in viewing the plight of African-Americans and the struggles of American Indians as separate issues. Indeed, a commander of government troops fighting the Seminoles at one point insisted, "This . . . is a negro, not an Indian war," an assessment that caused abolitionists to be blamed for the war (Rogin 238). With the hostilities in Florida, such strife was no longer framed as the familiar contest of savage against civilized; increasingly, such conflicts were framed, as in Thomas Hart Benton's words, as "the ravages of the colored races upon the white" (quoted in Horsman 205).

From the time of *Experiences* on, Apess's texts point out the analogous religious, juridical, and economic practices that underlay the

dispossession and/or genocide of Native populations and the enslavement of Africans. Subordination of both groups, he realized,
was buttressed by complex moral arguments, by legal sleight of hand,
by strong material incentives for certain segments of the population,
and, increasingly, by scientific discourse. Although originally the
"American savage" had been deemed a notch above the "African"
in the Anglo-Saxonist vision of racial hierarchy, by Apess's time that
slight advantage had been virtually erased. Americans had not only
begun to doubt whether Indians could ever be "elevated" to the
status of whites, but also speculated that indigenous peoples might,
in fact, be fated to move in the opposite direction. Georgia Governor
George M. Troup's letter to then Secretary of War John C. Calhoun
in 1824 demonstrates the perception that Indians would ultimately
"devolve" to the level of blacks:

> [T]he utmost of rights and privileges which public opinion
> would concede to Indians, would fix them in a middle station,
> between the negro and the white man; and that, as long as they
> survived this degradation, without the possibility of attaining
> the elevation of the latter, they would gradually sink to the
> condition of the former – a point of degeneracy below which
> they could not fall. . . . (quoted in Horsman 196)

Although intellectuals of predominantly northern European
American heritage (self-identified Anglo-Saxons) – even those generally sympathetic to both abolitionism and Indian reform – might
quibble over minute increments in the racial hierarchy, all agreed
that when compared with themselves, Africans and Indians were un-
deniably alike: Both groups were inferior to Anglo-Saxons. For a host
of reasons, then, Apess's work continually highlights the common
legacy of people of color.[8] The parallels between those identified as
Native Americans and as African-Americans, in particular, are more
vividly, more explicitly drawn with each new publication. In this regard, Apess's position indeed anticipates prominent black nationalist
Martin R. Delaney's stance, progressive even in 1854: "[W]e [Afri-
can-Americans and Native Americans] are identical as subjects of
American wrongs, outrages, and oppression, and therefore one in
interest" (214–15).

Because their ultimate goal – the eradication of American racism
– was the same, abolitionism and Indian reform readily occupied the
same rhetorical terrain. Like others more commonly considered abolitionists, Apess pleaded his cause by way of Judeo-Christian teachings and Enlightenment ideals as put forward in the Declaration of
Independence. Apess's opening "appeal to the lovers of liberty" has

a decidedly abolitionist ring. The *Eulogy* commences by chronicling
an early-seventeenth-century incident in which thirty American Indians were taken captive by an English ship "to be sold for slaves
among the Spaniards," an "inhuman act of the whites," Apess maintains, "which caused the Indians to be jealous forever afterward"
(279). Thus he locates the historical roots of racial tensions between
Europeans and American Indians in an actual attempt to enslave.
Apess then implies that the colonial powers had forever after chron-
ically confused enslavement with religious conversion; he states,
"How they could go to work to enslave a free people and call it
religion is beyond the power of my imagination and outstrips the
revelation of God's word" (279). Further invoking Christianity as
the ground for his broad-spectrum antislavery appeal, Apess tells the
story of how the English, "those pretended Christians," captured
and subsequently sold into slavery King Philip's ten-year-old son. Un-
derscoring colonial hypocrisies, Apess asserts that the early European
settlers would "on the Sabbath day . . . gather themselves together
and say that God is no respecter of persons," even as they were
"hating and selling their fellow men in bondage" (301). Proclaim-
ing that "[he who would] advocate slavery is worse than a beast"
surrounded by "the most corrupt and debasing principles in the
world," Apess maintains that it was only violent resistance – including taking the lives of their own people – that saved Indians from
the same fate as Africans. Apess contends:

> And there is no manner of doubt but that all my countrymen
> would have been enslaved if they had tamely submitted. But
> no sooner would they butcher every white man that come in
> their way, and even put an end to their own wives and children,
> and that was all that prevented them from being slaves; yes, *all.*
> (301)

Apess must have perceived in the burgeoning Abolitionist movement
– a highly visible international movement with a sense of moral urgency, a movement with clearly defined goals, a movement bent on
revolutionary intervention in the existing social matrix – a powerful
ally for Indian reform. To link his own reform objectives with those
of abolitionists, however, Apess needed to render his cause visible.

* * * * * *

In 1789 Henry Knox, secretary of war (and thus in charge of Indian
affairs), pronounced New England Indians nonexistent:

It is . . . painful to consider, that all the Indian tribes, once existing in those States now the best cultivated and most popu-
lous, have become extinct. If the same causes continue, the
same effects will happen; and, in a short period, the idea of an
Indian on this side of the Mississippi will only be found in the
page of the historian. (quoted in Pearce 56)

Some forty years later, native historian William Apess – a mixed-
blood survivor of the "extinct" Pequots – asserted the continuing
presence of New England Native Americans. Congruent with Vanishing American ideology, non-Indians believed that the only authentic
Indian was the "wild Indian" of the frontier. As James Madison
stated on leaving office:

Next to the case of the black race within our bosom, that of
the red on our borders is the problem most baffling to the
policy of our country. (quoted in Rogin 319)

Although blacks in contact with whites would always remain blacks,
Indians mingling with whites ceased to be truly Indian. Indians who
coexisted with whites either degenerated (becoming less Indian) or,
in rare instances, assimilated (becoming less Indian). Either way,
prolonged contact eroded true Indianness. Thus, for most New England non-Indians, Native Americans in their midst could no longer
be considered "real" (noble) Indians, but merely degenerate "rem-
nants" of an admirable – though quickly fading – past, living out
the last days of their race in wantonness and squalor. Although, with
free blacks, New England Indians were among the most despised
people in New England (O'Connell lxii), their status was viewed differently from that of Indians on the frontier. Thus one of Apess's
objectives was to demonstrate that "wherever there are any Indians"
(307), the same legacy of colonial racism prevails. Focusing on the
racialist dynamics of Indian–white relations "from Maine to Georgia," Apess's writings redraw the frontier as the color line, and in
so doing lift the veil of invisibility that cloaks indigenous groups
remaining east of the Mississippi.

To rephrase Apess's own question: Where, then, shall we place
this hero of the wilderness? Arguably, Apess scholarship needs to
move further in the direction suggested by Apess himself, needs to
be examined outside the parameters of American exceptionalism,
outside familiar plots of How the West Was Won. Clearly, the complexity of his political project has not yet been fully appreciated. To
be sure, his Enlightenment discourse involves problematic language.

With his assertions that Indians are *as good as* whites and that Indians ought to be acknowledged "as men and as Christians," he appears to concede to white males prior claims to the universal human subject. And although he forcefully advocates "rights" and "liberty" for indigenous peoples, it is unclear just what practices would fulfill his objectives – an ambiguity perhaps politically necessary.

Although as a political advocate and a cultural nationalist Apess appears to be without peer in his era, it is perhaps his role as historian that is most suggestive for contemporary scholars. O'Connell states, "The best modern histories of the encounters between New England Native Americans and the Anglo-Americans confirm the interpretive stance Apess takes" (276). But the *Eulogy*, like other Apess texts, goes beyond Indian-situated counter-memory; all his writings raise profound questions about the tensions between provisional and absolute truth and the implications of such questions for immediate political urgency. As an Indian, as a Pequot – a group whose extinction was decreed by law and subsequently transcribed by historians as fact – Apess was well aware that both law and history are ideologically invested cultural products. Yet he knew that without consensual truth, there would be little hope for implementation of "one general law" for all. The *Eulogy on King Philip* repeatedly reminds us that past and present stand in dynamic relation.[9]

Notes

1. For a sustained analysis of this ideology, see Brian W. Dippie's *The Vanishing American: White Attitudes and U.S. Indian Policy.*
2. For examples of the tendency to characterize both Apess and his reform efforts through this ideological lens, see McQuaid (622–5), Nielsen (418–20), and O'Connell (xxxviii–xxxix). At the time of this writing, Apess is believed to have died in 1838.
3. Barry O'Connell notes that there are two editions of this text. The first edition (the one used here) represents the full text of the January 8, 1836, address; it was published in 1836. The second edition appears to be a shortened version of the original and was delivered orally on January 26, 1836; it was published in 1837 (325).
4. See O'Connell's conjecture regarding Apess's constituency among New England Native Americans and African-Americans.
5. The *Advocate* in fact promises a "full view" at the second lecture, owing to some "dissatisfaction at the previous one" (quoted in O'Connell).
6. Aptheker reiterates this point in a 1992 study of the continuing presence of antiracist movements in American society. See his "Abolitionism and Racism" in *Anti-Racism in U.S. History: The First Two Hundred Years* (129–46).
7. O'Connell points to the "unreliable identifications of people by race and

by ethnicity" in New England population records of the time, given the extent of intermarriage among groups (xxvi). Further, Jack D. Forbes argues that in the American population at large, mixed Native American-African heritage may be far more widespread than most contemporary readings of the evidence would allow. In regard to the extent of cultural exchange and intermarriage between these two groups, Forbes asserts that "a sound empirical and conceptual basis" establishes "beyond any doubt that old assumptions must be set aside" (5).

8. Apparently, "colored" was in the early nineteenth century no more stable a category than "Anglo-Saxon." Just as "Anglo-Saxon" was used at certain times to refer exclusively to those deemed direct descendants of the Saxon tribes (i.e., to exclude the Irish, French, Scots, and Welsh) and at other times more inclusively (i.e., to include all whites of European descent), so the term "colored" was used by some to mean only those of African descent and by others to designate all nonwhites. Apess commonly refers to himself and to other nonwhites collectively as "colored."

9. I wish to thank Michael P. Kramer and David Van Leer for their insights, advice and encouragement through successive drafts of this essay.

Works Cited

Apess, William. *On Our Own Ground: The Complete Writings of William Apess, A Pequot,* ed. Barry O'Connell. Amherst: University of Massachusetts Press, 1992.

Aptheker, Herbert. *Abolitionism: A Revolutionary Movement.* Twayne's Social Movements Past and Present Series, gen. ed. Irwin T. Sanders. Boston: Twayne, 1989.

"Abolitionism and Racism." *Anti-Racism in U.S. History: The First Two Hundred Years.* Contributions in American History, No. 143. New York: Greenwood, 1992: 129–46.

Delaney, Martin R. "The Political Destiny of the Colored Race." *The Ideological Origins of Black Nationalism,* comp. Sterling Stuckey. Boston: Beacon, 1972: 195–236.

Dippie, Brian W. *The Vanishing American: White Attitudes and U.S. Indian Policy.* Lawrence: University Press of Kansas, 1982.

Forbes, Jack D. *Black Africans and Native Americans: Color, Race and Caste in the Evolution of Red-Black Peoples.* Oxford: Blackwell, 1988.

Horsman, Reginald. *Race and Manifest Destiny: The Origins of Racial Anglo-Saxonism.* Cambridge, MA: Harvard University Press, 1981.

McQuaid, Kim. "William Apes, Pequot: An Indian Reformer in the Jackson Era." *New England Quarterly* 50.4 (1977): 605–25.

Nielsen, Donald M. "The Mashpee Indian Revolt of 1833." *New England Quarterly* 58.3 (1985): 400–20.

O'Connell, Barry. Introduction. *On Our Own Ground: The Complete Writings of William Apess, A Pequot,* ed. Barry O'Connell. Amherst: University of Massachusetts Press, 1992: xiii–lxxvii.

Pearce, Roy Harvey. *Savagism and Civilization: A Study of the Indian and the American Mind.* 1953. Rev. ed. Berkeley: University of California Press, 1988.

Rogin, Michael Paul. *Fathers and Children: Andrew Jackson and the Subjugation of the American Indian.* New York: Vintage Books, 1976.

5

"THEY OUGHT TO ENJOY THE HOME OF THEIR FATHERS"

THE TREATY OF 1838, SENECA INTELLECTUALS, AND LITERARY GENESIS

DANIEL F. LITTLEFIELD, JR.

When the Revolutionary War ended, both New York and Massachusetts claimed the Iroquois lands in New York. In 1786 New York was given jurisdiction over the land, but Massachusetts was granted the preemptive right to purchase it should the Iroquois decide to sell. This preemptive right was sold three times in the next few years, during which time its holders bought tracts of varying size from the Senecas, who under the Treaty of Big Tree (1797) were established on several small reservations in western New York (Abler and Tooker 508–9). Like the other Iroquois, the Senecas became demoralized; social structures broke down, and reservation life sapped the vitality from traditional rituals (Wallace, "Origins" 444–5). Also, like the other tribes, the Senecas were besieged by appeals from Christian missionaries to allow the establishment of mission stations on Seneca land, where there had been little mission work before the war. Although Quakers established a mission among the Allegany Senecas in 1798, other mission groups were not successful until the second and third decades of the nineteenth century. With the missions came schools as part of the machinery for "civilizing" the Senecas. Although there was a school on the Buffalo Reservation as early as 1811 and on the Cornplanter Grant by 1814, schools, like missions, did not gain a solid foothold in Seneca land until the 1820s (Abler and Tooker 509–10).

By that time, the Senecas were split into factions known as the "Christian party" and the "Pagan party." The former embraced the efforts of the missionaries and advocated adoption of lifestyles and institutions like those of the whites. The Pagans rejected the missionary influence, and many followed the teachings of Handsome Lake, the Seneca prophet. His visions in 1799 revealed his famous Code, which reflected obvious Quaker influence but which revitalized Seneca society and formed the basis of the Longhouse religion, still vital among modern-day Senecas.[1]

Factionalism was heightened by the sale of Seneca land. In 1823 and 1826 the Ogden Land Company, which had bought the preemptive right to Seneca land in 1810, purchased large Seneca tracts on the Genessee River and on the Buffalo Creek, Tonawanda, and Cattaraugus reservations. Like its predecessors, the Ogden Company continued to press the Senecas to sell more land. This pressure was increased by the Indian removal policy of Andrew Jackson's administration. The Senecas resisted until 1838, when, through intimidation, bribery, and other forms of corruption, about half of the Seneca chiefs were induced to sign a treaty in which they agreed to sell the remaining Seneca lands and emigrate to Kansas. Only some of the chiefs supported the treaty; the majority of Senecas were against it. Convinced that the Senecas had been defrauded, the Society of Friends and others made the treaty an issue of public debate and undertook to have it revoked (Abler and Tooker 511). The public debate initiated by the 1838 treaty lasted for more than a decade. As a first result, it brought a number of young intellectuals from the Seneca reserves to the forefront in Seneca affairs and led immediately to a number of polemical tracts, including works, pro and con, by the Seneca chiefs Maris Bryant Pierce and Nathaniel Thayer Strong. As the debate engendered by the Treaty of 1838 led to the Seneca governmental "revolution" of 1848, other intellectuals emerged, such as Peter Wilson and Ely and Nicholson Parker, and Seneca literature expanded to include not only polemical tracts but also oratory, essays, history, and ethnography. The decade following the Treaty of 1838, then, witnessed the genesis of Seneca literature in English.

The first Seneca to make a significant public response to the treaty was Maris Bryant Pierce (1811–74). Born on the Allegany Reservation, Pierce was educated in a Quaker primary school, at Fredonia Academy, at a college preparatory school in Thetford, Vermont, and finally at Dartmouth College, which he entered in 1836. By that time, he had converted to Christianity and was a member of the Presbyterian church (Vernon 22–3).

Even before he reached Dartmouth, Pierce had committed himself to use his education on behalf of his people. While in college preparatory school at Thetford in 1834, he was reminded by White Seneca and other chiefs at Buffalo Creek, where the Pierce family then lived, that he had sworn to "resist usurpation" and to "raise the tomahawk" whenever necessary. Pressure was mounting for the Senecas to sell their land and remove to the West.

The chiefs urged Pierce to come home and help them resist the latest assault on their domain. Stop in Albany, they directed him, and ask Governor Marcy his views on the extension of New York laws to the Senecas. Had the governor advised the late Seneca delegation to remove to the West? What was the feeling of the people in Albany concerning Indian issues? Pierce was to be discreet in order not to make the governor "suspicious and jealouse."[2] Again and again during the next few years, Pierce would use his time between sessions at Dartmouth to do the chiefs' bidding.

The confidence that the older chiefs placed in Pierce was echoed by his friend and confidant Geh-da-on-toh, or James Young, the Cayuga nephew of White Seneca, who lived with the Senecas at Buffalo Creek. In 1838 Young wrote Pierce at Dartmouth: "You seem to be more ambitious for improvement than ever, I am glad that you feel so, the means is within your reach; your situations & advantages have led me to hope that you might be one of the many that would make good use of your education among our people, & cause the hearts of our old men to be glad, and not occasion grief to their aged hearts." Too many had abused the advantages brought by education and had caused division and discord among their people.[3]

During the months preceding the signing of the Treaty of Buffalo Creek in 1838, Pierce and Young commiserated over the Seneca infighting. Political division and squabbling were rife among the chiefs at Buffalo Creek. Young's responses to Pierce's letters of anxious concern contained little to soothe him. "I have wept in sorrow," Young wrote, "when I considered the changes that have & are still taking place among our once united people." Where they were once great and lived in peace, where they were once strong and happy, now contention, strife, discord, and divisions beset the chiefs. Where once the chiefs agreed on all transactions, now three or four parties squabbled over such matters as timber. Sometimes, Young wrote, the chiefs' squabbling had led him "to fear that they will continue in this course, & the whites are aware of it, & take the advantage" (Young to Pierce, April 3, 1837; Pierce Papers).

His fears were realized. In late 1837, he urged Pierce to come home and accept his share of the "great responsibility" that had devolved on them. The welfare of the Seneca Nation was at stake. The treaty commission was determined to have a treaty, sign it who would, "few or many." Look at the treaty made with the Cherokees in 1835, Young wrote. A notice was given that a council would convene at New Echota, and a treaty was made with those present, a minority of the tribe. Did the same fate await the Senecas? All chiefs "true to the interest" of the Seneca Nation should be there to prevent it (Young to Pierce, December 26, 1837; Pierce Papers). And among "all chiefs" Young included Pierce.

Both of the young chiefs agonized over what course was best for the Senecas. After much uncertainty, Pierce signed the treaty during the council, apparently believing, momentarily, that the Seneca case was hopeless, and Young signed it later (Vernon 27; Peters 550–64). But they were disturbed by the intimidation, bribery, and fraud that surrounded its negotiation, and before Pierce returned to Dartmouth, they laid plans to draft a memorial to the U.S. Senate describing the manner in which the treaty council had been conducted and explaining their motives for signing. Young consulted with his uncle, White Seneca, and drafted the memorial, but they never sent it (Young to Pierce, April 10 and May 4, 1838; Pierce Papers).

The reason, perhaps, was that as time passed, the treaty became more objectionable to them and they rued the day they had signed the "fatal paper." Both now objected to its removal provision, and through their correspondence they fed each other's growing resentment at the treatment that not only the Senecas but Indians in general had received at the hands of the whites. Young wrote Pierce, who was always anxious for news from home, that "it is indeed to be deplored of the manner in which the aborigines of the Country are treated by the whites, the manner in which they are rewarded for their hospitality in receiving their forefathers when they were yet small & weak & strangers in this Country." He found appropriate language in the lines of the poet who described the Indian as the April snow:

> In the warm noon we shrink away;
> And fast they follow, as we go.
> Toward the setting day
> Till they shall fill the land, and we
> Are driven into the western Sea. (Young to Pierce, May 4,
>   1838; Pierce Papers)

Young apparently sensed that of the two, Pierce was destined to be the more effective spokesman for the Senecas. He urged Pierce to persevere in his studies, to ignore the common assertion that the "Natives cannot learn." Wisdom and reason, he asserted, "have told us, that by proper culture they can be *honour* to Country & an *ornament* to Empires in point of reason." The Great Creator had been as bountiful to the Indian as to "the white man in confering strength to his intellectual capabilities." Thus, Young wrote prophetically, "I hope that you will be very useful to our people whatever our destiny will be hereafter" (Young to Pierce, June 6, 1838; Pierce Papers).

Young had evidence that Pierce was emerging as a spokesman for the Senecas. In May 1838 Pierce had gathered his courage and addressed the whites on the subject of temperance. He understood well the power of oratory and knew the influence of great Seneca orators of the recent past, such as Red Jacket and Farmer's Brother. In style and delivery he was no match for them, but he recognized the speaker's platform as a vehicle for placing before the public the Seneca objections to the Treaty of Buffalo Creek. And he could draw strength from the Seneca tradition in diplomacy. On July 4, 1838, in another temperance speech at Canaan, he asserted that treaties had been made through the influence and aid of distilled spirits, and consent to the treaties had been extorted from signers under the influence of liquor. He told of the excitement, the actions of land speculators, and the electioneering that had surrounded the treaty council at Buffalo Creek. Among those urging the chiefs to consent had been "a certain notorious minister who preached Gen'l Jackson's *humane* policy of removal of the Indians." The treaty was obtained, Pierce said, by the signatures of a minority of chiefs, among whom were one or two "notorious drunkards" (Pierce, Speech on Temperance, July 4, 1838; Pierce Papers; Vernon 29).

Such speeches were rehearsals for the one that brought Pierce wide recognition and established him as a major spokesman not only for Seneca rights but for Indian rights in general. Delivered on August 28, 1838, at the Baptist Church in Buffalo, it was published and widely circulated as *Address on the Present Condition and Prospects of the Aboriginal Inhabitants of North America, with Particular Reference to the Seneca Nation.* Although Pierce's purpose was to argue against acceptance of the treaty of 1838, he did not attack the issue directly. Instead, he placed the Seneca crisis in the context of general attitudes of whites toward Indians and of the history of Indian–white relations. His complex argument deserves extended analysis.

In the published *Address* Pierce first addressed two basic premises whites held regarding the Indians: The Indians are doomed to disappear, and their natural constitution makes them incapable of comprehending and acquiring the habits of Christian civilization. History had furnished ample evidence to give the first premise credence. But Pierce, unwilling to accept the "bitter cup" as God's will, asked: "But *whence* and why are we thus doomed? Why must we be crushed by the arm of civilization, or the requiem of our race be chanted by the waves of the Pacific which is destined to engulph us?" (4) The Indian and "civilization" need not be incompatible, one destroying the other. Thus Pierce's response to the second premise was that the Indian was indeed capable of acquiring the habits of Christian civilization.

In shaping his argument in the *Address,* Pierce examined Indian responses to white contact. Those who believed that the Indian was "untamable" questioned why the Indian had not become Christian and "civilized" to any large extent as a result of contact with whites and of efforts by missionaries. To Pierce, the answer was not inability to understand but Indian distrust resulting from the ill effects of contact. What if some "beings from fairy land, or some distant planet" should come among the whites, he asked, and the whites offered the beings the hospitality of their homes and fruits of their labor? What if those beings should then "by dint of their *superior wisdom* dazzle and amaze you, so as for what to them were *toys and rattles* they should gain freer admission and fuller welcome, till finally they should claim the *right* to your possessions and of hunting you like wild beasts, from your long and hitherto undisputed domain, how ready would *you* be to be taught of *them?*" (5)

He continued with a rhetorical question: Would not such action make the whites distrustful of the beings? Just so the Indians regarded the whites. In light of the way in which the whites had "habitually dealt with the Indians," the wonder was not that the Indians had not "laid aside their own peculiar notions and habits, and adopted those of their civilized neighbors," but that their hatred had not "burned with ten-fold fury against them." It was not, then, that the Indians could not be civilized; they had simply chosen not to be.

Pierce asserted that Indians possessed naturally certain characteristics that were fundamental in civilized people. They were physically strong and susceptible to feelings of hatred, friendship, love, pity, gratitude, ambition, pride, and vanity. They possessed imagination, memory, judgment, and elements of a moral sense, and they were sensitive to honor and disgrace. Indian history was replete with those who possessed these natural characteristics: Philip, Tecumseh, Red Jacket, Osceola. In Pierce's view, the fundamental human elements were "susceptible of cultivation and improvement, so as to entitle their possessor, to the rank which civilization and christianity bestow" (7). He cited the examples of Pocahontas, Catharine Brown, and, finally, Brown's tribe, the "ill-starred Cherokees." The Cherokees belied the theory that Indians could not be civilized or Christianized. They had made rapid progress in education, literacy, and letters. Their leader was John Ross – a scholar, patriot, and honorable man – who possessed "a character both of intellect and heart which many of the white men in high places may *envy,* yet *never be able to attain*" (8). However, his Indian blood doomed even such a man "and his children and kin to be hunted at the point of the bayonet by those powers, from their home and possessions and country, to the 'Terra incognita' beyond the Mississippi" (8).

Pierce's choice of the Cherokees as an example was strategic. Because the Eastern press had covered the Cherokee conflicts with the state of Georgia, the long history of their legal and moral fight against removal to the West was well known to Pierce's audience. Much sympathy had been generated for the Cherokees during the several preceding years, and Pierce no doubt hoped that some of that sympathy might spill over to the Senecas. At the time he made his speech, the Cherokees were under military rule and were in the process of being removed to the West.

Like the Cherokees, the Senecas were not only capable of being "civilized and christianized," he argued, but desired to be so. He pointed to their recent "improvements" in agriculture, equipment, labor practices, homes, diet, dress, and medical practices. Many tried to keep informed of outside events, several subscribed to newspapers and magazines, and some of the young men had libraries. "All these improvements," said Pierce, "are advancing at a rapid rate *except when* they are *distracted with other cares and anxieties*" (10). Of course, the present distraction was the treaty of 1838. To Pierce, it was not a question of whether the Senecas could be "civilized" but how that end could be best achieved. The answer was for the Senecas to remain in New York. There their lands were as fertile as those they would receive in the West. New York was the burial place of their ancestors and the place where they had played out their history. There, close to settled white society, were opportunities for physical, intellectual, and moral growth. The land company agents argued that in the West, free from white encroachment, the Senecas could possess a virtual wilderness. To Pierce, New York was Eden enough if evil-minded whites could be kept off Seneca land. Realizing that history was repeating itself in the Seneca treaty, Pierce was convinced that the Indians might as well stand their ground in 1838 as later.

It was an old story. The Ogden Land Company, claiming to be generous, offered one to two dollars per acre for land that to the whites was worth much more. In an appendix to the published speech, Pierce published a contract made in 1837 between an agent of the Ogden Land Company and a Seneca chief securing the chief's influence in the upcoming treaty negotiations. Pierce charged that besides buying chiefs, the land agents and pro-treaty factions used money, brandy, and intimidation to secure the treaty (14–16).

But what if the Senecas accepted the offer and left? Pierce did not believe that they "could possess *such a territory* this side of the shores of the Pacific, with *safety, free of molestation and in perpetuity*" (12). He understood well the ramifications of the term "Manifest Destiny": " 'Westward the Star of Empire takes its way,' and whenever that empire is held by the white man, nothing is safe or unmolested or enduring against his avidity for gain."⁴ The whites had already passed the Mississippi and were looking toward the Rocky Mountains – "nay even for the surf beaten shore of the Western Ocean." If the Senecas removed to the West, the whites in time would want their lands there and ask them to remove farther west, where conflicts would be inevitable with "other and more warlike tribes." But worse still would be the class of whites the Senecas would meet there: "those *white borderers,* who infest, yes *infest,* the western border of the white population, will annoy us more fatally than even the Indians themselves" (12). Pierce had described a cycle of history often repeated during the two preceding centuries. He did not want the Senecas to be part of its repetition. Thus he ended his tract with an appeal to the whites to let them live on in New York and let those who were "converted heathen" continue to serve God.

Pierce's tract is a clear acceptance of a prevailing concept held by government officials and others concerned with Indian affairs at the time: Indians must assimilate in order to survive. If the Senecas desired to return to the manners and customs of their ancestors, it might be better to remove them. But Pierce believed they were culturally beyond the point of return and insisted that they desired to adopt "those modes of living, and acting and thinking, which result from the cultivation and enlightening of the moral and intellectual faculties of man" (12).

Although he accepted the inevitability of assimilation, Pierce rejected the official government policy aimed at achieving it. Ostensibly, government officials and bureaucrats told themselves and each other, removal was in the best interests of the Indians because it would give them time to acquire the habits of "civilization." Andrew Jackson and his policymakers had been thoroughly successful in implementing this policy; even the powerful Cherokees had succumbed. Now Pierce was urging the weak Senecas to resist. The Ogden Land Company might have the preemptive right to buy Seneca land, but it could not force the Senecas to accept its offers, and Pierce made a strong case that the Senecas' material or spiritual lot would not be better in the West. His reference to the "ill-starred" Cherokees and the "Terra incognita" to which they had been exiled was aimed at arousing public sympathy in order to save the Senecas from a similar fate.

Pierce's *Address* reveals a good deal about the author. His style is often flowery and heavy, almost bookish at times, probably the result of his reading. His references to poets and to Indian figures, both historical and contemporary, indicate wide knowledge of literature and history – probably acquired at Thetford and Dartmouth – as well as of current events. He was also politic. He played on the sympathy of the whites and espoused "civilization," the end sought by the white policymakers. Ultimately, however, the sentiments were a mask from behind which Pierce raised a loud native voice against the concept of Indian removal. And as the first polemic voice raised against the Treaty of 1838, it was a strong one.

Pierce's Buffalo speech gained him widespread attention. When he returned to Dartmouth the following month, his classmates formally congratulated him on the "eloquent and highly valuable address" (E. L. Stafton [?] in Behalf of the Junior Class, September 13, 1838; Pierce Papers). But Pierce did not simply sit and enjoy the praise heaped on him; he worked steadily to thwart ratification of the treaty. He helped to amass evidence that most Seneca chiefs opposed sale of the land and removal, and that fraud had been used in obtaining signatures.

In early September, he and thirteen other chiefs communicated to the president their opposition to the treaty and their determination not to remove. In January 1839 he was one of four Senecas appointed to act as attorneys representing the Tonawanda, Allegany, Cattaraugas, and Buffalo Creek reservations. In Washington, they drafted memorials to the president and to the Senate expressing Seneca opposition to the treaty. Much of this work fell to Pierce, the only educated member of the delegation. In August 1839, when the secretary of war called a meeting at Cattaraugus of the chiefs opposed to removal, the chiefs wrote Pierce, who was back at Dartmouth, "Now we wish that you will not fail to come home; for why should we lose our homes from so small a matter? We want you here in order if we should be defeated: we will not say we are defeated on your account, because you were not here." And in December of that year, he was ordered to go to Albany as part of the Seneca delegation.[5]

The Senecas were not alone in their efforts to defeat the treaty. Whites in Washington and elsewhere immediately joined them, publicizing the fraud, intimidation, and bribery that had surrounded the signing. Pierce's Buffalo address was published and widely distributed. In its wake came other polemical pieces. Reuben B. Heacock of Buffalo published a pamphlet titled *An Exposition of Some Frauds* in October 1839. Substantial support also came from the Society of Friends. The Quakers battled the pro-Ogden spokesmen in the press and through pamphlets, issuing in early 1840 their most significant pamphlet, *The Case of the Seneca Indians,* in which they attempted to sum up the case. Despite these and other efforts, however, the treaty was ratified on March 25, 1840, and proclaimed by President Martin Van Buren on April 4.

By then Pierce was in his last year at Dartmouth, where he had continued to make a name for himself as an orator. He apparently felt it important to inform the general public about the Senecas and to point out the wrongs done them. In March 1840 he spoke to a large audience at Parsipanny, New Jersey, on the manners and customs of the Six Nations Confederacy and displayed Iroquois handicrafts such as wampum and moccasins to demonstrate that Iroquois women were not indolent, as had been charged. In May he delivered an address on the same subject at Woodstock, Vermont, as he did in July before the Philomatheon Society at Meriden Academy. And at his graduation, he spoke on "The Destiny of the Aborigines of America" (Vernon 25, 32–3).

Pierce left Dartmouth in the summer of 1840 with fond feelings for the school and with doubts about the future. As Pierce prepared to leave, he asked himself where he should find his home: in the west, or where he was born? "Shall it be my native home and remain inviolate? I hope it was so, but alas, it was not so. Our people are in the state of a great dilemma – to go or stay – but must go, says the government of the U.S. Humanity speaks: they may stay. They ought to enjoy the home of their fathers" (Pierce to [?], July 20, 1840; Pierce Papers; Vernon 33). Thus, when Pierce left for Buffalo Creek in August, he was apparently convinced that right was on the Senecas' side.

The strong public case that Pierce and the Quakers had made to support charges of fraud and intimidation surrounding the Treaty of 1838 at length drew a major response from Senecas on the pro-removal side. It was drafted by the young Seneca chief Nathaniel Thayer Strong (1810–72). Although little is known of Strong's early years, he was well educated and in 1837 was working as a U.S. interpreter and assistant to James Stryker, subagent to the New York Indians at Buffalo. In the months leading up to the treaty, Strong and Stryker worked behind the scenes with agents of the Ogden Land Company to help secure the treaty and, after its signing, to obtain its ratification. There is also sound evidence that Strong was involved in the bribery efforts by the Ogden agents.[6]

Strong published his response to the Quakers in January 1841 as *Appeal to the Christian Community on the Condition and Prospects of the New York Indians*.[7] His avowed purpose was to answer the Friends' objections to the Treaty of 1838, as expressed in *The Case of the Seneca Indians,* and to call attention to the condition of the Senecas and the influence of the treaty on their future. Strong's *Appeal* was as much a defense of his own actions, and of the chiefs who had signed the treaty and remained pro-treaty, as it was an answer to the Friends' publication.

First, he argued that the treaty was the result of a general movement among the New York Indians to accept the concept of removal. For more than thirty years, long before the Ogden Land Company had been formed, he said, those tribes had resolved to seek new lands in the West. They had first considered lands on the White River in Indiana but had finally acquired lands in Wisconsin in 1832. Some of the Oneidas and all of the Brothertons and Stockbridges removed, but the other tribes hesitated. Still, the more "intelligent" chiefs, Strong said, realized the "increasing evils" of the encroachment of unprincipled whites who overran their lands and corrupted their people. With the government urging them to move, the Senecas had sent delegations to the West in 1834 and 1837 to explore the lands. The last delegation had brought a favorable report, and a treaty council was called.

Second, in the *Appeal* Strong defended the actions at the council. Here he was twice concerned, for he had not only signed the treaty but had also interpreted it. The Quakers had charged that the council was called at the instigation of the Ogden Land Company. Strong's weak rebuttal was simply this: "I am certain that they had no immediate agency in bringing about the council, nor in the selection of the commissioners appointed to hold it" (8).

There had also been questions regarding the signatures on the treaty. Strong insisted that the document had been duly interpreted and "regularly" signed by a majority of the chiefs according to the practices of the Six Nations. This latter point is debatable. Forty-three chiefs signed the treaty, and there is some evidence that the number eligible to sign was closer to eighty or ninety. Furthermore, those opposing the treaty argued that consensus, not majority rule, had been the mode of decision making among the Senecas. Strong also argued that before the signing there had been little interference by whites, but that between the signing and the time the amended

treaty was sent by the U.S. Senate for the chiefs' approval, the whites
had organized opposition. When the chiefs reassembled to approve
the amended treaty the whites were there, arguing against the treaty,
appealing to the Senecas not to sell, and saying that the government
would not honor its commitment and that the "wild" Indians of the
West would kill them. "In short," Strong said, "every argument,
which could be addressed to the fears, the passions and the prejudices of an ignorant and suspicious people was made use of" (*Appeal*
10; Manley 317–18). Strong charged that the whites opposed to the
treaty were a combination of dram sellers, lumbermen, lessees of
mills, holders of water privileges near Buffalo, holders of licenses to
live on Indian land, missionaries, and the Society of Friends. Only
the Baptists among the missionaries remained aloof from the affair.
The result, said Strong, was that the council ground became the
scene "of the worst passions of our nature," resulting in intimidation
and threats of death.

Third, Strong's *Appeal* answered the Quakers' charges of bribery.
Customarily, since the first land sale, he argued, the Seneca chiefs
had demanded and gotten personal allowances in negotiations.
Among those who had benefitted from former treaties were Cornplanter, Farmer's Brother, and Red Jacket. Some of those chiefs now
charging bribery had received allowances under the Treaty of 1826.
Strong related the allowances to the old practice of giving presents
to the Indians but observed that times had changed. In the nineteenth century the Indians realized that money was necessary, and
since white advisers were always ready to stimulate their cupidity, it
was "not strange that the chiefs should be disposed to make the
most of their official prerequisites." In William Penn's time, blankets, cloth, and trinkets had been sufficient; now the chiefs demanded more "substantial allowances of money." In Penn's time
the allowances were called presents; now they were called bribery.
"If a right to personal gratuities," he wrote, "be the *privilege* of chiefs
according to the general and well-understood usage of Indian communities, then the acceptance of them, being consistent with official
fidelity, involves no violation of duty, and the payment of them is
not *bribery.*" If the Senecas were satisfied with the sale price, he argued, then there should be no complaint about what the chiefs
could do for themselves (20). Strong's distinction between custom-
ary gifts and bribery is a fine one, but he was correct in maintaining
that the practice was accepted.

In defending the treaty and its legality and propriety, Strong re-
lied heavily on letters and statements by officials of the War Department and the Indian Office, as well as on senators who supported

the treaty. He played on emotion and on religious and political biases. Addressing his *Appeal* "To the Christian Public," he depicted the Society of Friends as hypocrites, doubly dangerous because of the quietistic posture they assumed. In this case, he said, under the "false banner of friendship and good will," they had published "gross abuses, garbled statements, and repeated misrepresentations," which were "as incompatible with the law of Christian charity, as with the rules of candor and fair discussion" (3–4). He labeled the Quaker charges that the Senecas had been defrauded an "envenomed arrow shot from the bow of the meek and gentle Quakers." At the end of his *Appeal,* Strong called attention to the Quakers' stand for abolition, although they were not for freeing the Indians, who were "more effectively shut out from all the privileges which render freedom a blessing, than are the negroes!" It was true that the Indians were not forced to labor, as slaves were, but when they were hungry, sick, or old, he said, they could not ask the whites to take care of them (63–4).

Despite Strong's close attachment to the War Department bureaucracy and his questionable relationship to the Ogden Land Company, his *Appeal* offers ample evidence that he held genuine convictions regarding the future not only of the Senecas but of Indians in general. He generally agreed in one respect with polemicists such as Pierce on the other side of the issue: that since their first contact with Europeans, the aboriginal peoples of America had been victims of colonization. But unlike Pierce, he did not believe that the New York Indians were ready to "progress" toward adopting Christian civilization or that the nearby white settlements had a positive effect. Every attempt by either legislators or religious workers, he said, "to produce a radical and enduring change in the manners, habits and pursuits of Indian communities, has proved utterly abortive" (26). Certainly, there were some moral, industrious, and intelligent men among the Senecas, but most were poverty-ridden, ignorant, and degraded. These latter were demoralized by the proximity of the white settlements. They had acquired only the vices of the whites. They were cheated and debauched with drink. The women were prostituted, and venereal disease was widespread (26).

To Strong, removal was the possible salvation of the Senecas. He called it "a great and humane system of policy" by which to rescue his "perishing race from moral and physical ruin," basic to which policy was their "removal from the corrupting influences of associations with the white population" who surrounded them (24). Strong had apparently fully accepted the protestations of Andrew Jackson's administration that removal was a benevolent policy.[8] The significant point, however, is that Strong was putting forth the official view; his comments echo strongly those concerning Indian removal in Jackson's farewell address to the American public on March 4, 1837 (*A Compilation of the Messages . . . of the Presidents,* 1512–13).

Strong apparently believed in the benevolence of the government's removal and "civilization" policy. At least, according to the arguments in the *Appeal,* he believed that so-called civilization was basic to the Indian's survival and that to be "civilized," he must achieve four basic American goals: settlement in areas conducive to agriculture; sufficient land in fee simple, subject to no preemptive claims, to be held in severalty; elementary education and training in agriculture and mechanical skills; and self-government (6). The crux of Strong's social theory for Indians was the Indians' "rights and privileges of person and property, which are the common inheritance of the white man" (27).

According to the argument in Strong's *Appeal,* the greatest obstacle to acquiring these rights and privileges in the East was land title. He saw no difference between William Penn and the Ogden Land Company. Both were preemptive owners of Indian land. The Seneca title was "comparatively worthless," and as far as personal rights went, he wrote, "we are placed under restrictions equally severe and humiliating. We are shut out from all political privileges, and in the country of our birth, are regarded as aliens, being incapacitated from acquiring and holding any other, even by purchase from white men" (28). During the preceding fifty years, Strong explained, poor whites had come into the Genesee country and prospered, whereas the nearby Indians, living on better land and subjected to missionary efforts, had not progressed toward "civilization" because they were "deprived of the incentives and rewards which animate the freeman" (32). Without them, the Indians would never succeed. African slavery, he argued, could not be abolished without "subverting private rights, whilst national policy sustained by public opinion, encourages and facilitates efforts for *Indian emancipation*" (63). Such emancipation could come only with individual ownership of land, and that could succeed only in the West.

Thus, in many respects, Strong's writing is in philosophical agreement with the federal Indian policy of the Jacksonian era. His acceptance of the need for civilization and his belief in the benevolence of removal may grate on the modern reader, but he was not simply parroting the official view. Ownership of land in severalty was not much talked of in that day, and Strong's advocacy of it was prophetic of the significant turn federal policy would take nearly fifty years later with the Dawes Severalty Act of 1887. Although we must keep in mind the personal stake that Strong had in the Treaty of 1838, we must assume, too, that Strong apparently arrived at his own conclusions after long study. His work clearly indicates that he had read widely in both British and American, especially Indian, history and that he was politically astute enough to weigh the odds for Indian survival east of the Mississippi. Finally, we should read his work against the backdrop of factionalism that afflicted the Iroquois after 1797. He freely admits that the Senecas had been divided on the issue of removal since 1832; the majority of the Christian party and the most educated favored removal while the so-called Pagan party opposed it. He also charges that some opposed removal because they were afraid that they would lose their political power. There was no doubt truth in what he said. Factionalism would plague the Senecas for decades to come.

Opponents of the treaty could not let Strong go unchallenged. It appeared to some that Pierce might be the one to answer him. Pierce, who apparently was largely responsible for mobilizing Seneca resentment against the treaty, had entered the law office of Tillinghast and Smith at Buffalo on his return from Dartmouth. In the intervening months, he had served as translator and secretary for the chiefs and continued to work to have the treaty set aside. He was serving as secretary to the chief's delegation in Washington when Strong's pamphlet appeared. He was urged to see the new president, William H. Harrison, and his secretary of war shortly after the inauguration in order to become acquainted. He was also urged to compose a reply, written in his own style, to Strong's pamphlet, "correcting some of the misstatements" (Mrs. Maris B. Pierce to M. Comstock, undated; Jacob Harvey to Pierce, February 13, 1841; Pierce Papers).

Pierce apparently declined, for the Quakers responded in a pamphlet titled *A Further Illustration of the Case of the Seneca Indians,* which appeared the following July. In the main, the pamphlet brought the history of the controversy up-to-date and refuted Strong's major arguments with evidence amassed by the writers, including detailed analysis of documents relating to Senate and executive considerations of the treaty. In addition, they defended William Penn's record at length, berating Strong as the first and only Indian to attack not only Penn's good name but that of the Society of Friends as well. They also challenged Strong's credibility and questioned his motives, pointing out his ties to the Ogden Land Company. As a chief, he had violated his duty as a representative of the Seneca Nation and had perverted the authority conferred on him. He was a traitor to his country, they charged. His purpose was "to *veil* from the public

eye" the true condition of the Senecas and "to enlist the sympathy
of religious professors" in an unholy cause. He had become the
instrument of "selfish and cruel men," his conduct "perhaps more
the result of weakness than wickedness." Strong's "*literary* attain-
ments," they argued, refuted the basic argument of the Ogden
forces that the Senecas were not civilized and should therefore be
removed (6–7).

Although Maris Bryant Pierce had declined to answer Strong's
pamphlet, his mark was on the Quaker response. In refuting Strong's
arguments, the Quakers had quoted extensively from Pierce's Buffalo *Address* of 1838 (40–1). Also appended to the Quaker pamphlet
was a memorial from eighty-six Seneca chiefs and headmen to John
Tyler, who had become president following the sudden death of
William H. Harrison. Benjamin Ferris, who had a hand in drafting
the pamphlet, supposed that Pierce had written the memorial. In it,
the chiefs appealed to the president to request reconsideration of
the treaty on a number of grounds. One was that former treaties
obligated the government to protect the Senecas from such evils.
That obligation had not been forfeited:

> We have fought in common with your own soldiers, and shed
> our blood for the United States; and, from our youth, have
> loved the free republican institutions of your country. We were
> born within your limits, and though called savages by those who
> would dispossess us, we feel this movement a vastly deeper in-
> terest in every thing which concerns the welfare of the country
> than the hosts of foreigners, who, with all their imported no-
> tions of government and religion, have so easily become nat-
> uralized and obtained the rank and appellation of citizens.
> From our intercourse with such men, we fear they bear the
> name in many instances without the feeling of citizens. We
> imbibed that feeling with our earliest breath, and yet we must
> be driven off beyond the limits of civilization, because we lack
> the name. (*A Further Illustration* 75)

Across the river in Canada there was potential refuge:

> The land is fertile there. Our friends there are numerous. Our
> language is correctly spoken there, and it would seem that by
> casting our lot amongst them we might be happy. But the spirit
> of improvement, the genius of your free institutions, the energy
> of your republican government are wanting there, and we
> should deplore the stern necessity which would compel us to
> seek a home across the river. Still, it would be far preferable

to emigrating beyond that distant river, where, habituated as we are for a more northern climate, death or ills which would embitter the richest inheritance, would be our certain portion. (76)

"Whoever wrote the memorial," said Ferris, "has produced a document, which it seems to me, for classical elegance, in regard to language and arrangement – in perspicuity and force has seldom been equalled."[9]

The public debate that had raged over the treaty for four years finally led to a compromise. In early 1842 there was a meeting of the secretary of the interior, agents of the Ogden Land Company, and a Friends delegation. The Ogden Company agreed to the writing of a supplemental treaty whereby the Senecas retained title to the Cattaraugus and Allegany reservations but gave up Buffalo Creek and Tonawanda. The Senecas approved this agreement as the best arrangement they could make under the circumstances (Kelsey 123; Abler and Tooker 511).

The intense public debate over the Senecas subsided, but the political divisions that had caused opposing tribesmen to take up the pen did not. The events of 1838–42 had eroded Seneca faith in the old chiefs. Growing bitterness, heightened by the treaty-bound abandonment of Buffalo Creek and Tonawanda in 1845, led to demand that the old chiefs be overthrown and that leaders popularly elected replace them.[10]

One of the strongest pro-constitutional voices was that of Wa-o-wa-wa-na-onk, or Peter Wilson, a Cayuga living with the Senecas at Cattaraugus.[11] Although he had signed the treaty in 1838, Wilson, like Pierce, had worked earnestly to prevent its ratification by the Senate. In a speech before the annual meeting of Friends at Baltimore on October 29, 1848, Wilson defended efforts by constitutional advocates to wrest control of Seneca affairs from the hereditary chiefs. In the published version of the speech, he charged the chiefs with bad management and a betrayal of trust in their mishandling of affairs in 1838. He condemned removal as a failed policy and argued that the Senecas could achieve their destiny in New York. Despite the social disruption and catastrophic losses incurred following the treaty, he asserted that the Senecas had made progress during the decade. The political revolution then occurring was but a manifestation of the spirit of liberty that was sweeping the Western world. "The political agitation among our people," Wilson wrote, "is but the onward and upward progress in the scale of civilization, and it is hoped that ere long the people will arrive at the elevated position of your people, where the friends of the Indians have long desired to welcome them" (*Speech of Wa-o-wa-wa-na-onk* 3–11).

The Treaty of 1838 was a turning point in Seneca culture and history. Although the literature it generated first was polemical, the next generation of writers, whose careers were beginning to take shape between 1838 and 1848, moved beyond the debate to consider not only the present condition and future prospects of the Senecas but also their history and culture. In the process, they would expand the Seneca canon to include other literary forms such as oratory, the essay, ethnography, and biography.

At the center of this movement were members of the Parker family, the best known of whom was Ha-sa-no-an-da, or Ely (1828–95). About 1842 he entered Yates Academy in Orleans County, New York, where he worked to achieve fluency in English, mastery of Greek and Latin, and good oratorical skills. Because of his facility with English, at age fourteen he began to serve the Tonawanda chiefs as an interpreter and scribe in their official dealings with Washington (Armstrong 18–20). The Tonawanda Senecas maintained that they had not agreed to the Treaty of 1838 and refused to accept it as binding. They persisted in efforts to have themselves excluded from its provisions and in 1845 refused to abandon their lands, as the treaty required. As a result, they were ultimately, in 1857, allowed to retain, through purchase, a small portion of their former reserve. In their struggle to retain their homeland, the chiefs often called on the youthful Ely Parker. On one of his many trips with them to Albany in 1844 he met Lewis Henry Morgan. They began a collaboration that resulted in Morgan's monumental work on the Iroquois, *League of the Ho-de-no-sau-nee, or Iroquois* (1851).[12] In addition to his ethnographic work, Parker wrote a number of essays, speeches, and historical pieces.[13] Also prolific, but little known, was Ely's older brother Ga-yeh-twa-gth, or Nicholson H. Parker (?–1892). A lecturer and translator, he began writing in the 1840s and generated a large body of literature in the form of essays and speeches, addressing contemporary issues as well as Indian history and lore.[14]

Thus the debate that followed the Treaty of 1838 formed the backdrop for the beginnings of Seneca literature in English. Of the first generation of writers, only Strong continued to write, joining the Parkers and others in documenting Seneca culture and history, including a substantial life of Red Jacket.[15] Although little known to the outside world, Pierce, Strong, and Wilson enjoyed a local reputation as orators throughout their lives. Pierce was the last to die, and on that occasion a local editor wrote:

Thus has departed the last survivor of the first generation of educated Iroquois. First Wilson and then Strong, were stricken down in the maturity of their powers, when their vigorous native intellects seemed to have just become fully developed for usefulness to their people. Born orators, they also cultivated the graces of eloquence without acquiring the artificial trammels of the schools, and adorned what they touched with the imagery derived from those native fountains from which true genius draws perpetual inspiration.[16]

It was the Treaty of 1838 that caused them to tap "those native fountains" and to create the first chapter in the history of Seneca literature in English.[17]

Notes

1. Wallace, "Origins" 445–8. Handsome Lake and the Longhouse religion are the subject of Wallace's *The Death and Rebirth of the Seneca.* For an account of religious factionalism among the Senecas, see Berkhofer 135–6.
2. White Seneca *et al.* to Pierce, June 27, 1834; Maris Bryant Pierce Papers, Buffalo and Erie County Historical Society, Buffalo, New York. Items in this collection are cited parenthetically in the text as Pierce Papers.
3. James Young to Pierce, June 6, 1838, Pierce Papers. The Cayugas had scattered after the Revolutionary War, some going to Canada and others remaining with the Senecas in New York. See White, Engelbrecht, and Tooker 500–4.
4. *Address* 12. Pierce is quoting from Adams's Oration.
5. Asher Robb to Pierce, September 13, 1838; Pierce to Joel R. Poinsett, January 29, 1839; Pierce to the Honorable Mr. Sevier, February 2, 1839; George W. Paterson to Pierce, April 8, 1839; Pierce's Statement of Expenses, March 19, 1839; Daniel Two Guns to Pierce, August 5, 1839; Seneca White to Pierce, December 18, 1839; Pierce Papers. See also *The Case of the Seneca Indians in the State of New York* 123–7, 133–7, 138, 144–6; and "Journal of Henry A. S. Dearborn" 89, 92–3, 118–19.
6. *Buffalo Express,* January 10, 1872; Manley 314–23; "Journal of Henry A. S. Dearborn" 67, 89, 94, 102–3, 211, 124–215, 222.
7. The *Appeal* was published in Buffalo and New York; the Buffalo printing is followed here.
8. Prucha has demonstrated what he thinks was a genuine belief in the benevolence of the removal policy on the part of Jackson and others (527–39); but see Satz's article, which examines "the differences between the rhetoric and the reality of removal policy" (72).
9. Benjamin Ferris to My Dear Friend, August 16, 1841; Indian Collection, Buffalo and Erie County Historical Society.

10. Abler, "Seneca National Factionalism" 25–6; "Friends, Factions, and the Seneca Nation Revolution of 1848" 74–9; Abler and Tooker 511–12.
11. Wilson signed the Treaty of 1838 as a principal Cayuga warrior, not as a chief; see Peters 556 and also "Journal of Henry A. S. Dearborn" 118–19.
12. For information on Parker and Morgan's collaboration see Armstrong 3–13, 40–6; also Abler and Tooker 512.
13. A bibliography of Parker's published works appears in Armstrong 223–4. His manuscript works can be found in the Ely Parker Papers and the Arthur C. Parker Papers at the Buffalo and Erie County Historical Society. His diary can be found in the American Philosophical Society Library, Philadelphia. For a guide to other repositories containing Parker materials, see Armstrong 216–19.
14. Biographical information on Nicholson H. Parker can be gleaned from Arthur C. Parker, *The Life of General Ely S. Parker*. His manuscript works can be found in the Arthur C. Parker Papers, Buffalo and Erie County Historical Society.
15. Strong's manuscript works, including his life of Red Jacket, can be found in the Nathaniel T. Strong Papers, Buffalo and Erie County Historical Society.
16. *Buffalo Commercial Advertiser*, August 17, 1874.
17. Archival materials drawn on here are on deposit at the Buffalo and Erie County Historical Society, Buffalo, New York. Other collections that might yield additional useful information for this era of Seneca literature include the Maris Bryant Pierce letters, Dartmouth College; Arthur C. Parker Papers, University of Rochester; William Clement Bryant Papers, Columbia University; Ogden Papers, New York Historical Society; and various collections in the Friends Historical Library, Swarthmore College, and at the American Philosophical Society, Philadelphia.

Publications Cited

Abler, Thomas S. "Friends, Factions, and the Seneca Nation Revolution of 1848." *Niagara Frontier* 21 (Winter 1974): 74–9.
———. "Seneca National Factionalism." *Iroquois Culture, History, and Prehistory: Proceedings of the 1965 Conference on Iroquois Research*. Albany: University of the State of New York/State Education Department/New York State Museum and Science Service, 1967.
Abler, Thomas S., and Elisabeth Tooker. "Seneca." In Trigger.
Adams, John Quincy. *An Oration Delivered at Plymouth, December 22, 1802*. Boston, 1802.
Armstrong, William H. *Warrior in Two Camps: Ely S. Parker, Union General and Seneca Chief*. Syracuse, NY: Syracuse University Press, 1978.
Berkhofer, Robert F., Jr. *Salvation and the Savage: An Analysis of Protestant Missions and American Indian Response 1787–1862*. Lexington: University of Kentucky Press, 1965.

The Case of the Seneca Indians in the State of New York. Philadelphia: Merrihew and Thompson, 1840.

A Compilation of the Messages and Papers of the Presidents. Vol. 4. New York: Bureau of National Literature, 1897: 1512–13.

A Further Illustration of the Case of the Seneca Indians in the State of New York, in a Review of "An Appeal to the Christian Community, &c. By Nathaniel T. Strong, A Chief of the Seneca Tribe." Philadelphia: Merrihew and Thompson, 1841: 6–7.

"Journal of Henry A. S. Dearborn, a Record of Councils with the Seneca and Tuscarora Indians at Buffalo and Cattaraugus in the Years 1838 and 1839." *Publications of the Buffalo Historical Society* 7 (1904): 33–225.

Kelsey, Rayner Wickensham. *Friends and the Indians, 1655–1917*. Philadelphia: Associated Executive Committee of Friends on Indian Affairs, 1917.

Manley, Henry S. "Buying Buffalo from the Indians." *New York History* 28 (July 1947): 313–329.

Parker, Arthur C. "The Life Of General Ely S. Parker." *Publications of the Buffalo Historical Society* 23. Buffalo, NY: Buffalo Historical Society, 1919.

Peters, Richard, ed. *The Public Statutes at Large of the United States of America*. Vol. 7. Boston: Charles C. Little and James Brown, 1846.

Pierce, Maris Bryant. *Address on the Present Condition and Prospects of the Aboriginal Inhabitants of North America, with Particular Reference to the Seneca Nation. Delivered at Buffalo, New York, by M. B. Pierce, a Chief of the Seneca Nation, and a Member of Dartmouth College*. Philadelphia: J. Richards, 1839.

Prucha, Francis Paul. "Andrew Jackson's Indian Policy: A Reassessment." *Journal of American History* 56 (December 1969): 527–39.

Satz, Ronald N. "Indian Policy in the Jacksonian Era: The Old Northwest as a Test Case." *Michigan History* 60 (Spring 1976): 71–93.

Speech of Wa-o-wa-wa-na-onk, an Indian Chief. Baltimore [?], 1848.

Strong, Nathaniel T. *Appeal to the Christian Community on the Condition and Prospects of the New York Indians, in Answer to a Book Entitled the Case of the New York Indians, and Other Publications of the Society of Friends*. Buffalo: Press of Thomas & Co., 1841. New York: E. B. Clayton, 1841.

Trigger, Bruce G., ed. *Northeast*. Vol. 15 of *Handbook of North American Indians*, ed. William C. Sturtevant. Washington, DC: Smithsonian Institution, 1978.

Vernon, H. A. "Maris Bryant Pierce: The Making of a Seneca Leader." *Indian Lives: Essays on Nineteenth- and Twentieth-Century Native American Leaders*, ed. L. G. Moses and Raymond Wilson. Albuquerque: University of New Mexico Press, 1985.

Wallace, Anthony F. C. *The Death and Rebirth of the Seneca*. New York: Vintage Books, 1972.

"Origins of the Longhouse Religion." In Trigger.

White, Marian E., William E. Engelbrecht, and Elisabeth Tooker. "Cayuga." In Trigger.

6

"I AM JOAQUIN!"

SPACE AND FREEDOM IN YELLOW BIRD'S THE LIFE AND ADVENTURES OF JOAQUIN MURIETA, THE CELEBRATED CALIFORNIA BANDIT

JOHN LOWE

Christopher Newman, that quintessential American abroad, opens Henry James's *The American* by occupying a huge circular divan at the Louvre; he sits, spreads his arms and legs, and fills up all the space he possibly can. He is, of course, from the West (where else?), where his prodigious energy and WASP identity have given him direct access to the American dream. A French aristocrat quite rightly nominates him for the title of "Duke of California."

The word "California" has always had a certain poetic resonance for Americans, partly because of the state's tremendous size but also because of its unique and abundant beauty. It is the original dream of the New World garden magnificently enlarged and gilded. Indeed, the term "golden republic" refers not only to the native grasses, themselves emblematic of the state's general fecundity, but also to the mother lodes of gold discovered in the mid-1800s, images that underline the tensions inherent in the state's identity. Aware of these ironies, Yellow Bird (John Rollin Ridge), in *The Life and Adventures of Joaquin Murieta, the Celebrated California Bandit,* gives us a saga of space and freedom set in the golden republic's halcyon days of the 1850s. It is, to be sure, a story with a didactic purpose that pushes a moral message, and much of it is mediocre and slack. At its best, however, it is a powerful reminder of how the metaphysics of access to the American dream have always depended on the appropriation of space for the concept of identity, and how the politics of displaced and relocated peoples can give rise to heroic and sometimes mythical folk literature. Increasingly, it has been the important task of those denied the benefits of American life – the poor, the dispossessed, blacks, Native Americans, and immigrants – to remind all Americans of who they are as a people, and of what America says it is and should be. Fighting a battle for equality, armed with an awareness of our stated national principles and the demand that they be extended to all, disadvantaged Americans keep a national dynamic alive.

John Rollin Ridge (Yellow Bird was his tribal name) was born in Georgia to one of the most powerful families in the Cherokee Nation. The Ridges saw the inevitability of the federal government's plan to relocate the Nation and urged a negotiated acceptance, thus pitting themselves against the equally powerful Ross family. The issue had really been resolved, however, when gold was discovered in north Georgia.

When the Rosses killed Yellow Bird's father and grandfather, the family fled; Yellow Bird killed a man himself in a dispute and subsequently went to California to mine gold. Failing at that, he embarked on a literary career but remained obsessed with getting revenge for his relatives' murders. Meanwhile, he vented his spleen by indirectly damning U.S. imperialism in California. He did this by writing a romantic novel based on the contemporary and compelling legend of Joaquin Murieta, seeing an affinity between that figure's wronged ethnic, familial, and sexual honor and his own. Yellow Bird's publishers obviously saw the parallel, too; the "Publishers' Preface" to the original edition prominently announced that the author was "a 'Cherokee Indian' born in the woods – reared in the midst of the wildest scenery – and familiar with all that is thrilling, fearful, and tragical in a forest life" (2). The author of this minibiography seems intent on establishing a romantic yet forbidding association between Yellow Bird and the preexisting tradition of the noble savage. This latter figure had long been connected, in the popular imagination, with the mastery of treacherous space, that is, the forest, forever linked in the Eurocentric mind with the moral "wood of error," the labyrinth, and the abode of the devil. The physical Western American counterpart of these images could easily be found in the desert, the plains, and the mountains, and all of these function in Joaquin's narrative; indeed, the expulsion from Eden/home is a constant theme.

Joaquin Murieta, branded as Cain and made to wander, unlike Christopher Newman but like Ridge himself, has had the American dream snatched from under him; a Mexican, his homestead in California has been seized by the American government. The narrative seems intent on reversing this imposed typology, on making us see Joaquin as more of an Abel/victim figure. Still, we must be careful in building this parallel; as his biographer notes, Ridge paradoxically favored assimilation as the ultimate answer to the "Indian question," and eagerly pursued wealth and position for himself and his family (Parins 2). Ridge seems to have been caught in limbo, neither inside nor outside a secure American identity; his writing resonates with that tension, which helps account for what seems his exuberant relief in the expansive spatial metaphors of Murieta's story.

The Joaquin myth was a composite of several bandits' careers. In *Joaquin*, Ridge faithfully follows the basic facts but interweaves them with details suggested by his own life; as noted, his family was originally driven, along with most other Cherokees, from northern Georgia, where the discovery of gold led to a land rush for Indian property. Ridge arrived in California in 1850, the same year that, in the novel, Joaquin rides up from Mexico. Just as Ridge's family was driven from Georgia, Joaquin is driven from his gold field claim by both predatory Anglo marauders and an equally unjust set of laws that persecuted foreign-born miners with an outrageous tax. Unlike Ridge, however, Murieta terrorizes most of California, and he is pursued and finally killed by a crude gang of deputies under the leadership of Captain Harry Love. His head and the hand of Three-Fingered Jack, his sidekick, are preserved in alcohol and then go on display for years in the sideshows and "museums" of the state as a warning to others. Rumor has it that the body parts were lost in the great San Francisco fire and earthquake, which would seem to be an appropriate coda to a heroic and brutal tale that takes much of its power from that of nature.

We might further note the metonymy involved here. The spatial confinement of the robbers' bodily parts backfires, for as the subsequent display of Joaquin's head and Three-Fingered Jack's hand across the state indicates, the "relics" are rather considered icons, retaining tremendous power. Although the bandits are dismembered and "caught" in glass jars, the meaning of their lives radiates endlessly.

What makes Ridge's Joaquin story different from its many other variants, and adds to the residual power of the myth, is his realization of this power. In his romantic and poetic evocation of Joaquin and his enchanted progress through the edenic spaces of the golden republic, Ridge similarly "caught" Joaquin and his men in the confined space of the novel but found a means to make their magical powers work anew for the readers. This aspect of the text perhaps accounts for its popularity in California, for in addition to providing the state with a heroic myth, it sets it against what Gaston Bachelard calls images of "felicitous space," which grow out of a kind of "topophilia," a mapping of space we love, space "that may be defended against adverse forces," and also space that may thus also be "eulogized" and therefore further "poeticized" (Bachelard xxxi). Anyone familiar with the similar topophilia of almost all Native American literature will immediately see the usefulness of Bachelard here, and of the centrality of *Joaquin Murieta* to that pattern. I make broad use of his theories here in an attempt to portray the meaning of Ridge's apparently random semiotics of landscape, as well as to demonstrate their metaphysical and political implications.

The Life and Adventures of Joaquin Murieta begins, traditionally but significantly, with the narrator's words: "I sit down to write somewhat concerning the life and character of *Joaquin Murieta*" (7). The sedentary stance of the author, a trite commonplace, here becomes an effective contrast to an extraordinarily mobile hero. The narrator then refers to Joaquin as a "truly wonderful man" who was nothing more or less than the "natural production of the social and moral condition of the country in which he lived, acting upon certain peculiar circumstances favorable to such a result, and consequently, his individual history is a part of the most valuable history of the State" (7). The narrator is interested in establishing Joaquin's amazing ability to range freely and quickly through the vast spaces of California. He therefore claims that although there were supposedly at least five "sanguinary devils" named Joaquin ranging the country at the same time, there was really only one: Joaquin Murieta.

Our omniscient guide then quickly sketches in the series of outrages that transformed Joaquin into an outlaw. Here the story has much in common, in a symbolic sense, with more current explorations of imperialism and empire, such as *The Jewel in the Crown* and David Lean's film of *A Passage to India,* for all three feature a cry of rape, which signifies what has been done to a country and a people. Daphne Manners, in *Crown,* actually is gang-raped, but the crime is falsely ascribed to Harry Kumar, an Indian. In *Passage,* the hysterical Adela Quested accuses her Indian friend, Dr. Aziz, of attempting to rape her. Both novels, written by Englishmen, ironically focus on unjust charges against men who represent whole cultures that have been "raped" by the British Raj. Here, the rape of Rosita (Joaquin's mistress) by Anglo-Americans similarly and ironically comments on the "rape" of displaced Hispanics in California and, obliquely, on the "rape" of the Cherokees, whose tragic story of displacement and disintegration is surely on Ridge's mind as he maps out parallel events in California.

In *Joaquin,* after the title figure has been ousted from successful ventures in mining and farming, he is forced to witness Rosita's rape, which is soon followed by the murder of his half-brother by a crazed vigilante mob. These events have a catastrophic affect on Joaquin, which is expressed in a spatial metaphor: "His soul swelled beyond its former boundaries, and the barriers of honor, rocked into atoms by the strong passion which shook his heart like an earthquake, crumbled around him. Then it was that he declared . . . he would live henceforth for revenge and that his path should be marked with blood" (12–13). Joaquin's circle of self, thwarted in its effort to grow via the traditional American way (hard work, enterprise, and democratic comradeship), has burst through into a new and larger circle through the passion of anger. His vow to cut a "bloody path" through the state as he avenges the wrongs done to him and his family presages ever-widening circles of spatial/criminal conquest. His path echoes several principles set down in the 1840s by Ralph Waldo Emerson in his seminal essay "Circles." In one of literary Transcendentalism's prime expressions, Emerson gives space and confinement elemental circular forms, first in the human eye and then, significantly, in nature, for the "horizon" formed by the eyes is the second circle man knows, a "primary figure" that is repeated "without end" in nature (263). Here and in his other essays, Emerson maps out an imperial self that properly seeks expansion and power, a process generated from and paralleled by nature itself. The concept of the self expressed by ever-expanding concentric circles has a demonic side as well; at one point in "Circles," Emerson relates his expanding circles of self to explosive anger, the kind Ridge's readers see expressed by Joaquin: "But the heart refuses to be imprisoned; in its first and narrowest pulses it already tends outward with a vast force and to immense and innumerable expansions" (Emerson 265).

Theories of "self-reliance" and the "imperial self" fed into the ideology of manifest destiny. These ideas would find magnificent expression in other key works of the period, particularly in Hawthorne's exploration of the "magic circles" of the self in *The Scarlet Letter* (1850) and in Melville's critique of unleashed darker elements of Emersonian and capitalist ideology, *Moby-Dick* (1851), books published only a few years before *Joaquin*. Although it is beyond the scope of this essay, *The Life and Adventures of Joaquin Murieta* surely demands to be studied alongside these books and other masterworks of what we have called the "American Renaissance," as well as with the works of newer members of the canon such as Frederick Douglass, Harriet Beecher Stowe, and Harriet Jacobs. As in many of those narratives, in *Joaquin Murieta* we follow a somewhat romantic and poetic evocation of a hero through edenic spaces, but it is a vision that coexists with a gruesome litany of murders, robberies, and tortures. Yellow Bird was able to achieve this fusion, perhaps, because he was taking folkloric materials and transforming them into narrative virtually at their moment of formation. Bakhtin has demonstrated that the novel's roots must ultimately be sought in folklore, where the object of artistic representation is degraded to the level of a contemporary reality; the fluid periods of history are ideal for furnishing such material (Bakhtin 39).

Furthermore, as is often the case with an American 'classic,' *Joaquin's* narrative charts a key moment in American history, a time when prospectors from all over the world converged on the mother lode. The gold rush as mined by Mark Twain, Bret Harte, and others quickly became the stuff of legend and literature. What has been left out of the literature, however, is the displacement of Mexican-Americans. The victory of the United States over Mexico in 1848 coincided almost exactly with the discovery of gold in California. Two years later, the state's legislature passed a "Foreign Miners' Tax Law"; ironically, Germans, French, and, for a time, Chinese were permitted to stay, but Latino miners were forced out. The great Mexican ranches in the state, with their hundreds of dependents, contributed a vast displaced population; some of these displaced individuals became outlaws who were supported by others in the Hispanic community.

The force of history seemed to accelerate drastically during these years, and *Joaquin's* hectic narrative keeps fictional pace. As the narrator points out, one of the most amazing things about the ensuing and terrifying assassinations of the men who had brutalized Joaquin and his family is the swiftness with which the miscreants are dispatched. Throughout the tale, the banditti act swiftly; celerity works hand in hand with mastery of space. Joaquin's apparent ability to be everywhere is partially explained in the text, as the narrator conflates another Joaquin story by having the actual Joaquin Valenzuela (one of the five Joaquins) function as Joaquin's lieutenant. This also implies that Joaquin operates as part of a long line of Mexican bandits, for Valenzuela, we are told, rode with the famous guerrilla chief Padre Jurata in Mexico and presumably schooled Joaquin in the tricks of the trade.

Physical security conceived in terms of spatial refuge, frequently set as nature's bosom, also finds expression in material goods that answer immediate temporal needs. Joaquin's only safety is said, for instance, to lie "in a persistence in the unlawful course which he had begun. It was necessary that he should have horses and that he should have money" (13–14). Soon the local newspapers are full of accounts of attacks on ranchers, coaches, and travelers:

> The scenes of murder and robbery shifted with the rapidity of lightning. At one time, the northern countries [sic] would be

suffering slaughters and depredations, at another the southern,
and, before one would have imagined it possible, the east and
the west, and every point of the compass would be in trouble
... the country ... was so well adapted to a business of this
kind – the houses scattered at such distances along the roads,
the plains so level and open in which to ride with speed, and
the mountains so rugged with their ten thousand fastnesses in
which to hide. (15)

As Joaquin's mastery of space expands, that of the public at large
shrinks, for "all dreaded to travel the public roads" (22), a fact that
contributes powerfully to the Americans' growing anger and resentment.

Joaquin's most impressive feat comes when he is surprised by a
band of men in a canyon:

His only practicable path was a narrow digger-trail which led
along the side of a huge mountain, directly over a ledge of
rocks a hundred yards in length, which hung beatling [sic] over
the rushing stream beneath in a direct line with the hill. . . . It
was a fearful gauntlet for any man to run ... [there was] danger of falling 100 feet ... [he] must run in a parallel line with
his enemies ... with their revolvers drawn. He dashed along
that fearful trail as if he had been mounted upon a spirit-steed,
shouting as he passed, "I am Joaquin! Kill me if you can!" (87)

It is hardly surprising that this is the moment in the book that artists
have most often depicted (it appears on the cover of the 1955
Oklahoma Press edition), for as Ridge remarks, "It was perfectly
sublime to see such super-human daring and recklessness" (87). We
may read the scene's spatial semiotics both ethnically and politically.
Murieta, belonging to neither the Indian nor the Anglo-American
world, nor even to the community of law-abiding but oppressed Mexicans, rides a razor-thin ridge (also the author's last name) of marginality throughout the book, boldly outlined against nature, riding
on it, across it, against it, supported yet threatened by the abyss.
Politically, he is alien, outlaw, racial and religious other; but all this
is transcended through his "sublime" mastery of American space(s),
much of it forbidden. Again and again, the narrator refers to Joaquin's lightning-like ability to range across the land as "magical."
He is also careful, however, to provide a counterpoint of realistic
reasons for Joaquin's success, such as the general support and encouragement the protagonist receives from the rest of the Mexican
community, the unsettled condition of the country, and the isolation

of the mining regions. Joaquin also, like Robin Hood, deals gently with those who support him, and many ranchers buy protection by sheltering the band for the night and keeping quiet about it later.

Yellow Bird takes care to authenticate space. He understands the value time has in setting the boundaries of place, so when Joaquin is in a specific vicinity, the narrator frequently gives the precise date, quotes local newspapers for details of the location, and specifies towns, rivers, mountains, and even gullies. One may easily chart Joaquin's course across the state by following Yellow Bird's narrative mapping. Arroyos, rocks, and other prominent features in the terrain are also added, not for scenic effect but to reify the landscape. Two men are traveling on a road, specifically the one "that leads up Feather River, near to the Honcut Creek, which puts into that stream" (21). Similarly, the complementary grid of temporal reality is laid over the natural. When Joaquin is said to be in a specific locale, Ridge includes sentences supposedly taken from newspapers in passages like this: "*The Marysville Herald* of November 15, 1851, speaking of the horrible state of affairs, has the following remarkable paragraph: 'Seven men have been murdered within three or four days in a region of country not more than twelve miles in extent' " (21). All this is necessary. Joaquin's mastery of space will not be magical unless the land itself is realistic and believable.

The most important statement of this central theme comes when Joaquin relocates to a spot near Mount Shasta in the northern part of the state. The mountain, Ridge maintains, "serves at a distance of two hundred miles to direct the course of the mountain-traveler, being to him as the polar star to the mariner" (23). Mount Shasta awesomely "rears its white shaft at all seasons of the year high above every other peak . . . in its garments of snow like some mighty archangel, filling the heaven with his solemn presence" (23). This rather trite description nevertheless parallels Yellow Bird's main themes, for like Joaquin, Mount Shasta towers above its peers, is unassailable and unavoidable, and extends into space both horizontally and vertically.

The mountain creates a peak of sorts in the narrative as well, for Yellow Bird inserts into the novel his two-and-a-half-page poem, "Mount Shasta, Seen from a Distance." At first the mountain is personified as a proud blasphemer, a tower of pride that defies the storms of heaven that beat against it in wrath. Mount Shasta, however, is not static: "age by age" it is "still rising higher / Into Heaven!" (23). In an abrupt turn, Yellow Bird reveals that the mountain, far from being the blasphemous rebel that it seems to be, was created by God and symbolizes the higher law of God that humans should strive to attain. "And well this Golden State shall thrive, if, like / Its own Mounta Shasta, sovereign law shall lift / Itself in purer atmosphere – so high / That human feeling, human passion, at its base shall lie subdued. . . . Its pure administration shall be like / The snow, immaculate upon that mountain's brow!" (25). In his poem, Ridge points to the discrepancy between what the law should be and what it actually is.

This long apostrophe to the mountain enables Yellow Bird to take us as readers high above the state to share this lofty monarch's view of "the fertile / Vale, and undulating plains below, the grass" (25). From this vantage point we understand the purifying effect that Mount Shasta has on the land, for from its flanks come cool breezes and vapors which "guarantee . . . health and happiness" to the farms and farmers below. Even better, and more romantically, the mountain inspires "loftier feelings . . . nobler thoughts" for the humble plowman; little children, asking who made the mountain, learn from their mothers that it is God's creation. We thus, like the spotted hawk in Walt Whitman's similarly conceived *Song of Myself* (1855), aspire to "the eagle's cloudless height" and the clear-eyed perspective on American nature and the law that should proceed from the continent's grandeur and majestic space. The poem ends, in fact, by transforming this "blasphemous" Babel-like natural phenomenon into a symbol of law, a pure white shaft that towers above humanity's activities as a moral guide. It is in the shadow of this peak that Joaquin and his men take refuge for several months, descending at intervals into the valley below to steal horses with the aid of the Indians.

How does all this work in the overall scheme of the novel? Mount Shasta suggests the doubled nature of Joaquin, who as rebel against an unjust set of laws that discriminate against Mexicans actually represents a purer law. Like Mount Shasta, his freedom in space gives him a kind of vertical presence in the society of humans as well; as with most mythical bandits, his actions, which take place during hard times for many people, offer heroic and poetic imaginative space and freedom for the oppressed and the weak, who lack Joaquin's resourcefulness and courage. The fact that the mountain's base in earthly nature is frequently obscured by clouds aligns with Joaquin's mythical stance, one much like the trickster's, between God and humanity. Moreover, the cooperation with California's Indians underlines Yellow Bird's doubled role as narrator and begins a long skein of references to the shameful treatment Native Americans have received in the Golden State, both as victims and as scapegoats. Ridge will charge, in fact, that "The ignorant Indians suffered for many a deed which had been perpetrated by civilized hands. It will be recollected by many persons who resided at Yreka and on Scott's River in the fall and winter of 1851 how many 'prospecters' [sic] were lost in the mountains and never again heard from; how many were found dead, supposed to have been killed by the Indians, and yet bearing upon their bodies the marks of knives and bullets quite as frequently as arrows" (27).

Joaquin's role as trickster and his alignment with Indians dovetail in the episode where he and his men are robbed by the Tejons. The trickster, as mediator between God and humanity, usually has his way, but if he did so always, he would be too close to the status of God; therefore he, too, must occasionally come to grief, as Coyote, Raven, and Brer Rabbit all do from time to time. Moreover, it is often true that a weaker creature tricks the trickster, and that is precisely how the Tejons function here. As masters of the region's terrain and as silent, superb hunters, the Tejons have little difficulty surprising Joaquin and his band, stripping them naked, and beating them soundly with willow rods. The episode is a version of the "trickster tricked" motif that Paul Radin has identified in trickster narratives, one also found in African-American folktales and confirmed by Ridge's statement that "The robbers were robbed" (40). Joaquin, however, laughs off the episode and refuses to take revenge on Old Chief Sapatarra and his band. He knows, as we do, that they were inspired to this mischief by a wealthy white rancher, who sought their aid in retrieving stock the bandits had stolen. Moreover, when Joaquin's band, men and women alike, are stripped naked by the Tejons, the men find new clothing but the women hide themselves in the brush "like mother Eve"; the phrase points both to the regenerative nature all around them and to the parallels between their retreats and the Garden of Eden/mythical nest.

It should not be supposed, however, that Ridge is in close consort with California Indians. His portraits of them are quite mixed, perhaps because of his own ancestry in a supposedly more civilized tribe, the Georgia Cherokees, who had their own alphabet, had adopted white modes of production, and had established thriving businesses before the forced march to the West. In a later scene, he paints the Tejon Nation in lazy poses as they eat acorns and worms, and he charges them with treachery and cowardice. When they succeed in robbing Joaquin and his band, Ridge comments, "The poor, miserable, cowardly Tejons had achieved a greater triumph over them than all the Americans put together!" (38). Nor are the Tejons the only Native people who operate against Joaquin; later, some Cherokees aid the American pursuers and kill two of Murieta's band. Presumably, Ridge had in mind those renegades who sided with the

Ross faction rather than with his own family; there were no good Indians, per se, for Ridge, even in his own tribe.

Similarly, Ridge's verdict on the "Digger" Indians is mixed. Like the Mark Twain of *Roughing It,* he has contempt for their supposedly low standard of living and their employment in menial positions (the term "Digger" was a derogatory label imposed by white settlers), but he admits that in their capacity as runners bearing mail, they are "very expeditious on foot and willing to travel a considerable distance for a small piece of bread, fresh meat, or a ragged shirt. I have known them to swim rivers when the waters were high and dangerous in order to carry a letter to its destination. They are exceedingly faithful in this business, having a superstitious dread of that mysterious power which makes a *paper talk without a mouth*" (130). However, although they are admired for their mastery over time and space, their ignorance, superstition, and servile natures undercut this quality. In short, Joaquin's ability to achieve his own rough version of justice in an unjust world is a beacon of hope for all oppressed Californians – exemplified in his frequent but sometimes problematic alliance with the Indians.

Joaquin and his band cannot be continually in motion; such a plot would be as exhausting to the reader as it would be to the men and would violate the traditional pattern in the Robin Hood genre that Ridge follows. Like Robin, Joaquin has a mistress, Rosita, who travels with him, like Maid Marian; his gang is full of idiosyncratic desperados; and, most important for this discussion, Murieta's band has a multitude of natural hideouts to return to for rest and recuperation. The rugged arroyos are their Sherwood Forest. Bachelard would term these hidden strongholds "nests," and indeed, that is the way Yellow Bird describes them. The most beautiful is the Arroyo Cantoova, fenced in by impenetrable mountains. It contains rich pasturage for the many animals Joaquin and his band steal from the ranchers. Entrance is limited to a narrow pass that can be guarded and defended by only a handful of men; even better, the arroyo is at least 150 miles from any human habitation. Despite these rather forbidding facts, the "nest" is attractive. "Embosomed" by the mountains, the retreat abounds in wild game and features a luxurious grove of evergreen oaks that Joaquin and his "still blooming companion," Rosita, inhabit. The refuge is the band's bower of bliss, roofed by "rich foliage," "carpeted" with grass and flowers (28).

The various nest/sanctuaries of the novel operate as many other features of Yellow Bird's poetic landscapes do; as Bachelard would say, they give us back the situations of our dreams –, in this case, the dream of security. This idea is as old as Theocritus and the pastoral tradition, where a simplification of setting and character enables the poet/writer to reduce complex ideas to essences. Attic shepherds and shepherdesses, whether inhabiting Virgil's *Eclogues,* Shakespeare's Arden Forest, or Faulkner's bucolic Mississippi, may introduce probing aesthetic and moral arguments and propositions effortlessly and clearly against the untroubled rural backdrop, whose "bosom" shelters but also nourishes the body and the spirit. An alternative to the tradition has always been the hidden refuge of the bandit, which popular novels and operas often feature; Blackmoore's *Lorna Doone,* Scott's *Rob Roy,* Bizet's *Carmen,* and Verdi's *Il Trovatore* all feature hidden banditti mountain paradises. They are places to go when someone cries, "Flee, all is discovered!" Readers can relate to this idea of refuge; as Bachelard notes, nests are the imaginative and supremely safe childhood spaces we yearn for in daydreams (99). In political terms (and we should not forget that Murieta represents a persecuted and exiled minority and a kind of proto-guerrilla movement), the retreats are reminiscent of those of the montagnards of Vietnam or the freedom fighters in Afghanistan.

Yellow Bird, however, makes this "nest" uniquely and unforgettably American. The thrust of nature, the interplay between Mexicans and Indians, the guns and horses and sweeping rides over the vast plains of Western narrative – all these qualities and several more, linked indelibly with American republican iconography, stimulate shocks of recognition for the American reader. It is here, in this natural "house," that Joaquin promises Rosita that one day he will soon complete his revenge, take his booty, and retire to a peaceful ranch where he will build her a "pleasant home," the ultimate sacred space for Yellow Bird's domestic readers. Just three years earlier, in *Uncle Tom's Cabin,* Harriet Beecher Stowe had created parallel domestic nests for runaway slaves in properly Victorian American homes, homes purposely delineated as identical to those of her readers.

Part of Joaquin's revenge lies in the invasion of precisely this domestic space: Many of the murders he commits take place in the homes of his victims, and he delights in secret penetration of other social spaces as well. In one of the novel's most famous scenes, Joaquin, in disguise, is playing monte in a saloon in Mokelumne Hill when his fellow players begin a discussion about the dreaded Joaquin. One of them boasts that he would "just like once in his life to come across Joaquin, and that he would kill him as quick as he would a snake," whereupon Joaquin jumps up on the table, brandishes his pistol, and shouts "I am Joaquin! if there is any shooting to do, I am in" (31). He has impishly "become the game," and as so often happens in the book, his action ruptures the narrative; it precipitates a chase, hurling the reader into yet another whirlwind across the landscape. But Joaquin's escape into vast space is underlined by his preceding ability to puncture the restricted space, the "temple" of the profane urban world, the saloon. Murieta is not content merely to penetrate this sanctum sanctorum of the patriarchs; the poker table, a doubled altar with the gods of money above and guns below, is literally trampled and profaned by Joaquin's muddy boots.

However, Joaquin is not a blasphemer of the truly sacred. He and his colleagues are befriended by the Catholic Church and take shelter for weeks at a time at places like San Gabriel Mission, thereby appropriating sacred as well as secular space and adding yet another nest for rest and recuperation. More often, however, Joaquin returns to the maternal embrace of the arroyos, moving back and forth between his multidirectional raids and his secret mountain dens, "so rugged with their ten thousand fastnesses in which to hide" (15).

Who can stop this "outrageous" bandit? Clearly, only a man such as Captain Harry Love, who is as masterful as Joaquin in transcending space and time. That is exactly how the bandit's ultimate nemesis is introduced, quite early in the book, long before he is to kill Joaquin:

> Love had served as an express rider in the Mexican war and had borne dispatches from one military post to another over the most dangerous tracts of Mexico. He had traveled alone for hundreds of miles over mountains and deserts. . . . Riding fleet horses and expert in the use of the lasso, it required a well-mounted horseman to escape [bandits] on the open plains, and many a hard race with them has the Captain had to save his neck and the valuable papers in his charge. (34)

Similarly, the real Love's men succeeded in tracking Murieta partly because, as Edwin Corle has observed, they were "expert horsemen, superb marksmen and perfectly capable of handling themselves in any terrain, be it the coastal valleys, the dry deserts or the High Sierras" (Corle 270). Furthermore, Love comes from a pioneer background, and is thus suited to the hardships and dangers of border life. Finally, in his role as deputy sheriff of Los Angeles County, he is a representative of the law that Joaquin scorns.

Still, Love has difficulty finding the charmed Murieta. Throughout the book Ridge creates the impression that Joaquin is enclosed in a magical space, making him immune to legal retribution, no matter how desperate the situation has become. This theme frequently becomes interwoven with concepts of moral space as well. One evening, Joaquin, riding alone, meets Joe Lake, a friend of his "more happy and honest days." After the men exchange greetings, the text quickly becomes sentimental. Joaquin weeps, confesses that he is not the man he once was, admits that he hates almost all Americans but still loves Joe, and thus implores Joe not to betray him. "Lake assured him there was no danger, and the two parted, for the wide gulf of dishonor yawned between them, and they could never again be united" (51). Lake, unaware of Joaquin's uncanny ability to be everywhere at once, immediately betrays his friend to Americans in Ornetas while a serape-clad Mexican listens; this bystander, Joaquin's spy, reports to the master himself, who is just outside. Charging that "you have lied to me," Murieta shoots Lake dead. An instant later, he is seen on top of a nearby hill with fifty men, once again protected by "the magical luck which pursued this man, following him like an invisible guardian fiend in every hour of his peril" (51). The passage reaffirms our sense of Joaquin's magical mastery of space, but adds the sense of moral distance and the gulfs opened up by imperialist history.

Such passages – and there are several – are more than merely adventures. They exemplify the ballooning myth of Joaquin in the state that Ridge was chronicling. As Joseph Henry Jackson has stated, "Hardly a town along the Mother Lode is without its cavern, cellar, or tunnel, in or through which Murieta dodged the law," and the tales that relate these episodes are repeated "solemnly as truth," as great myths always are (110–11). Harry Hansen's *Guide to the Golden State* lists many "shrines" to Joaquin across the state, including a resort called Murietta [sic] Hot Springs, a museum claiming to have his red sash, and various others, typified by the town of Murphys: "The town has the usual Joaquin Murrieta [sic] legend: here the ubiquitous bad man is said to have been a three-card monte dealer in 1851 and to have begun his bloody career when his brother, unjustly . . . was hanged" (446, 447, 491–4, 524). Although the various versions of the tale over the years have taken many liberties, there is one quality they all share: mastery of space. When Edwin Corle published his study of banditry in 1949, he emphasized that Joaquin's "forays ranged throughout the gold towns in the High Sierras and up and down the Royal Highway, and nobody could be sure just where he was, what he was planning or where he would strike next" (267).

One explanation for this magical space comes from the concept of banditti solidarity. Together, the band is strong, but if their principle of *e pluribus unum* falters, disaster ensues. For instance, when

Joaquin and his band need to move through the Los Angeles section
of the state, Love's home territory, they separate so as not to be
detected. It is here that Reyes, Joaquin's friend and Rosita's brother,
is captured and hanged shortly after Love has found and murdered
Gonzalez. As Joaquin's band fragments and is reduced, so are his
powers; it seems important that this process begins in an area where
land has been massively appropriated from Hispanics and where pre-
modern life presents obstacles, physical, social, and psychic, to the
unfettered movements of the banditti. Twenty men are lost in one
fight alone, including the valued lieutenant Claudio. Soon afterward,
Mountain Jim is hanged in San Diego.

The differing locales for these events indicate the sweep of Joaquin's network across the state once again but also demonstrate the
menace that increasing settlement and urbanization pose to space
and freedom – and not just for outlaws. Joaquin astutely sees these
events as an evil omen, one dictating the need to act swiftly and
conclusively.

Once back in Arroyo Cantoova, he announces a master plan of
destruction that will end his days as a bandit. Now that he commands
2,000 men spread over the state, he intends to make a clean sweep
of the southern counties, killing and burning as he goes on toward
the refuge of Sonora. "When I do this, I shall wind up my career.
My brothers, we will then be revenged for our wrongs, and some
little, too, for the wrongs of our poor, bleeding country. We will
divide our substance and spend the rest of our days in peace" (75).
This last campaign begins in earnest with a strategic attack by Joaquin's full forces on Calaveras County, which is described by Ridge
in edenic terms. The gang's terrifying assault brings on the final
conflict with Captain Love, which is made possible by Joaquin's in-
explicable decision to travel apart from his band and with only three
followers.

Joaquin in these last pages is not the man he was, as is suggested
earlier in the scene with Lake. His decision to leave a trail of
scorched earth behind him actually masks what amounts to his surrender. What causes this change? Bachelard suggests that a true poetics of space is based in simple images of felicitous space; he also
stresses the concepts of interiority and exteriority that exist in the
human imagination, depending on how the person in question reacts to the spaces that surround him. Joaquin, an outcast in the
world of people, initially poeticizes the world of nature positively in
the mode of Bachelard's topophilics; he has not been "cast into the
world" since he has opened it through his actions. As a master of
space, he is a master of nature, and in its subservience it is beautiful

proof of his identity. In his interior daydreams, the vast landscapes of California that he effortlessly covers are corresponding symbols of his interior immensity. Like a poet cited by Bachelard, Joaquin might say, "As I stood in contemplation of the garden of the wonders of space I had the feeling that I was looking into the ultimate depths, the most secret regions of my own being; and I smiled, because it had never occurred to me that I could be so pure, so great, so fair! My heart burst into singing. . . . All these constellations are yours, they exist in you" (189). It would be easy to find similar passages in Ridge's contemporaries, like Cooper, Emerson, Whitman, and Thoreau, and in other Native American writings, but let us continue in a French vein. Baudelaire writes, "In certain almost supernatural inner states, the depth of life is entirely revealed in the spectacle, however, ordinary, that we have before our eyes, and which becomes the symbol of it," thereby permitting intimate grandeur to unfold (cited in Bachelard 195). Moreover, as Bachelard suggests, movement within vastness magnifies this feeling: "When the dreamer really experiences the word immense, he sees himself liberated from his cares and thoughts, even from his dreams. He is no longer shut up in his weight, the prisoner of his own being" (195).

Unfortunately, perceptions can change. Joaquin's feeling of transcendence eventually becomes a trap; the originally authenticating sense of identification with the powers of vast landscapes pales. Bachelard quotes the poet Jules Supervielle's reactions to similarly endless rides on the South American pampas: "Precisely because of too much riding and too much freedom, and of the unchanging horizon, in spite of our desperate gallopings, the pampa assumed the aspect of a prison for me, a prison that was bigger than the others" (221). Joaquin, however, as I have suggested, possibly understands that even the vast sweep of wild California will have to submit to the American imperialist enterprise; *his* "pampas," unlike Supervielle's, are not "unchanging." Moreover, no matter how big the space, if it offers no sanctuary except in hidden enclaves, is it not still a prison, no matter how vast? Finally, of course, the ever-constricting wild landscape, always a metaphor for the mind itself, mirrors the internal constriction of identity, and the possibilities of topographic transcendence collapse.

We can only go so far, however, in reading Murieta's sensibilities. Ridge created a composite hero to command our attention but was unable to develop his psychology. To Ridge's credit, however, our interest in and frustration with the narrative are related to more important issues than the character of Joaquin. Murieta's story, calculated for popular appeal, has more to tell us than we suspect. A parallel version, the 1936 movie *The Robin Hood of El Dorado* (which, ironically and predictably, cast the Anglo Warner Baxter in Joaquin's role), was made in an escapist mode. It was also crafted, however, to speak to mainstream American concerns during a grim economic decline, when crime, be it Bonnie and Clyde's or Joaquin Murieta's, sometimes seemed justified, romantic, and peculiarly American. The movie was based on Walter Noble Burns's history/novel of the same title (1932); as Kent Steckmesser notes, Burns was following the same formula he had used in his wildly successful and historically inaccurate *Saga of Billy the Kid* (1926). Although the topic is outside the scope of this essay, one must be struck by the way Ridge inserts into the American outlaw narrative the assertion that ethnicity constitutes an affront to society, as surely as do broken laws. Joaquin speaks not only for the poor but also for the racially and ethnically oppressed, all denied "space" at the feast of America. He becomes a necessary mythic hero, who, like Robin Hood and Rob Roy, has been generated from and supported by the folk. As Lukacs has noted, both Goethe and Scott were interested in this kind of figure as demonstrative of the possibilities for "human upsurge and heroism" that are widespread among the masses (52–3); the ruptures of history, and their consequent patterns of dislocation and relocation, thus provide revolutionary possibilities for heroic behavior.

The Joaquin legend is in many ways the chief mythic nugget from the mother lode created by the birth of the state of California. For Californians, Murieta's story has become more than folklore; we may surely call it an epic. Bakhtin felt that the epic genre echoed a world of beginnings and peak times, a shared heroic past that speaks to the present. Joaquin also seems generated and nurtured by a threatened but still untamed nature. His very exteriority and marginality ironically locate him in the magical realm of spatial and imaginative freedom, and he thus personifies the dream that was felt but rarely experienced by actual miners, whose faces were averted into the mud as they panned for gold. The Chilean Pablo Neruda, one of the more recent writers to set this tale, ends his lyric poem, *Splendor and Death of Joaquin Murieta,* with a passage redolent of both Joaquin's link to the people and Bachelard's formulations. Neruda seems to suggest that Joaquin's poetic spaces still exist, most particularly in the souls of people still yearning to be free:

> Joaquin, return to your nest: gallop the air toward the south
>   on your blood-colored stallion.

The streams of the country that bore you sing out of silvery
   mouths. Your poet sings with them.
Your fate mingled bloodshed and gall, Joaquin Murieta; but
   its sound
is still heard. Your people repeat both your song and your
   grief, like a tolling bell struck underground. The people
   are million. (175)

Works Cited

Bachelard, Gaston. *The Poetics of Space,* trans. Maria Jolas. Boston: Beacon
   Press, 1969.
Bakhtin, Mikhail. *The Dialogic Imagination: Four Essays by Mikhail Bakhtin,* ed.
   Michael Holquist and Caryl Emerson. Austin: University of Texas Press,
   1981.
Corle, Edwin. *The Royal Highway.* Indianapolis: Bobbs-Merrill, 1949.
Emerson, Ralph Waldo. *Selected Writings of Emerson,* ed. Donald McQuade.
   New York: Modern Library, 1981.
Hansen, Harry, ed. *A Guide to the Golden State.* New York: Hastings House,
   1969.
Jackson, Joseph Henry. *Anybody's Gold: The Story of California's Mining Towns.*
   San Francisco: Chronicle Books, 1970.
Lukacs, Georg. *The Historical Novel,* trans. H. and S. Mitchell. London: Merlin,
   1962.
Neruda, Pablo. *The Splendor and Death of Joaquin Murieta,* trans. Ben Belitt.
   New York: Farrar, Straus and Giroux, 1972.
Parins, James W. *John Rollin Ridge: His Life and Works.* Lincoln: University of
   Nebraska Press, 1991.
Radin, Paul. *The Trickster: A Study in American Indian Mythology.* New York:
   Schocken Books, 1972.
Ridge, John Rollin (Yellow Bird). *The Life and Adventures of Joaquin Murieta,
   The Celebrated California Bandit.* 1854. Rpt. Norman: University of
   Oklahoma Press, 1955.
Steckmesser, Kent. *The Western Hero in History and Myth.* Norman: University
   of Oklahoma Press, 1965.

7

"THIS VOLUMINOUS UNWRITTEN BOOK OF OURS"

EARLY NATIVE AMERICAN WRITERS AND THE ORAL TRADITION

WILLIAM M. CLEMENTS

Leslie Marmon Silko's dedication of *Storyteller* to "the storytellers as far back as memory goes and to the telling which continues and through which they all live and we with them" signals her sense that her written verbal art derives from and builds on a long-standing tradition of spoken verbal art in her community, Laguna Pueblo. This facet of Silko's work has received attention from commentators who note how she both incorporates traditional themes and motifs from Laguna oral tradition[1] into her fiction (Ruoff, "Ritual") and views her work as a link in the chain of transmission that extends from the past and into the future (Lucero; Ruppert; Wong 186–96). Silko's connectedness with oral tradition parallels that of many authors who have shaped the "Native American Renaissance" of the late twentieth century (Lincoln). Scholars have often noted that the American Indian writers whose work has generated that renaissance represent the continuation of tribal traditions of verbal art and participate in expressive cultures rooted in the spiritual and intellectual contexts of their own local communities.

Not as much attention, though, has been paid to the ways in which writing by Native Americans in the nineteenth and early twentieth centuries relates to the oral tradition.[2] In fact, many students of this writing, especially of the autobiographical works, have instead emphasized its parallels with Euroamerican literature. Arnold Krupat, for example, views the self-definition emerging from William Apess's *A Son of the Forest* as "deriving entirely from Christian culture" (145). The voice Apess assumes in this autobiography, according to Krupat, reflects "very closely a voice to be heard commonly in the early nineteenth century" among Euroamerican writers, that of "salvationism" (144). Similarly, H. David Brumble has focused on how social Darwinism, a force in late-nineteenth-century Euroamerican letters, informs Charles A. Eastman's *Indian Boyhood*. This account of the famous Santee physician's first sixteen years concludes with his removal into the Euroamerican society of his acculturated and assimilated father, a personal "passage into adulthood" that begins the process of evolutionary cultural development (162).

Krupat, Brumble, and others who have emphasized how Euroamerican ideologies and literary attitudes color the works of nineteenth- and early-twentieth-century American Indian authors have correctly identified important features of those works. Indeed, early Native American written literature generally drew on European and Euroamerican literary models. But another body of material also influenced some of these authors. Indigenous oral traditions, particularly storytelling, had an effect on many Indian writers, even those who wholeheartedly adopted Euroamerican, Christian values. Although some of them may not have shared the deep sense of continuity between their own writing and the literatures of their communities that a contemporary author such as Silko articulates, many nevertheless drew on oral tradition and perceived their writing in relation to it.

The ways in which early Native American authors approached their tribal heritages of verbal art varied. For those writers who wrote histories and ethnographies of their nations, oral tradition provided a source of data that were unavailable elsewhere. Examples include nineteenth-century histories by David Cusick and Elias Johnson, writing on the Iroquois (the latter more specifically on the Tuscarora), and those by William W. Warren and George Copway treating the Ojibwa, as well as William Jones's ethnographic studies of the Fox published in the early 1900s. For writers who advocated special personal and cultural concerns, oral tradition helped to validate the legitimacy of those special interests. Warren, for example, cited oral tradition to prove that the Ojibwas and other "Algic" peoples were descended from the ten lost tribes of Israel (54–75). Copway used oral tradition to counter the argument that his plan for a "perpetual reserve for all the Northwest Tribes this side of the Rocky Mountains" did not take into account the heterogeneity of Native American cultures (*Indian Life* 256–8; "American Indians"; see also Smith 19–20). "The traditional stories which are related by our forefathers, indicate that our common stock was one," he wrote (*Indian Life* 260) in support of a shared homeland for the native peoples of the Old Northwest. More partisanly personal, Simon Pokagan used accounts from Potowatomi oral history to validate his family's long-standing prominence in tribal affairs, as well as their tactful diplomacy ("Massacre" 649, 653, 654). The proof in oral narratives that his father, Leopold, had enjoyed status among the Potowatomis since early in the 1800s justified Simon's participation in legal actions to reclaim Chicago's lakefront for the tribe (Clifton, *Pokagans* 55, 57; "Sandbar").

Three other uses of oral tradition, though, suggest even more forcefully how important the indigenous literary heritage remained even for highly acculturated writers: Early Indian authors who wished to emphasize the "essential humanity of Indian people" (Ruoff, "Three" 258) might cite evidence from traditional oral literature in support; writers who accepted the image of the Indian as "vanishing American" (Dippie) drew on oral literature to reactualize a way of life that they believed to have disappeared; and in the manner of Silko, some writers saw oral literature and its creators/performers as the foundation of an ongoing literary tradition in which they and their writing were assuming a place.

Oral Tradition as Evidence of Shared Humanity

As A. LaVonne Ruoff has noted ("Three" 252), early American Indian writers and African-American slave autobiographers shared the task of establishing themselves as members of the human race whose ideas were worth the attention of Euroamerican readers. Such a perceived need to demonstrate common humanity figures in one of the earliest ethnographic works written by a Native American, Hendrick Aupaumut's late-eighteenth-century "History of the Muh-he-con-nuk Indians." A fairly straightforward account of his people's way of life, the essay carefully suggests parallels between their values and those of Christianity. For example, "before they ever enjoyed the Gospel revelation" (28), the Mahicans believed in a monotheistic high god whose precepts were conveyed to children through careful instruction by each family head. Those precepts strikingly paralleled both the Ten Commandments and the ethical teachings of Jesus (28–30). Although Aupaumut admits that some parents failed in their obligation to instruct their children, he notes that similar "bad examples" may be found "among civilized nations" as well as among the Mahicans (30). Aupaumut's ethnography portrays a people who are not all that different from the Euroamerican Christians for whom he was writing, a commonality shown by other Native American writers, in part, through their oral tradition.

The title of Charles Eastman's second volume of autobiography, *From the Deep Woods to Civilization,* seems to summarize the evolutionary social theory that came to dominate the second half of the nineteenth century and persisted in some quarters well into the twentieth.[3] Although now the idea, which placed European and

American civilization at the apogee of human development, seems blatantly ethnocentric, in its day it represented enlightened opinion. Belief in cultural evolution usually meant an acceptance of human psychic and spiritual unity. That which separated "primitive" Native Americans such as Ohiyesa (Eastman's Santee name) from "civilized" Europeans and Euroamericans such as Eastman became was not an innate racial difference but diversity of cultural development. In fact, according to many evolutionists, the lifeways of primitive peoples represented how the ancestors of civilized humanity had once lived.

Early Native American writers accepted the idea that Indians had the inherent potential to be civilized. After all, their own examples proved the point. Johnson, who wrote his history of the Tuscarora in order to "animate a kinder feeling between the white people and the Indians," believed in "our capabilities for future elevation" (7) and was certain that there existed "the presence of an element in our character which must eventually lead to important results" (8). Early Native American writers might reinforce the idea that, in Pokagan's words, "nature has placed no impassable gulf between us and civilization" ("Future" 705) by presenting evidence of similarities between Native American and Euroamerican cultures and by demonstrating the essential humanity of American Indians. Oral narratives proved to be effective in doing this.

In an autobiography published in 1883, Sarah Winnemucca, for example, articulated the case for her Paiute people by citing accounts from tribal lore that stressed their human kinship with Euroamericans. In the book's first chapter, "First Meeting of Piutes and Whites," she quotes her grandfather's telling of a myth that traces the origin of the two peoples from a common set of parents (Hopkins 6). She later recounts a Paiute tradition concerning "a small tribe of barbarians who used to live along the Humboldt River." These people, from whom she clearly distances her people, engaged in cannibalism, a practice that caused her ancestors to destroy them (73–5) and thus define themselves in terms that her Euroamerican readers would accept as "human."

Simon Pokagan also countered the familiar image of Indians as bloodthirsty subhumans, dedicated to erecting the barrier of savagism to the advance of civilization through brutal violence, by citing a "tradition among our fathers" that explained the enmity that Native Americans felt for Europeans:

an armed band of Wau-be-au'-ne-ne-og' (white men), gorgeously clad, came on the war-path from the East, reaching the

Dakotas, which then extended south as far as the mouth of the
Arkansas River; . . . they were vindictive and cruel, destroying
the natives wherever they went with Awsh-kon-tay' Au-ne-me-
kee' (thunder and lightning). They were looking for gold, their
Man-i-to (god), and, not finding him, went down Mi-che-se-pe
(the great river) and were seen no more. Those cruel adven-
turers, who came among us by sea and land, must have awakened hatred and revenge in the hearts of our fathers, which
may have been transmitted to their children. ("Future" 701)

Pokagan's motive for presenting this narrative and other evidence
showing that savagery in warfare was not exclusive to Indians, but
generally human, was "not to censure, but to show that *cruelty and
revenge are the offspring of war, not of race*" ("Future" 705).

Pokagan also suggested that human nature rather than Indian
identity accounted for "superstitious" beliefs and legends among
Native Americans. He noted, for example, the belief in unlucky days
among his classmates at Oberlin as evidence that his own people
were no more prone to irrational beliefs than Euroamericans ("Indian Superstitions" 240). Similarly, in what may be his earliest publication, an essay on the "Sioux mythology," published in 1894,
Eastman notes the common human "inborn consciousness of the
highest goodness or *God*" (212), which found expression in the concept of *Wakantanka*, the Great Mystery, among his ancestral people,
as it was also manifested in the Christian concept of god. Even in
his straightforward, "scientific" presentation of Fox texts, William
A. Jones conveyed something of the essential humanity of his Native
American sources. He noted, for instance, that their religious principles were as sacred to them as the Bible was for Christians. Ridi-
culing either would be "profane" (2).

Those Native American writers who actually published textuali-
zations of oral narratives from their storytelling heritages often did
so to emphasize the humanity they shared with Euroamericans. Eastman and his wife, Elaine Goodale Eastman, offered such a collection
in 1910 when they retold twenty stories from Santee Sioux oral tradition in *Smoky Day's Wigwam Evenings*.[4] They recognized that a literal
rendering of the stories would not meet the expectations of their
intended juvenile audience and consequently took "occasional liberties . . . to fit them to the exigencies of an unlike tongue and to
the sympathies of an alien race" (iii). But they also noted the fundamental human unity between the original audiences for the stories
and their young Euroamerican readers. In an appendix to the volume, entitled "Suggestions to Teachers," they couch this idea in

evolutionary terms: "As all educators know, there is a period in the development of the child, usually reaching its height from about the eighth to the tenth year, which corresponds in many respects to the stage of primitive culture reached by the American Indian" (143). Eastman had noted the educational value of the stories he heard while growing up according to the traditional manner (*Indian Boyhood* 51, 122, 137, 150), and the Eastmans suggest that the same stories can have similar value for Euroamerican children once superficial differences in language and culture disappear.

About a decade earlier, another product of the northern Plains, Zitkala-Šă (Gertrude Bonnin), a Lakota, had anticipated these views in a collection of stories, many dealing with the trickster figure Iktomi. In the preface to her *Old Indian Legends,* published in 1901, she had noted that these stories, once told to the "little black-haired aborigine," had come now to belong just as much to "the blue-eyed little patriot." The study of Native American storytelling and other oral literary behavior, she claimed, "strongly suggests our near kinship with the rest of humanity and points a steady finger toward the great brotherhood of mankind." The particular stories that she retold clearly showed that the Native American "seems at heart much like other peoples" (vi).

Although exposure to Euroamerican civilization did not necessarily convince these writers of its superiority, many nevertheless believed that the displacement of their own way of life was inevitable. That Indians as individuals could make the adjustment to civilization required them to share the basic humanity of Euroamericans. Oral tradition proved that they did.

Oral Tradition as Reactualization of an Idyllic Past

Many early Native American writers accepted – albeit grudgingly – the view that they were "vanishing Americans," doomed at best to assimilation. As Simon Pokagan wrote of his people's future, "by the middle of the next century all Indian reservations and tribal relations will have passed away. Then our people will begin to scatter; and the result will be a general mixing up of the races. . . . [G]enerations yet unborn will read in history of the red men of the forest, and inquire, 'Where are they?' " ("Future" 708). But grudging acceptance of their collective cultural fate did not mean that Indian writers had to forget about their past. Oral tradition allowed some of them a way to recapture that past – to reactualize it. That was particularly the case with Eastman, but even writers less conscious of the problems of Euroamerican life, of which Eastman's education and activism had reinforced his awareness, used oral literature as a way to return to the past and to revive in the imagination what they perceived as now only a "memory culture."

George Copway, for example, devoted much of his adult life to winning Indians to the Christian way of life and to establishing his own success in Euroamerican terms. But his autobiography, published when he was especially relishing his notoriety as a Christian Indian missionary, comes most alive when he recounts his preconversion life. And his *Traditional History* rises above its rather cursory presentation of data about Ojibwa history when Copway describes verbal art performances:

> These legends have an important bearing on the character of the children of our Nation. The fire-blaze is endeared to them in after years by a thousand happy recollections. By mingling thus, social habits are formed and strengthened. When the hour for this recreation arrives, they lay down the bow and the arrow and joyously repair to the wigwam of the aged man of the village, who is always ready to accommodate the young. (*Indian Life* 98–9)

Copway includes the texts of five "Legendary Stories and Traditional Tales" in order "to give you some idea of the manner in which my people amuse themselves in their wigwams" (98): an account of the etiology of the water lily, a historical legend of Ojibwa–Iroquois hostilities, a thunderbird story, a narrative of the origins of the North Star and the echo, and a story about an alcohol-induced murder. For the first, he provides enough of the storytelling context to afford a sense of the experience that he had apparently appreciated so much as a child: "An old chieftain sat in his wigwam quietly smoking his favorite pipe, when a crowd of Indian boys and girls suddenly entered, and with numerous offerings of tobacco, begged him to tell them a story" (99). That Copway successfully reactualizes the past in this passage may be an exaggeration, but that seems to be the direction in which he is going.

Although informed by romantic nostalgia, Charles Eastman's writings exemplify more clearly the use of oral tradition as a way of recreating a past, of making a heritage perceived as defunct come alive again in the imagination. Eastman's biographer has suggested that *Indian Boyhood,* the physician's first volume of autobiography, conveys "an unconscious longing to return to a world he viewed as naturally good" (Wilson 132). Using other methods as well, Eastman fulfills that longing by recalling performances of oral literature, especially by the storyteller Smoky Day and by the grandmother who reared him. Smoky Day, Eastman recalls, was "widely known among us as a preserver of history and legend. He was a *living* book of the traditions and history of his people" (115; emphasis added). Moreover, the stories that Smoky Day told served even to reactualize a heroic past that predated the childhood of Ohiyesa. Through his tales, "[o]ur heroes are always kept alive in the mind of the nation" (118), Eastman writes. In a volume on Indian lore for Boy Scouts and Campfire Girls, Eastman described how the storyteller was able to make the past come alive for his or her listeners:

> True stories of warfare and the chase are related many times over by actors and eye-witnesses, that no detail may be forgotten. Handed down from generation to generation, these tales gradually take on the proportions of heroic myth and legend. They blossom into poetry and chivalry, and are alive with mystery and magic. The pictures are vivid, and drawn with few but masterly strokes. (*Indian Scout* 174–6)

Oral literature represents one of the principal devices through which Eastman "conjured up" an Indian life that "was more romantic than real. . . . [It was] the Eden Eastman pictured" (Wilson 192).

Reactualization of an idealized past seems to define the aims of another book by Eastman. *The Soul of the Indian* outlines Dakota spirituality, implies that other Native American groups accepted much the same viewpoint, and emphasizes how Euroamerican influences have corrupted that spirituality. The essence of Dakota spirituality had come to the young Ohiyesa through oral literature. Tribal elders, Eastman recalled, repeated "time-honored tales with dignity and authority, so as to lead him [the young man] into his inheritance in the stored-up wisdom and experience of the race" (34). He describes the moral lessons he had learned from the stories told by his grandmother: "Long before I ever heard of Christ, or saw a white man, I had learned from an untutored woman the essence of morality. With the help of dear Nature herself, she taught me things simple but of mighty import" (87). Raymond Wilson suggests that Eastman's purpose in writing *The Soul of the Indian* may have been "his need to reaffirm his identity with the past rather than to explain that past to white society" (135). And David Reed Miller defines the book as Eastman's "text for understanding himself" (63). The volume exhibits Eastman's pride in being Indian and in the "ancestral religious beliefs, which seemed to give meaning and perspective to his life" (Wilson 135).

Eastman and Copway knew their Native cultures only after contact with Euroamerican culture. The precontact culture endured for them only in the stories they had heard. These stories allowed them to participate imaginatively in that precontact culture, and when they retold the stories and recounted the experience of hearing them performed, they made that imaginative experience available to their readers.[5]

Oral Tradition as Foundation for Literary Expression

One distinction that marked the men who rose to leadership among the northern Plains groups treated in Eastman's *Indian Heroes and Great Chieftains* was oratorical ability. Spotted Tail, for example, was known for "his remarkable speeches" (37), American Horse was noted "for his eloquence" (174), and texts of the subjects' speeches appear in biographies of Red Cloud, Tamahay, and Sitting Bull. William Warren also noted the oratorical powers of Ojibwa leaders, especially Shosh-e-man, "the most eloquent man the Ojibways have ever produced" (335). Copway described how Ojibwa orators "have filled the forest with the music of their voices, loud as the roar of a waterfall, yet soft and wooing as the gentle murmur of a mountain stream." He continued, "We have had warriors who have stood on the banks of lakes and rivers, and addressed with words of irresistible and persuasive eloquence their companions in arms" (*Indian Life* 126). The image of the "noble eloquent savage" (Sorber), of course, has been a familiar one since as early as the seventeenth century.

In writing autobiography and history, early Native American writers were bound to rely on Euroamerican models. Although oral narratives such as coup tales might provide indigenous precedents for such writing (Brumble 22–30), the extension of a plotted narrative that covers a significant portion of a life or the collation of material from diverse sources into a sustained historical narrative had no real forerunners in Native American literary heritages. But their recognition that the ability to manipulate language characterized prominent figures in their cultures must have affected these early writers. Some of them perceived their written work as a manifestation of this admired ability. Like Leslie Marmon Silko, they saw themselves continuing the verbal artistry that extended from the oral literature of the past through their own writings.

Eastman again emerges as most explicit in this approach to relating the oral tradition to his work.[6] The role of the storyteller was an important one among his people, since one who could "portray a character or a situation truthfully, yet with just a touch of humorous or dramatic exaggeration," became "not only an entertainer in demand at all social gatherings, but an honored schoolmaster to the village children" (*Indian Scout* 176).

In *Indian Boyhood,* Eastman emphasizes that the Santee youth's education involved learning verbal artistry:

> Very early, the Indian boy assumed the task of preserving and transmitting the legends of his ancestors and his race. Almost every evening a myth, or a true story of some deed done in the past, was narrated by one of the parents or grandparents, while the boy listened with parted lips and glistening eyes. On the following evening, he was usually required to repeat it. If he was not an apt scholar, he struggled long with his task; but, as a rule, the Indian boy is a good listener and has a good memory, so that the stories were tolerably well mastered. The household became his audience, by which he was alternately criticized and applauded. (51)

Eastman's purpose in presenting this description of apprenticeship in eloquence is to emphasize that verbal art skills came not from instinct or inheritance but from education. He was obviously pleased that this education had been successful in his own case and recalled an instance of being "generously praised" for his storytelling ability (201). Moreover, he believed that early training in verbal art had continued to bear fruit. During the early decades of the twentieth century, he spent much of his time in speaking engagements. He attributed his successes in that role to sharing and developing "the native gift of oratory in some degree" (*Deep Woods* 186).

Also, when it came time to present written versions of oral narratives – as he did in *Indian Heroes and Great Chieftains* and (with his wife, Elaine Goodale Eastman) *Smoky Day's Wigwam Evenings* – he felt well within his rights, as a product of the same storytelling tradition that had produced the people from whom he heard the material, to make whatever changes might be warranted by the particular audience and context. The Preface to the folktale collection – written by Elaine Eastman but presumably with her husband's endorsement – outlines the rationale behind their retelling of the material:

> we hope and think that we have been able to preserve in the main the true spirit and feeling of those old tales – tales that have been handed down by oral tradition alone through many generations of simple and story-loving people. The "Creation myths" and others rich in meaning have been treated very simply, as their symbolism is too complicated for very young readers; and much of the characteristic detail of the rambling native

story-teller has been omitted. A story that to our thinking is
most effectively told in a brief ten minutes is by him made to
fill a long evening by dint of minute and realistic description
of every stage of a journey, each camp made, every feature of
a ceremony performed, and so on indefinitely. True, the attention of his unlettered listeners never flags; but our sophisti-
cated youngsters would soon weary, we fear, of any such
repetition. (iv–v)

Perhaps Eastman did indeed view himself as a " 'rememberer' much
like . . . his grandmother, and Smoky Days [sic]. . . . In this sense he
saw himself to be a folk historian or recorder rather than an academic" (Miller 64).

A similar justification – that she participated in an ongoing storytelling tradition – may have informed Zitkala-Ša's handling of Lakota stories in *Old Indian Legends*. Her prefatory comments reveal her
awareness of the flexibility of oral tradition, since she had heard the
same stories from different narrators and found "the renderings varying much in little incidents" (v–vi). Her goal was to "transplant the
native spirit of these tales – root and all – into the English language"
(vi). Although such changes as she and the Eastmans made represent standard practice for adapters of oral literature into print, their
rights to transform what they heard instead of reproducing verbatim
texts lie in their being part of the same dynamic heritage of verbal
art in which the stories had been developing for generations.

A sense of being part of an ongoing literary heritage may have
figured in the motivations of other Native American writers who
tried to capture in print the oral literatures of their cultures. One
suspects that David Cusick perceived his role in presenting Iroquois
oral literature as ethnographic more than as participatory. Perhaps
only William W. Warren, among the writers discussed here, did not
have such a self-perception. Despite his own Ojibwa connections, he
consistently uses "them" in reference to his mother's people and
employs "us" and "our" when referring to Euroamericans (e.g., 23,
48).

* * * * * *

These approaches to using oral tradition employed by selected Native American writers from the early period only suggest the significance of tribal literary heritages for these authors and their
contemporaries. Yet they remind us that the early writers, like their
spiritual descendants who have shaped a Native American literary
renaissance in the late twentieth century, represent a continuation

of the verbal art that begins with orally performed stories, songs, orations, and ritual texts. On and alongside this oral literature, Native American writers developed a verbal art that used Euroamerican forms and themes but did not abandon the indigenous oral heritage.[7]

Notes

1. The quotation in the title comes from Charles A. Eastman's *The Soul of the Indian* (143). The term "oral tradition" refers to the process of orally performed verbal art that has characterized most (probably all) Native American communities and to the material that has been created during oral performances and has often been reperformed by different storytellers, singers, and orators throughout successive generations. Although oral tradition as a process seems to have some common features cross-culturally, each community (or tribe or nation) may have a distinctive oral tradition in terms of both the features of the process and the nature of the material performed orally. My argument here is that early Native American writers drew on the distinctive oral traditions of the communities in which they were enculturated (their indigenous heritages), as well as on European and Euroamerican literary models.
2. There are some notable exceptions to this generalization, including portions of books by Brumble, Murray, and Wong.
3. For an examination of this work that demonstrates that Eastman's acceptance of his own identity as a civilized person and of the whole concept of cultural evolution was not clear-cut, see Peterson's essay in this volume.
4. Eastman's biographers and critics have noted that although this is the only one bearing her name, Elaine Goodale Eastman probably contributed significantly to all of her husband's published work (Miller 66; Wilson 191; Wong 140–2). However, without contrary evidence, we must assume that Eastman himself endorsed fully any ideas that were published under his name.
5. This is essentially what N. Scott Momaday suggests about his experience of precontact Kiowa culture. It had ceased to exist – in Momaday's view – as an integral entity in 1890, but survived first in the memories of those who had been alive at the time and then in the stories they and their descendants told. Momaday, born in 1936, knew Kiowa culture imaginatively through those stories. See *The Way to Rainy Mountain*.
6. This point regarding Eastman has been explored by Copeland, by Stensland, and by Wong 139–52.
7. Some of the research for this essay was carried out while I participated in Arkansas State University's Research Reassignment Program. I am grateful for the opportunities afforded by that program and to the Interlibrary Loan Department of the Dean B. Ellis Library at Arkansas State University for valuable assistance in obtaining materials.

Works Cited

Aupaumut, Hendrick. "History of the Muh-he-con-nuk Indians." *The Elders Wrote: An Anthology of Early Prose by North American Indians 1768–1931*, ed. Bernt Peyer. Berlin: Dietrich Reimer Verlag, 1982: 25–33.

Beauchamp, W. M. *The Iroquois Trail, or Foot-Prints of the Six Nations, in Customs, Traditions, and History, in Which Are Included David Cusick's Sketches of Ancient History of the Six Nations*. Fayetteville, NY: H. C. Beauchamp, 1892.

Brumble, H. David III. *American Indian Autobiography*. Berkeley: University of California Press, 1988.

Clifton, James A. *The Pokagans, 1683–1983: Catholic Potawatomi Indians of the St. Joseph River Valley*. Lathan, VA: University Press of America, 1984.

———. "Simon Pokagan's Sandbar: Potawatomi Claims to Chicago's Lakefront." *Michigan History* 71.5 (September–October 1987): 12–17.

Copeland, Marion W. *Charles Alexander Eastman (Ohiyesa)*. Western Writers Series No. 33. Boise, ID: Boise State University, 1978.

Copway, George [Kah-ge-ga-gah-bowh]. "The American Indians." *American [Whig] Review* 9 (June 1849): 631–7.

———. *Indian Life and Indian History, by an Indian Author. Embracing the Traditions of the North American Indians Regarding Themselves, Particularly of That Most Important of All the Tribes, the Ojibways*. Boston: Albert Colby, 1860.

———. *The Life, History, and Travels, of Kah-Ge-Ga-Gah-Bowh (George Copway), a Young Indian Chief of the Ojebwa Nation, a Convert to the Christian Faith, and a Missionary to His People for Twelve Years*. . . . Albany, NY: Weed and Parsons, 1847.

Dippie, Brian W. *The Vanishing American: White Attitudes and U.S. Indian Policy*. Middletown, CT: Wesleyan University Press, 1982.

Eastman, Charles A. *From the Deep Woods to Civilization: Chapters in the Autobiography of an Indian*. 1916. Rpt. Boston: Little, Brown, 1936.

———. *Indian Boyhood*. Boston: Little, Brown, 1902.

———. *Indian Heroes and Great Chieftains*. Boston: Little, Brown, 1918.

———. *Indian Scout Talks: A Guide for Boy Scouts and Camp Fire Girls*. Boston: Little, Brown, 1914.

———. "The Sioux Mythology." *Popular Science Monthly* 46 (November 1894): 88–91. Rpt. *Native American Folklore in Nineteenth-Century Periodicals*, ed. William M. Clements. Athens: Ohio University Press, 1986: 211–16.

———. *The Soul of the Indian, An Interpretation*. Boston: Houghton Mifflin, 1911.

Eastman, Charles A., and Elaine Goodale Eastman. *Smoky Day's Wigwam Evenings, Indian Stories Retold*. Boston: Little, Brown, 1910.

Hopkins, Sarah Winnemucca. *Life Among the Piutes: Their Wrongs and Claims*, ed. Mrs. Horace Mann. Boston: Cupples, Upham, 1883.

Johnson, Elias. *Legends, Traditions and Law, of the Iroquois, or Six Nations, and History of the Tuscarora Indians*. Lockport, NY: Union, 1881.

Jones, William A. *Fox Texts*. Publications of the American Ethnological Society No. 1. Leyden, the Netherlands: E. J. Brill, 1907.

Krupat, Arnold. *The Voice in the Margin: Native American Literature and the Canon*. Berkeley: University of California Press, 1989.

Lincoln, Kenneth. *Native American Renaissance*. Berkeley: University of California Press, 1983.

Lucero, Ambrose. "For the People: Leslie Silko's *Storyteller*." *Minority Voices* 5 (1981): 1–10.

Miller, David Reed. "Charles Alexander Eastman, The 'Winner': From Deep Woods to Civilization." *American Indian Intellectuals, 1976 Proceedings of the American Ethnological Society*, ed. Margot Liberty. St. Paul, MN: West, 1978: 61–73.

Momaday, N. Scott. *The Way to Rainy Mountain*. Albuquerque: University of New Mexico Press, 1969.

Murray, David. *Forked Tongues: Speech, Writing and Representation in North American Indian Texts*. Bloomington: Indiana University Press, 1991.

Peterson, Erik. "An Indian, an American: Ethnicity, Assimilation and Balance in Charles Eastman's *From the Deep Woods to Civilization*." *Studies in American Indian Literatures* 4.2–3 (1992): 145–60.

Pokagan, Simon. "The Future of the Red Man." *Forum* 23 (1897): 698–708.

"Indian Superstitions and Legends." *Forum* 25 (1898): 618–29. Rpt. *Native American Folklore in Nineteenth-Century Periodicals*, ed. William M. Clements. Athens: Ohio University Press, 1986: 237–52.

"The Massacre of Fort Dearborn at Chicago. Gathered from the Traditions of the Indian Tribes Engaged in the Massacre, and from the Published Accounts." *Harper's* 98 (March 1899): 649–56.

Ruoff, A. LaVonne Brown. "Ritual and Renewal: Keres Traditions in the Short Fiction of Leslie Silko." *MELUS* 5.4 (1978): 2–17.

"Three Nineteenth-Century American Indian Autobiographers." *Redefining American Literary History*, ed. A. LaVonne Brown Ruoff and Jerry W. Ward, Jr. New York: Modern Language Association, 1990: 251–69.

Ruppert, Jim. "Story Telling: The Fiction of Leslie Silko." *Journal of Ethnic Studies* 9 (1981): 53–8.

Silko, Leslie Marmon. *Storyteller*. New York: Seaver, 1981.

Smith, Donald B. "The Life of George Copway or Kah-ge-ga-gah-bowh (1818–1869) – and a Review of His Writings." *Journal of Canadian Studies* 23.3 (Fall 1988): 5–38.

Sorber, Edna C. "The Noble Eloquent Savage." *Ethnohistory* 19 (1972): 227–36.

Stensland, Anna Lee. "Charles Alexander Eastman: Sioux Storyteller and Historian." *American Indian Quarterly* 3 (1977): 199–208.

Warren, William W. *History of the Ojibways, Based Upon Tradition and Oral Statements. Collections of the Minnesota Historical Society* 5 (1885). Rpt. St. Paul: Minnesota Historical Society Press, 1984.

Wilson, Raymond. *Ohiyesa: Charles Eastman, Santee Sioux*. Urbana: University of Illinois Press, 1983.

Wong, Hertha Dawn. *Sending My Heart Back Across the Years: Tradition and Innovation in Native American Autobiography*. New York: Oxford University Press, 1992.

Zitkala-Sa. *Old Indian Legends*. 1901. Rpt. Lincoln: University of Nebraska Press, 1985.

8

"A TERRIBLE SICKNESS AMONG THEM"

SMALLPOX AND STORIES OF THE FRONTIER

HELEN JASKOSKI

I

Histories of North America have largely ignored, marginalized, or discounted the contributions of Native North American historians. As a result, the official story has been, as Annette Kolodny says, "univocal and monolingual, defining origins by what later became the tropes of the dominant or conquering language" (12). Kolodny calls for a reopening of the frontier, a reassessment "thematizing frontier as a multiplicity of ongoing first encounters over time and land, rather than as a linear chronology of successive discoveries and discrete settlements.... There can be no paradigmatic first contact because there are so many first encounters. And there can be no single overarching story" (13). Richard White's detailed exploration of the history of the Great Lakes area from 1650 to 1815 is a step in the direction Kolodny proposes, but even this impressive revisionist account of the *pays d'en haut,* as he calls it, omits the work of Native historians. However, White's paradigm of the eighteenth-century northwest frontier as a space defined by multi-interest negotiation, compromise, and improvisation provides a useful framework for examining the ways in which nineteenth-century historians, writing in the context of literary romanticism, conceptualized the frontier of the previous century.

Colonial history of the Western Hemisphere fascinated American historians a hundred years later. Francis Parkman, George Bancroft, and Willard Motley perceived conflicts like the conquest of Mexico or Peru as the working out in the hemisphere of the destinies of the European world powers. Parkman, in his multivolume series on the French and British in North America, returned again and again to the area around the Great Lakes, Canada, and the Ohio valley.

During the time Parkman's works were being published, between

1840 and 1900, a number of American Indian authors also wrote histories of the Great Lakes area. LaVonne Ruoff mentions some half dozen of these histories, devoted to accounts of the Tuscaroras, Ojibwas,[1] Wyandots, Iroquois, and Ottawa. Not surprisingly, the Native historians gave little attention to the European balance of power as acted out on the North American continent. Their agenda was different and more complex. They addressed a dual audience of Indians and non-Indians, and their texts reflect that mixed reception. Their aims were several: to preserve and explain their nations' pasts; to correct erroneous or biased ideas about Indians; to argue for compliance with treaty obligations; to present themselves as models contradicting stereotypes of savagism; and to promote better treatment, especially better education, for Indians.[2]

These works belong to a genre that Mary Louise Pratt, borrowing a term from Françoise Lionnet, calls "autoethnographic texts." Applying the term to works by indigenous Latin American authors, Pratt says that an autoethnography is

> a text in which people undertake to describe themselves in ways that engage with representations others have made of them. . . . [These texts] involve a selective collaboration with and appropriation of idioms of the metropolis or the conqueror. These are merged or infiltrated to varying degrees with indigenous idioms to create self-representations intended to intervene in metropolitan modes of understanding. Autoethnographic works are often addressed to both metropolitan audiences and the speaker's own community. Their reception is thus highly indeterminate. (35)

Such texts offer the possibility of recovering a less one-sided story of the frontier experience. The focus of this essay is a specific set of such contact stories: accounts of the coming of smallpox among the eighteenth-century Great Lakes Native peoples.

Contagious disease decimated the Western Hemisphere's indigenous populations on a scale that far outweighed military conquest. Of all the plagues carried with the conquest, smallpox was the most devastating; "war, famine and all other causes of death combined could not be compared to smallpox" (Sheehan 229). Comparison of Native American and colonizers' accounts of smallpox permits a unique insight into that liminal, chaotic geographical and psychological space known as the "frontier."

Three nineteenth-century historians who wrote about the colonial Great Lakes area recorded accounts of smallpox epidemics and their origins. The most widely known smallpox story comes from Francis

Parkman's *The Conspiracy of Pontiac* (1870). Ottawa political leader Andrew J. Blackbird relates a similar story from the same period of the French and Indian War in his *History of the Ottawa and Chippewa Indians of Michigan* (1887). William Whipple Warren, a Minnesota Ojibwa historian and legislator, offers two very different accounts of an epidemic that took place in Minnesota in the 1780s in his *History of the Ojibway People* (1885). Comparison of these historians' smallpox stories enlarges our understanding of the history and epidemiology of the disease in the particular period. The smallpox stories also offer insight into alternative conceptualizations of the experience that historians a century later envisioned as the "frontier." One other Ojibwa historian, George Copway, who does not tell a smallpox story, offers in his *Indian Life and Indian History* (1860) such a paradigm for understanding events of the time – including smallpox epidemics – as they were experienced by the native communities.

II

The first of these smallpox stories to be published, and the most well known, is in the sixth edition of *The Conspiracy of Pontiac* by Francis Parkman. Parkman excerpts the correspondence of July 1763 between General Jeffery Amherst, commander-in-chief of British forces, and Colonel Henry Bouquet, who was on his way from Philadelphia to relieve the besieged garrison at Fort Pitt. Parkman's treatment of the episode offers insight into his method and his self-perception as a historian. He says that Amherst, writing to Bouquet,

> finds fault with Captain Ecuyer at Fort Pitt for condescending to fire cannon at [the Indians]. . . . This despicable enemy had, however, pushed him to such straits that he made, in a postscript to Bouquet, the following detestable suggestion: –
> "Could it not be contrived to send the *Small Pox* among those disaffected tribes of Indians? We must on this occasion use every stratagem in our power to reduce them."
> (Signed)   J.A.

> Bouquet replied, also in postscript: –

> "I will try to inoculate the ____ with some blankets that may fall in their hands, and take care not to get the disease myself. As it is a pity to expose good men against them, I wish we could make use of the Spanish method, to hunt them with

English dogs, supported by rangers and some light horse, who would, I think, effectually extirpate or remove that vermin."

Amherst rejoined: "You will do well to try to inoculate the Indians by means of blankets, as well as to try every other method that can serve to extirpate this execrable race. I should be very glad your scheme for hunting them down by dogs could take effect, but England is at too great a distance to think of that at present."

(Signed)   J.A.

There is no direct evidence that Bouquet carried into effect the shameful plan of infecting the Indians, though, a few months after, the small-pox was known to have made havoc among the tribes of the Ohio. Certain it is, that he was perfectly capable of dealing with them by other means, worthy of a man and a soldier; and it is equally certain that in relations with civilized men he was in a high degree honorable, humane, and kind. (2:43–7)

Parkman footnotes Amherst's last "J.A." signature with a discussion of the state of the manuscripts. He then adds that the reports of the subsequent smallpox outbreak came from a Gershom Hicks (2:45).[3]

The passage offers a specimen of Parkman's self-presentation as historian and a window into his strategy as author. Elsewhere in *The Conspiracy of Pontiac* his method is to present his story as a polyvocal text in which he weaves together the voices of eyewitnesses, participants, and contemporary commentators to produce a highly dramatic rendering of the events described. However, in this instance Parkman does not trust his texts to speak for themselves, and his handling of them suggests ambivalence and distress at the news his research has uncovered.

His narrator is caught throughout the passage between conflicting loyalties and judgments. The proposal to infect the Indians with smallpox is "detestable," but Amherst has been "pushed" to make it; the plan is "shameful," but Bouquet is honorable when dealing with "civilized men"; there is no evidence that Bouquet actually distributed infected blankets, but a smallpox epidemic did break out. Amherst's and Bouquet's words are inserted into both the text proper and the footnotes, and the narrator's comments appear in both places as well. Up to this point in his history, Parkman has been framing his story as part of a master narrative recounting a civilizing project (British colonization) that has been momentarily interrupted

by a doomed uprising (Pontiac's war). Now that narrative falters as
evidence of the colonizers' corrupt intentions and despicable means
comes to light. The historian's language conveys his attempt to distance himself from means that he finds repugnant, even while he
approves the end – the colonizing project.

Parkman's smallpox story illustrates a concept of frontier ideology
outlined in Miller and Savage's discussion of Roman stereotypes of
Germanic peoples. Characterizing an indigenous population as sub-
human or animallike is necessary, they say, in order to define the
region as "uninhabited" and thereby to justify settlement by the
occupying power. In a footnote, Parkman offers just such reasoning,
expressed in another of Amherst's letters: "I wish there was not an
Indian Settlement within a thousand miles of our Country, for they
are only fit to live with the Inhabitants of the woods: (i.e., *wild beasts*),
being more allied to the *Brute* than the *human* Creation" (2:44).
The emphases are Amherst's; his language, together with Bouquet's
reference to the Indians as "vermin," serves the function assigned
to stereotyping: "Frontier stereotypes justify behavior that would
normally be defined as illegal or immoral but which, on the frontier,
directed toward the aboriginal people, becomes a predictable norm.
Such behavior assumes that the aboriginal people are something less
than human and reflects a radical human-versus-subhuman dichot-
omy" (Miller and Savage 131).

Francis Parkman was not critiquing frontier ideology, however,
but (as Levin shows) offering it as a grand romantic drama. The
smallpox episode compelled his imagination: He cites this "sufficiently startling . . . proposal of the Commander-in-Chief to infect
the hostile tribes with the small-pox" (1:viii) as information important enough to justify issuing an extensively revised text in the sixth
edition of *The Conspiracy of Pontiac*. The presentation of the smallpox
episode is a melodramatic minidrama: Amherst and Bouquet take
the main stage to carry on their blustering dialogue, and Parkman
as narrator retreats to pedantic editorializing and footnotes.

This dramatic conceptualization emphasizes the psychology of individuals, which was Parkman's abiding interest as a historian. He
outlines his view in the introduction to the second volume of *The
Conspiracy of Pontiac*, where he confidently addresses a homogeneous
audience sharing his own values:

> We have followed the war to its farthest confines, and watched
> it in its remotest operations; not because there is anything es-
> pecially worthy to be chronicled in the capture of a backwoods

fort, and the slaughter of a few soldiers, but because these acts exhibit some of the characteristic traits of the actors. (2:3)

Notwithstanding his long stays among the indigenous peoples of the Pacific Northwest, Parkman looks exclusively through the lens of his elite New England upbringing. The designation of the "farthest," "remotest," "backwoods fort" reiterates the notion of the frontier as a wild and uninhabited space, a void or chaos awaiting an act of creation – that is, settlement – and locates it at the margins of the civilized, creating center. The emphasis on the "characteristic traits" of important men (as opposed to "a few soldiers") corresponds with those nineteenth-century historical theories that held "great men" to be the most important makers of history. To understand the character and psychology of the man behind the event would be to understand the event itself.

This theory can explain why Parkman not only includes but dwells on the blanket episode. As history, the Amherst–Bouquet conspiracy is inconclusive: Whether the British were actually responsible for the epidemic is never established. Seen as literary narrative, it lacks action and closure; the tale remains truncated and incomplete, dwelling on motivation and never establishing execution or consequences. However, although inconclusive as event or incomplete as narrative, the story is fascinating as psychology and character study, a revealing interlude in colonial history conceived as romantic drama.

III

A different perspective on a smallpox epidemic during the French and Indian War appears in Andrew J. Blackbird's *History of the Ottawa and Chippewa Indians of Michigan*. Blackbird, Chief Mack-e-te-be-nessy, was a member of a distinguished Ottawa family from the northwest shore of the Michigan lower peninsula. He wrote his *History* late in life, after a long career in education, politics, and public service.

Blackbird's book, like many similar autoethnographic texts, is a combination of autobiography, history, ethnography, and polemic. He opens with a conventional reference to inaccuracy in current histories. In the course of correcting the record he relates the story, preserved by elders of his nation, of a smallpox epidemic during the height of the French and Indian War, about 1757. Blackbird's story is unique because of the unusual disease vector.

It was a notable fact that by this time [1763] the Ottawas were greatly reduced in numbers from what they were in former times, on account of the small-pox which they brought from Montreal during the French war with Great Britain. This small pox was sold to them shut up in a tin box, with the strict injunction not to open the box on their way homeward, but only when they should reach their country; and that this box contained something that would do them great good, and their people! The foolish people believed really there was something in the box supernatural, that would do them great good. Accordingly, after they reached home they opened the box; but behold there was another tin box inside, smaller. They took it out and opened the second box, and behold, still there was another box inside of the second box, smaller yet. So they kept on this way till they came to a very small box, which was not more than an inch long; and when they opened the last one they found nothing but mouldy particles in this last little box! They wondered very much what it was, and a great many closely inspected to try to find out what it meant. But alas, alas! pretty soon burst out a terrible sickness among them. The great Indian doctors themselves were taken sick and died. The tradition says it was indeed awful and terrible. Every one taken with it was sure to die. Lodge after lodge was totally vacated – nothing but the dead bodies lying here and there in their lodges – entire families being swept off with the ravages of this terrible disease. The whole coast of Arbor Croche . . . was entirely depopulated. . . . It is generally believed among the Indians of Arbor Croche that this wholesale murder of the Ottawas by this terrible disease sent by the British people, was actuated through hatred, and expressly to kill off the Ottawas and Chippewas because they were friends of the French Government or French King. (9–10)

The story's function within Blackbird's history and its relationship to other sources of information about contemporary smallpox epidemics show Blackbird to have been a careful historian, as well as a subtle shaper of narrative and a dedicated polemicist.

Before relating the smallpox story, Blackbird alludes to the relationship the British sought to establish with the Ottawas after the British victory over the French:

The British Government made such extraordinary promises to the Ottawa tribe of Indians. . . . They should receive gifts from her sovereign in shape of goods, provisions, firearms, ammunition, and intoxicating liquors! Her sovereign's beneficent arm should be even extended unto the dogs belonging to the Ottawa tribe of Indians. And what place soever she should meet them, she would freely unfasten the faucet which contains her living water – whiskey, which she will also cause to run perpetually and freely unto the Ottawas as the fountain of perpetual spring! (8)

The account parallels the smallpox story that is narrated next. In both instances, delegations of Ottawas visit Montreal; the Ottawas hear extravagant promises; and a commodity that is proffered as having almost magically beneficent properties turns out to be an agent of horrible destruction. Trade becomes treachery. The secret of both flowing fountain and magic box is invisible death and long-lasting deterioration.

The striking image in each vignette is the gift: bountiful fountain, nested boxes. However, the rhetoric in the two passages contrasts in tone and technique. Sarcasm pervades the catalog of British-provided "goods, provisions, firearms, ammunition, and intoxicating liquors" and continues in the hyperbolic metonymy of the "sovereign's beneficent arm . . . extended unto the dogs" of the Indians and the metaphorical "faucet which contains her living water." Figurative language is enriched with biblical echoes in fountain and spring.[4] The box of smallpox described in the subsequent paragraphs might be another powerful figure of speech, recalling legends of hidden evil in caskets and Pandora's box. The description of the box, however, proceeds in a tone of factual understatement and journalistic reporting: The passage lacks rhetorical ornamentation of any kind, and events are reported as fact, not allegory.

The distinction between fact and trope, history and legend, is consistent with Blackbird's treatment of legend, myth, and history throughout his book. In describing a massacre on Mackinac Island, he distinguishes the massacre story, which he considers to be historical, from a romantic legend about the two survivors. The romance "may be considered, at this age, as a fictitious story; but every Ottawa and Chippewa to this day believes it to be positively so" (21). The chapter in which this episode is related begins with a headnote that reinforces the distinction by contrasting the "Earliest Possible Known History of Mackinac Island" and "Its Historical Definition" with "The Legends of the Two Who Escaped."

Other passages in Blackbird's *History* appeal to conservative Christian readers and support his careful distinction between belief and evidentiary proof. Chapter 9 retells two of the great myths of "Ne-

naw-bo-zhoo," the stories of the flood and the earth diver and of
the hero swallowed by the water monster; in doing so, Blackbird
points out parallels between these traditions and the biblical stories
of Noah and Jonah. Blackbird's claims are positive, unapologetic,
and undefensive: "These are some of the legends told among the
Ottawa and Chippewa Indians, as related in their own language,
which are in some things quite similar to the records of the Bible"
(78). Later, he comments on popular theories that Indians were
descended from the "lost tribes" of Israel: "From evidence of working in metals and from the many other relics of former occupants,
it is evident that this country has been inhabited for many ages, but
whether by descendants of the Jews or of other Eastern races there
is no way for us to determine" (96). In his skepticism Andrew Blackbird was ahead of many respected scientists of his day. In general,
the narration of the smallpox story corresponds with his depiction
of historical events as distinguished from legend, myth, or specula-
tion.[5]

External evidence also supports the hypothesis that the box of
smallpox was probably real. In the period Andrew Blackbird was writing about, the last fifty years of the eighteenth century, smallpox
inoculation had gained widespread acceptance in England and was
also practiced in France. Edward Jenner first derived smallpox vaccine from cowpox, which is harmless to humans and produces immunity to smallpox. However, until Jenner's vaccine was adopted in
the latter part of the eighteenth century, immunization against smallpox was accomplished through inoculation, a very different proce-
dure. Inoculation involved deliberate infection of a subject with live
smallpox virus taken from an infected individual. The method produced immunity, but it was risky. The rates of death from inoculation were estimated at one in fifty, compared to one in six when the
disease was contracted fortuitously (Miller 117–23, 125); however,
among Indian populations the success rate for inoculation tended
to be lower (Duffy).

The practice of smallpox inoculation is dated to the eleventh century in China and was known in Africa and the Middle East. Translations of Chinese medical treatises were a major means of
promoting smallpox inoculation in eighteenth-century Europe and
the Americas.[6] The "mouldy particles" that Andrew Blackbird says
caused an infection among the Ottawa Indians sound remarkably
like the infectious matter introduced in the process of inoculation.
Chinese medical textbooks offer descriptions of classic inoculation
procedures. The *Golden Mirror of Medicine*, for instance, describes four
methods of smallpox inoculation; two of them are as follows:

(1) The nose is plugged with powdered smallpox scabs laid on cotton wool . . . (2) . . . The powdered scabs are put into the end of a silver tube which is about six or seven inches long and curved at the end. The scabs are blown into the nose. (Hume 140)

Is it possible that a container of smallpox matter collected for purposes of inoculation was available in Montreal, and that it came into the hands of a group of Indians from Michigan, who carried the infection home? Is it possible that whoever gave the box to the Ottawas had benign motives, hoping to enable them to become immunized against this terrible plague?

Jesuit missionaries in China were much involved in studying and translating classical Chinese treatises of all kinds, and were important agents in introducing Chinese knowledge and culture into Europe. Jesuits had been active in carrying out inoculation campaigns among indigenous peoples in Latin America. There was a Jesuit mission at L'Arbre Croche (Henry 47). Individual links for such a connection exist, but it is precisely the nature of the *pays d'en haut* as an "abyss" between cultures undergoing "contact" that precludes certainty on these questions. White refers to the history of this time and place as "a fractured society . . . preserved in fractured memory. . . . The fragments are the history" (2). Blackbird's box of smallpox is one such fragment: Its matching or contiguous pieces are missing in the interstices of those fractures.

The dating of this epidemic is also both problematic and revealing. Other records indicate that Blackbird's smallpox story actually conflates two different events. The opening sentences, dating the epidemic to the last years of the French and Indian War, allude to the great epidemic that passed throughout New France from 1755 to 1757. This plague was so devastating that military campaigns were aborted and trade had to be abandoned (Duffy 336; Stearn and Stearn 43–4); it decimated the populations around Fort Mackinac and on the islands of the straits connecting lakes Michigan and Huron. However, the destruction of L'Arbre Croche, a fifteen-mile-long town on the northwestern shore of the lower Michigan peninsula, which Blackbird mentions at the end of his story, took place some fifty years later, around 1799, in a different pandemic that swept through the former French territories from upper Canada as far south as Louisiana (Stearn and Stearn 51–2).[7] It appears that Blackbird has synthesized the two episodes into a single narrative.

This collapsing of temporal distinctions between events that are related thematically but separate in time is characteristic of oral traditions. In the Preface to his history of the western Ojibwa, William Warren notes it as a difficult issue for the historian: "Through the somewhat uncertain manner in which the Indians count time, the dates of events . . . may differ slightly from those . . . endorsed by present standard historians as authentic" (26). Blackbird's rhetorical strategy serves an autoethnographic design. If his agenda is to "intervene" in the official story, then documenting chronology takes second place to the more pressing need to convey the instability, disruption, and devastation that characterized the frontier.

The story of the introduction of smallpox into the Ottawa population is an origin story, an account of a paradigmatic event that was reenacted many times. Its character as paradigm, however, does not conflict with the possible existence of the objects described in it. Furthermore, Blackbird's smallpox story displays a literarily satisfying wholeness lacking in Parkman's: There is a beginning, a middle, and an end, plausible (although speculative) motivation, and tragic consequences out of proportion to the actions that precipitate them.

IV

Two more smallpox stories, from William Warren's *History of the Ojibway People,* extend our understanding of historians' construction of the events of the period. During the 1840s William Whipple Warren, a young Ojibwa educated in New York and at mission schools, began collecting oral histories from Indians, traders, and settlers in Minnesota. After his election in 1850 to the Minnesota legislature, Warren reworked his stories with more material into a history of the western Ojibwa, which remained in manuscript at the time of his death in 1853. Warren's book, *History of the Ojibway People,* was eventually published by the Minnesota State Historical society in 1885. The *History* offers two different stories to explain a smallpox epidemic in the 1780s that decimated the Pillager band of Ojibwas of Leech Lake, Minnesota.

The first story opens in the summer of 1781, when the Leech Lake Ojibwas were camped on the Red River. A trader came upriver from the Mississippi; he was ill and could not leave his boat, but his assistants put out a lot of rain-soaked cloth to dry in the sun. The temptation was finally too much for the Ojibwas, Warren says; preparing for "their grand medawe rite . . . when they are accustomed to display all the finery of which they are possessed, caused them doubly to covet the merchandise of the sick trader" (257–8). Eventually all of the trader's stock, including a substantial amount of liquor, was appropriated. In the ensuing chaos "the rifled trader was obliged quickly to embark in his empty canoe, and leave the inhospitable camp of the Ojibways to save his life. It is said that he died of the sickness from which he was suffering, at Sauk Rapids, on his way down the Mississippi" (259). This event, Warren says, gained the Pillager band their name. It also precipitated the censure of other Ojibwas who predicted that traders would stay away.

Accordingly, the following spring (1782), a group of Pillagers took a supply of beaver skins to Fort Mackinac. There the British commandant gave

> their leader a medal, flag, coat, and bale of goods, at the same time requesting that he would not unfurl his flag, nor distribute his goods, until he arrived into his own country.
>
> With this injunction, the Pillager chief complied, till he landed at Fond du Lac, where, anxious to display the great consequence to which the medal and presents of the British had raised him in his own estimation, he formally called his followers to a council, and putting on his chief's coat, and unfurling his flag, he untied his bale of goods, and freely distributed to his fellows. Shortly after, he was taken suddenly sick, and retiring to the woods, he expired by himself as the discovery of his remains afterwards indicated. (260)

His companions also died, and the sickness – smallpox – spread to many villages. Warren concludes that "it is a common saying to this day [the 1840s], that the white men purposely inflicted it on them by secreting bad medicine in the bale of goods, in punishment for the pillage which the Leech Lake band had committed on one of their traders" (257–60).

This is a tale of theft and retaliation, greed and revenge, and it makes sense of the epidemic in terms of retributive justice and punishment for transgression. It offers literary symmetry and moral paradigms: The invisible trader sick in his boat parallels the invisible infection later distributed in the bundles of trade goods; the cloths stolen for ceremonial finery are followed by infected textile goods; the trader's death alone on a remote river has its counterpart in the Pillager chief's death alone in the woods. Like Andrew Blackbird's story, it has a satisfying completeness as to motives, actions, and consequences.

However, William Warren was as uncomfortable as Francis Parkman when it came to believing the worst of British officers, and he searched out a different explanation of the same epidemic. This second smallpox story begins on Dead River, to the west of Leech Lake, among a war party of Kenistenoe, Assiniboine, and Ojibwa

warriors. The men traveled west to the banks of the Missouri, where
they attacked a Gros Ventre village. There was little resistance, and
the raiders took a number of scalps, one of them "a giant in size
. . . as large as a beaver skin" (261). The oversized scalp was believed
to have special powers, and when on the fourth day of the party's
homeward journey a man died, the victors threw away "the fearful
scalp . . . every day, however, their numbers decreased, as they fell
sick and died" (261). Only four Ojibwas survived to reach their village at Dead River, where the disease then killed almost the entire
population. Refugees fleeing this plague

> spread the contagion to Rainy Lake . . . from thence by the
> route of Pigeon River it reached Lake Superior at Grand Por-
> tage, and proceeded up the lake to Fond du Lac, where its
> ravages were also severely felt, and where the Pillager party on
> their return from Mackinaw caught the infection, and tak-
> ing it to Sandy Lake, but a few of their number lived to reach
> their homes at Leech Lake, where it is said to have stopped.
> (261–2)

This story satisfies a modern understanding of the etiology of smallpox; in contrast to Warren's first story, it emphasizes empirical theories of epidemiology, with themes of contamination and contagion
plotted through a causal chain realized in the series of villages falling, one by one, to the fearsome disease. The two stories meet in a
particular place and moment: at the village of Fond du Lac[8] in 1882,
when the presence of the Ojibwas fleeing the scourge at Dead River
coincides with the Pillager chief's precipitate distribution of his
bounty.

However, although it is scientifically plausible, this revisionist story
offers neither the narrative completeness nor the well-wrought fit of
motive, action, and result that characterize both Blackbird's story
and the first (and more popular) story that Warren relates. Tracing
the course of the disease back through the villages it destroyed offers
no closure, but only open-ended potential for infinite regress back
through ever more remote sources. Indeed, the story never does
reach the original European vector. This is a story of motiveless ma-
lignity, of a terrible chain of effects without cause.

Warren's inclusion of both stories enables him to present his
methodology as a historian. In a transition paragraph between the
two smallpox stories, Warren explains – in language reminiscent of
Parkman's – that the belief that the British commandant had purposely given the Pillagers infected goods

was a serious charge, and in order to ascertain if it was really entertained by the more enlightened and thinking portions of the tribe, I have made particular inquiries, and flatter myself that I have obtained from the intelligent old chief of the Pillagers, a truthful account of the manner in which the smallpox was, on this occasion, actually introduced among the Ojibways. (260)

Here Warren uses the smallpox stories – much as Blackbird discriminates between history, legend, and allegory – to portray himself as a skeptical, judicious historian. Unwilling to credit sensational tales, he delves deeper, makes "particular inquiries," and finally accepts an explanation on the authority of an "intelligent old chief" who represents the "enlightened and thinking portions of the tribe." The result is a "truthful account" of how things "actually" happened, and the writer can even indulge in a little self-congratulation: "I . . . flatter myself."

The presentation of competing stories is not characteristic of Warren's *History* as a whole. Apparently, the smallpox stories fascinated and disturbed him, just as similar information had troubled Parkman, and both authors reveal a personal engagement with their materials more transparently in these episodes than elsewhere in their respective works. Where Parkman dwells on psychology, Warren effaces individual identities and thereby emphasizes the archetypal shape of his first story and the relation of both stories to the locations where they take place. While Warren's second story purports to be the credible, the truly historical account, inclusion of the first, discredited, smallpox story fulfills several functions: It accounts for the Pillager name, it permits the author to display and validate his method, and it offers an almost mythlike paradigm of culture contact.

V

These three books have a curious intertextual relation – or lack of relation – to each other. William Warren's *History of the Ojibway People* was written in the 1850s but was not published until 1885, more than thirty years after the author's death at the age of twenty-eight. In collecting Ojibwa traditions during the 1840s, Warren could well have received eyewitness accounts of the 1780 epidemic. In any case, he was the first English-speaking historian to record for publication the supposition that smallpox was deliberately introduced by colonizers as a weapon of war or revenge. It is tempting to speculate whether, if Warren had written thirty years later, or if he had seen Parkman's documentary sources, he might have been less eager to defend the commander of Fort Michilimackinac.

The 1870 edition of Parkman's *The Conspiracy of Pontiac* is the first of these three books to make public the evidence of a deliberate intention to spread smallpox among the Indians. If Parkman had been able to see Warren's earlier notes, would he have considered the Amherst–Bouquet plan such an anomaly? Andrew Blackbird singles out "the history of the life of Pontiac . . . written by a noted historian" from "a number of writings by different men who attempted to give an account of the Indians" (7) as a work to which he responds; however, he makes no mention of Parkman's infected-blanket story, even though it offers striking parallels to his own remarkable account of the infectious box. Did Blackbird see an earlier edition of Parkman's history or was he alluding to a book by another author? Besides being the subject of popular memoirs and histories, Pontiac's war was – as Flynn notes – a major motif in the Indian dramas of the nineteenth century; Blackbird could well have encountered any of these popular representations of colonial history. With the discovery of archival sources, other possibilities give rise to tantalizing speculations. What confirmation might Blackbird have found for his theory of motive if he had seen the British generals' correspondence?

Francis Parkman's smallpox record and William Warren's second smallpox story are incomplete but complementary; Parkman's is all intention, Warren's all results. As narration, each supplies the other's lack: Parkman offers confirmation for the deliberate introduction of contagion that is missing in Warren, and Warren details the conclusion of such an action. There is no middle – or rather, the middle is indefinite, an abyss – between the two different epidemics separated by seventeen years in time and hundreds of miles in distance. Beginning and ending, motive and result, remain unconnected. There is no turning point, no critical moment of opening and discovery. The fragmentariness itself expresses the disruption and conflict of the frontier. Neither the individual stories nor any attempt to collate them provides a congruent reconstruction of the period. Only tantalizing parallels remain, suggesting possible, unprovable, connections. The fragmentation that White says characterized the era persists a hundred years after the events as individual historians attempt, from the isolated fragments available to them, to construct a coherent story of the past.

VI

The Ojibwa historian/autoethnographers do not invoke the romantic mythos that governs Parkman's story of creation out of chaos, civilization displacing wilderness. Warren's first story and Blackbird's narrative embody a Native American paradigm, a different kind of origin story and one that centers on expiation as a response to violence and on healing instead of conquest as a resolution of disorder. A third Ojibwa historian of the period, George Copway, presents the archetypal myth.

Born in Canada in 1818, George Copway had a varied career. Missionary, newspaper editor, and friend of James Fenimore Cooper, he lived at different times in the United States and in Canada. In 1850 Copway published a history of the Ojibwa Indians, *The Traditional History and Characteristic Sketches of the Ojibway Nation* (Littlefield and Parins 35). In 1858 the book was reissued under the title *Indian Life and Indian History, by an Indian Author...*, and subsequent reprintings carried this title. In the course of outlining Ojibwa religious traditions, always an important task for Indian historians, Copway relates the origin myth of "Me-day Worship" (160), the central healing ritual of the Ojibwa people. (This is the same ceremony that Warren calls "medawa"; conventional spelling today is usually Midewiwin.)

The myth begins by describing an edenic existence at the beginning of time: "When Keshamonedoo made the red men, he made them happy. The men were larger, were fleeter of foot, were more dexterous in games, and lived to an older age than now. The forest abounded with game, the trees were loaded with fruit" (163–4). God watched over the people, and powerful otherworldly beings, called *Manitou,* traveled between heaven and earth on a vine that humans were forbidden to climb. However, one young man, singled out by these beings for favors, determined to escape the envy of his fellows by moving to the heavens. His deserted grandmother climbed to the sky to bring him back, and the village was punished for her transgression. People complained of pain; "some were unable to walk, and others equally unable to speak. They thought some of these fell asleep, for they knew not what death was. They had never seen its presence. . . . There was no more hunting, no more games, and no song was sung to soothe the sun to its evening rest. Ah, it was then a penalty followed transgression. Disease was the consequence of the breaking of the vine. Death followed" (167). The people punished the old woman by burning her cabin and appealed to the Manitou, who told the Ojibwas that death was to be a part of their world, but that they would be initiated into the medicinal uses of plants. This wisdom would be transmitted thereafter through the "Medwiwin" medicine ceremony (163–7).

Like many other Native American tales, this is an origin myth for a ceremony, framed as a story of transgression, quest, insight, and reintegration. In such stories, orderly intercourse exists between the human world and the world of the powerful Other in a homogeneous, harmonious universe. Transgression of a boundary or violation of a prohibition produces chaos, violence, death, and disruption – that is, a liminal, borderland condition where laws no longer operate. Finally, after expiatory negotiations, the original ideal state can be recovered temporarily by being re-created in ceremony.

Aware of his non-Indian audience's Christian frame of reference, Copway refers to the beings from the world of the other as "spirits"; this was a common shorthand that many Indians used to explain such concepts to Europeans. The designation suggesting angels, however, misses the sense of participatory exchange present in Native American peoples' cosmogonies. What the Native person could have seen as a process involving risk, education, discipline, and enlightenment in an encounter with a terribly powerful master could be misread by Europeans as propitiation and appeasement of a divine being. Put another way, for the Ojibwa the Other was more relatedly natural than alien divine, and to be reckoned with in terms of power that could be appropriated or acquired as well as appeased. Seeing that they themselves were encountered in terms the Indians used to designate a powerful Other, Europeans sometimes made the mistake of assuming that the Indians thought they were gods. This was not true; as is clear from the smallpox stories just considered, Europeans were recognized as human. Yet they were Other, and in making sense of their contact with these Others, the Native Americans had available paradigms from tradition.[9]

There are striking parallels between George Copway's version of the Midewiwin origin myth and William Warren's and Andrew Blackbird's smallpox stories. All the stories involve a world of the Other, and all show protagonists who travel into this liminal, borderland world: The Ottawas travel to Montreal, and the Pillagers visit Fort Mackinac. There is a prohibition in each, and Warren's story involves transgression of the prohibition (echoing the earlier transgression of stealing the goods). Disorder and disruption ensue, followed by chaos and death, in each case interpreted as retaliation by the Other. In Warren's story, the Midewiwin ceremony itself is what the Pillager band was preparing for when the original trader visited them. Blackbird's story emphasizes the theme of the dubious value of getting too close to the Other and the ambiguous relationship of death and medicine, both issuing from the same source. Indeed, if Blackbird's polluted box really existed as a container for smallpox inoculation, the event would emulate the myth in a remarkable way. Each story explains how death and possible annihilation came to the people.

If the myth is a paradigm for stories of the introduction of small-pox among Indians, then it shows that discovery is a two-way enterprise, not the sole prerogative of the invader or colonizer. The central figures of Blackbird's and Warren's stories are not passive victims waiting to receive an inexorable plague. They are discoverers: They go out to the dangerous, borderland region of the Other and they return with power. The power is destructive, but the myth explains that such power can eventually be appropriated and reconstituted with expiation and the proper ritual.

Blackbird, Warren, and Copway were themselves like the protagonists they wrote about. Each of these men wrote explicitly with the intention of dis-covering to a non-Indian audience the hidden, unnamed, silenced side of the frontier story. Their books may be seen as having a function similar to that of the *Manitou* of the myth: Like the tutelary beings who guide and teach humans (and unlike Parkman's narrative, which is addressed exclusively to the colonizers), the autoethnographies offer the prospect for a reweaving of communication and relationship across an abyss of misunderstanding and violence. Their project of intervening in the master narrative is profoundly optimistic, resting on assumptions that a receptive audience can be found and that a ceremony of education and healing can occur.

This essay began with the hypothesis that the story of the American frontier is incomplete if it considers only the perspective of the colonizer. Examination of these smallpox stories and the histories from which they come suggests that there is no single story. The frontier, by definition, belongs to the colonizer. So Parkman's dismissal of events in "backwoods forts" will always be a different story from Warren's and Blackbird's careful delineation of places that are named, known, and meaningful. Both Blackbird's and Warren's texts portray a society that resembles the *pays d'en haut* White describes: a conflicted – but not a chaotic – place that is defined by negotiation, compromise, and attempts to work out differences through solutions that approximate desiderata for either side. To the colonizer the frontier may be a "liberated zone" where, far from central authorities, no laws can be made to apply. To the colonialist historian it may be a wilderness waiting to be tamed. To the Native peoples, by contrast, frontier lawlessness originates in the disruption of an ordered existence by a catastrophe of virtually demonic appearance and dimension. Frederick Jackson Turner's definition of the frontier as "meeting point between savagery and civilization" (quoted in Hudson 13) may be true from either side, but the application of the terms will be reversed depending on whose point of view governs the story.

Francis Parkman's and William Warren's smallpox stories of infected blankets and infected scalps, no matter how complementary they are in their narrative structures, cannot be synthesized to make a coherent history. There is no "master narrative"; there is no omniscient viewpoint; there are only multiple stories of the frontier. This is the point at which frontier stories acquire contemporary relevance, for this condition of mutually exclusive stories of the American space still prevails. Smallpox is gone,[10] the frontier is not: The frontier condition of multiple visions of the North American space persists. To understand that condition requires attention to the multiple constructions of it.[11]

Notes

1. The current spelling is Ojibwa. Variant spellings in the titles and texts of individual works are retained in title citations and quotations (e.g., Chippewa, Ojebway, Ojibway).
2. See Clements' essay in this volume for an overview of the aims of early autobiographers and historians.
3. Knollenberg, working with archival sources unavailable to Parkman, offers further evidence that the plan was indeed carried out.
4. Blackbird, a devout Protestant convert from Catholicism when he wrote his *History*, would have found several allusions in the Revised Standard version of the New Testament, among them the Gospel of John 4.4 ("But whosoever drinketh of the water that I shall give him shall never thirst; but the water that I shall give him shall be in him a well of water springing up into everlasting life") and Revelation 7.17 ("For the Lamb which is in the midst of the throne shall feed them, and shall lead them unto living fountains of waters; and God shall wipe away all tears from their eyes"). Blackbird's implicit contrast of the ideals of Christianity with the actions of Christians belongs to a tradition that includes much abolitionist literature, as well as writings by other nineteenth-century Native North American authors (see the essays by Murray, Dannenberg, and Peterson in this volume).
5. For contrasting analyses of the relationship of myth and history in two other smallpox stories, see Feer, and Marriott and Rachlin.
6. Several accounts point out that African slaves taught European coloniz-

ers in the Western Hemisphere how to inoculate for smallpox. Catholic missionaries carried out inoculation campaigns among Indians in Latin America, which were moderately successful when they were accepted, although not as effective as among Europeans. British colonists evidently did not attempt to inoculate Indians to prevent smallpox. Later, with the introduction of Jenner's vaccination method, Jefferson promoted the first of a number of U.S. government campaigns to immunize Indian populations against smallpox (Duffy; Sheehan; Stearn and Stearn).

7. Tanner's map of smallpox and other epidemics shows a major smallpox epidemic in the islands of the straits in 1757–8 (as well as in 1670–1 and 1681–2) and another in the Little Traverse region, where L'Arbre Croche was located, in 1800–1 (170).

8. This Fond du Lac is at the western tip of Lake Superior; present-day atlases show a Fond du Lac reservation at the site of the old village.

9. White points out that the Europeans, originally regarded as *manitou*, or grandfathers, suffered a demotion in rank when the French governor of Canada accepted the designation "father" (36). White also uses "manitou" as both the singular and the plural form, perhaps to avoid distracting English connotations of the Ojibwa plural "manidog."

10. Smallpox is almost gone. In probably the most impressive project of mutual cooperation ever undertaken, eradication of smallpox throughout the world was completed in 1979. There is presently a plan to destroy all remaining laboratory stocks of variola, the smallpox virus. This deliberate annihilation of a species has, paradoxically, raised questions in the scientific community as to the wisdom of doing away with any life form, no matter how invidious (Caldwell).

11. I am grateful to the American Philosophical Society for a grant that supported the initial research for this essay. A California State University Foundation grant also assisted production of the final essay.

Works Cited

Bible. Authorized (King James) Version. Philadelphia: National Bible Press, 1963.

Blackbird, Andrew J. *History of the Ottawa and Chippewa Indians of Michigan.* Ypsilanti, MI: Ypsilantian Job Printing House, 1887. Rpt. Petoskey, MI: Little Traverse Regional Historical Society, 1977.

Caldwell, Mark. "Vigil for a Doomed Virus." *Discover* (March 1992): 50–6.

Copway, George. *Indian Life and Indian History, by an Indian Author Embracing the Traditions of the North American Indians Regarding Themselves, Particularly of That Most Important of All the Tribes, the Ojibways.* Boston: Albert Colby and Company, 1860.

Duffy, John. "Smallpox and the Indians in the American Colonies." *Bulletin of the History of Medicine.* Vol. 25. Baltimore: Johns Hopkins University Press, 1951.

Farris, Glenn J. "Recognizing Indian Folk History as Real History: A Fort Ross Example." *American Indian Quarterly* 13 (1989): 471–80.

Feer, Michael. "'The Skunk and the Smallpox': Mythology and Historical Reality." *Plains Anthropologist* 18 (1973): 33–9.

Flynn, Joyce. "Academics on the Trail of the Stage 'Indian': A Review Essay." *Studies in American Indian Literatures* 1st ser. 11.1 (1987): 1–16.

Henry, Alexander. *Travels and Adventures in Canada.* New York: I. Riley, 1809. March of America Facsimile Series Number 43. Rpt. Ann Arbor: University Microfilms, 1966.

Hudson, John C. "Theory and Methodology in Comparative Frontier Studies." *The Frontier: Comparative Studies,* ed. David Harry Miller and Jerome O. Steffen. Norman: University of Oklahoma Press 1977: 11–31.

Hume, Edward H. *The Chinese Way in Medicine.* Westport, CT: Hyperion Press, 1940.

Jacobs, Wilbur R. *Dispossessing the American Indian: Indians and Whites on the Colonial Frontier.* New York: Charles Scribner's Sons, 1972.

Jones, Peter. *History of the Ojebway Indians: with Especial Reference to Their Conversion to Christianity.* 1861. Rpt. Freeport, NY: Books for Libraries Press, 1970.

Knollenberg, Bernhard. "General Amherst and Germ Warfare." *Mississippi Valley Historical Review* 41 (1954): 489–94.

Kolodny, Annette. "Letting Go Our Grand Obsessions: Notes Toward a New Literary History of the American Frontiers." *American Literature* 64.1 (1992): 1–18.

Levin, David. *History as Romantic Art: Bancroft, Prescott, Motley, and Parkman.* Stanford, CA: Stanford University Press, 1959.

Lionnet, Françoise. "Autoethnography: The An-Archic Style of *Dust Tracks on a Road.*" *African American Autobiography: A Collection of Critical Essays,* ed. William L. Andrews. Englewood Cliffs, NJ: Prentice Hall, 1993: 113–37.

Littlefield, Daniel F., Jr., and James W. Parins. *A Biobibliography of Native American Writers, 1772–1924.* Metuchen, NJ: Scarecrow Press, 1981.

Marriott, Alice, and Carol K. Rachlin. *American Indian Mythology.* New York: Thomas Y. Crowell, 1968.

Miller, David Harry, and William W. Savage, Jr. "Ethnic Stereotypes and the Frontier: A Comparative Study of Roman and American Experience." *The Frontier: Comparative Studies,* ed. David Harry Miller and Jerome O. Steffen. Norman: University of Oklahoma Press, 1977: 109–37.

Miller, Genevieve. *The Adoption of Inoculation for Smallpox in England and France.* Philadelphia: University of Pennsylvania Press, 1957.

Parkman, Francis. *The Conspiracy of Pontiac and the Indian War After the Conquest of Canada.* 2 vols. 1870. Frontenac ed. vols. 14 and 15. Rpt. New York: Charles Scribner's Sons, 1915.

Pratt, Mary Louise. "Arts of the Contact Zone." *Profession 91.* New York: Modern Language Association, 1991: 35–9.

Ruoff, A. LaVonne Brown. *American Indian Literatures: An Introduction, Bibliographic Review, and Selected Bibliography.* New York: Modern Language Association, 1990.

Sheehan, Bernard. *Seeds of Extinction: Jeffersonian Philanthropy and the American Indian*. Chapel Hill: University of North Carolina Press, 1973.

Stearn, E. Wagner, and Allen E. Stearn. *The Effect of Smallpox on the Destiny of the Amerindian*. Boston: Bruce Humphries, 1945.

Tanner, Helen Hornbeck. *Atlas of Great Lakes Indian History*. Norman and London: University of Oklahoma Press, 1987.

Warren, William W[hipple]. *History of the Ojibway People*. Minneapolis: Minnesota Historical Society, 1885. Rpt. with Intro. by W. Roger Buffalohead, 1984.

White, Richard. *The Middle Ground: Indians, Empires, and Republics in the Great Lakes Region, 1650–1815*. Cambridge: Cambridge University Press, 1991.

9

"A DESIRABLE CITIZEN, A PRACTICAL BUSINESS MAN"

G. W. GRAYSON – CREEK MIXED BLOOD, NATIONALIST, AND AUTOBIOGRAPHER

ROBERT F. SAYRE

In the development of American Indian autobiography the first two decades of the twentieth century were a turning point. In 1902 Charles Eastman published *Indian Boyhood,* his story of growing up in what he claimed was the vanished traditional world of the Santee Sioux. In 1906 S. M. Barrett published *Geronimo's Story of His Life,* the last or nearly the last of the popular dictated autobiographies of famous war chiefs. And in 1920 Paul Radin published the first autobiography written at the request of an anthropologist, *The Autobiography of a Winnebago Indian.* In between, Eastman published his second volume, *From the Deep Woods to Civilization* (1916), telling of his assimilation into the white world; the Dutch businessman-ethnologist William Wildschut began his interviews with Two Leggings, which would be the basis of Peter Nabokov's later volume, and various memorialists like Joseph Dixon published collections of autobiographies which were intended to be records of the end of the noble redman (*The Vanishing Race,* 1913).

This was, therefore, a period of significant endings and beginnings: the end of autobiographies of war chiefs dictated to journalists, the beginning of lives of supposedly ordinary or representative Indians written for anthropologists, and many stories of the "end" of traditional practices and "beginning" of new ones along "the white man's path" (as Eastman called it). Moreover, these stories coincided, as David Brumble has pointed out, with the triumph of social Darwinism as a national ideology and the implementation of the Dawes Act (148–55). Although the Dawes Act had been passed in 1887, the actual fulfillment of its goals of breaking up reservations by allotting farm-size acreages to individual Indians took years to accomplish. Indeed, it was never enforced on all reservations, but it did express the intent of Federal policy and so marked a new era in U.S.–Indian relations.

158

One of the last tribes to be affected by the Dawes Act was the Creek, or Muscogee, who along with the other "Civilized Tribes" (the Cherokee, Chickasaw, Choctaw, and Seminole) had been exempted from the original bill. After removal from their native lands in Georgia and Alabama, the Creek had reestablished themselves in Indian Territory. In land between the Arkansas and Canadian Rivers, in what is now east central Oklahoma, they had built farms and towns and reconstituted themselves as the Creek Nation. They also had built schools and churches and started newspapers, with the intention among some of their leaders of creating a modern, progressive Indian state. But in 1893 the U.S. Congress established the Dawes Commission, authorizing it to begin allotting the lands of the Creek and their neighbors. The Creek contested the policy and delayed its implementation as long as possible, but finally in 1901 their leaders agreed with the Commission to accept allotments and start to dissolve their tribal government.

George Washington Grayson was one of the Creek leaders who fought the allotment acts and dissolution of his nation, and his autobiography, written between 1908 and 1912, but not published until 1988, is another of the works from this critical period. Although only about 160 pages long and represented by its editor as a Civil War memoir, it does a great deal to help us realize the character of the "educated," "civilized," "mixed-blood" Creek leaders (as they were called and as they thought of themselves) who fought allotment. As such, it is a remarkably interesting and important document, and in this essay I want to attempt to explain why, by looking at its content and style as they illustrate Grayson's character and beliefs. By doing this, I also hope to add Grayson's autobiography to the growing list of original Indian autobiographies, a group of texts which is helping contemporary Indians to build their literary heritage and helping non-Indians to overcome prejudices and ignorance.

An initial difficulty in reading Grayson's autobiography is its title. *A Creek Warrior for the Confederacy: The Autobiography of Chief G. W. Grayson*, the title of the 1988 edition, was given it by its editor, W. David Baird (Letter), and it makes the reader expect a Civil War memoir. Grayson did serve in the War, rising from private to captain in a Creek Confederate regiment, but the War memories occupy only about a quarter of the book. Secondly, the term a "Creek Warrior" is at once too generic and too romantic. Mary Jane Warde, who has written a biography of Grayson, informs me that the title on the typescript of the autobiography was "Red Paths and White," but she adds that this may have been the title given it by Edward Everett

Dale, a scholar who began to prepare it for publication in the 1930s
(Letter). Thus, I prefer to call it simply "The Autobiography of G.
W. Grayson," leaving out the "Chief" since Grayson did not become
Creek Principal Chief until 1917, years after he wrote the autobi-
ography, by which time the title had become mainly honorific
(Baird, Preface 9).

The term autobiography was also used by Grayson. He begins his
narrative, "On several occasions as my inclinations led me, I have
while seated at our family meals related to the members of my family
incidents of my past life, many of them the results of conditions and
circumstances created by the late war between the states in which I
played a small part" (12). His family suggested that he record these
stories, he says, and "To accomplish such a task with a fairly satis-
factory approach to completeness, . . . it seemed to me that the work
should be given the form and character somewhat of an autobiography" (12). Such is Grayson's opening, with his reasons for writing
a full autobiography. But he then comes up with a curious admission, which he turns into a kind of boast: "I have no recollection of
ever having read an autobiography written by anyone else, and
hence have adopted no model by which to be guided in my effort,
and supposing that it would probably be conceded that each such
writer may justly be a law unto himself, I have proceeded to write in
my own way, and as suits me best" (12–3).

The very fact that Grayson was consciously writing his autobiography is a sign of what we today would call his acculturation. He did
not need a journalist or anthropologist to come propose it to him.
He already knew of the form and chose it for himself. He even says
he is writing to please his family – sounding like countless other
Victorian ladies and gentlemen politely reconciling their modesty
and their vanity. Yet this makes us instantly skeptical of his next
assertion, that he had never read any other autobiographies. How
could he be so familiar with the term and the genre's conventions
and not have read any examples? One answer is that autobiography
had by 1908 become a well-known genre and that he could have
read about it in many places, including William Dean Howells's first
essay on it in *Harper's Monthly*.[1] Another possibility is that the claim
itself is an autobiographical convention, used in one way or another
by Augustine, Rousseau, Wordsworth, and Whitman, and that Grayson was simply, like other autobiographers, asserting his right to act
as if he was naive and original, even if he were not. We need to know
more about Grayson's reading.[2] Whatever the case, Grayson does
seem like a man who wants the freedom to be different, to invent
and suit himself, and to be pleased with the whole process. He enjoys

his uniqueness, as he also loves speaking and writing and being the patriarch at his dinner table.

In the end such a sense of himself is justified because his story is significantly different. It is not the story of a religious conversion, like many white American autobiographies. It is only briefly the story of a Civil War soldier – then a very popular subject of American autobiographies. And it pays very little attention to the means and lessons, after the War, of Grayson's business success, a subject a non-Indian businessman would have been very proud of. Rather, Grayson's autobiography is about evenly divided into four parts: first, a long account of his ancestry; second, stories of his schooling; third, miscellaneous war stories; fourth, stories of his later tribal service. Each part is in turn recounted with a kind of confidence and polish which indicate that he had told about it many times before. Grayson does not seem like someone who was having an identity crisis and writing to determine who he was. On the other hand, the signs of repetition and polish do suggest that at earlier moments in his life Grayson had indeed had his conflicts and had learned the importance of being able to tell the world who he was. Someone of such a complex and unusual background could not let others whisper about his ancestry and character. He had learned to take charge of social occasions, by becoming an accomplished storyteller.

The topic of his ancestry, which Grayson immediately takes up, is one of those difficulties which probably confronted him and which certainly confront the modern reader trying to appreciate and characterize G. W. Grayson. We may now be able to call his book an autobiography, but what do we call him? An Indian or a white man? A mixed blood? A metis? A Creek? What or which? The problem is a major one because of the way both Indians and non-Indians have attached such ideological prejudice to "blood." On the one hand the "mixed blood" is considered nearer to "civilization" than the "full blood," and thus presumably more adapted and "advanced." This prejudice, masquerading as a kind of racial theory, has gained credence from the evidence that among the Creek and other "Civilized Tribes," mixed bloods like Grayson were usually the leaders. Yet during the implementation of the Dawes Act this fact was also used by opponents of Creek Nationhood in order to divide the Creek people. Mixed bloods were accused of not representing the full bloods, who, in turn, were implied to be more truly "Indian." Thus, glib progressivism assigned cultural superiority to the "Mixed," while a glib primitivism assigned greater cultural authenticity to the "Fulls." This left some one like Grayson in the paradoxical position of being able to benefit from being "Mixed," but also losing from it when he was discounted for not being "Full." Mary Jane Warde tells how in 1908 someone in the Government wrote on the back of a photograph of Grayson, "shows no trace of Indian blood," implying that though he was thus competent to manage his own affairs, he could not speak for the Creek "Full Bloods," and still less the "Freedmen," who were African as well as white and Indian. Grayson, however, was so conscious of these prejudices that he once held up a negotiation in Washington so that a Creek who looked Full Blood enough to satisfy Federal officials could come all the way East, to show the officials that Fulls and Mixeds were united (Warde, "George Washington Grayson" 318, 177).[3]

Grayson's way of handling this dilemma was to be proud of both his white and Indian ancestry. His earliest white ancestor, he says, was Robert Grierson, a Scotsman who by 1796 was "living in the Indian country, subsequently the state of Alabama, married to a Creek Indian woman of the name of Sin-o-gee" (15). Grierson had come as a trader, but by "good management . . . he amassed a considerable fortune; much greater perhaps than did any other one person in that locality" (15–6). He had a large house where both Indians and whites were welcome and owned at least seventy slaves. It was the slaves' pronunciation of Grierson which led to the name's being spelled Grayson, and "if there was anything in a name, I would move for a return to the original" (17). Yet what most mattered to Grayson was accomplishment, as his description of his great-grandfather Robert clearly reveals. "By example and precept [he] led the way toward the cultivation of habits of industry and thrift among the Indians" (20). He was "a desirable citizen, a practical business man . . ." (20). "He was not one of that restless low type of white men too often in evidence among the Indians, whose puny morals chafing under the restraints and responsibilities of civilized life impel him to sneak away into the Indian country where they may hunt, trap, fish and eke out an existence little removed from the life of the savage, and where their life and character are a blight to the Indians and not a blessing" (20). Instead, Grierson "was a trader belonging to that class of useful pioneers ever found in the van of progress, boldly and openly blazing the way for advancing civilization and empire . . ." (20).

Balancing this praise of Grierson as an agent of "progress" is Grayson's pride in his Indian great-grandfather, In-tak-fahp-ky. He was a Creek "magician or conjuror" who had a white wife, Mary Benson, and whose son Johnie Benson or Tul-wa Tus-tun-ug-gee married Grierson's and Sin-o-gee's daughter Katy Grayson. In-tak-fahp-ky "would sometimes amuse himself by the perpetration of in-

nocent practical jokes at the expense of his friends and intimates"
(21). He also played jokes on his wife, Mary Benson, who had been
captured by a war party, and Grayson's manuscript contained a long
account of one of them. Unfortunately, Baird cut this joke, from "a
concern for readability and chapter balance" (Preface xvi, 21n11),[4]
so we do not know what Grayson liked about it. Grayson does say,
however, that he admired In-tak-fahp-ky's and Mary Benson's son
Johnie because he fought heroically at the Battle of Horse Shoe
Bend, where the Creeks held out against the hated Andrew Jackson
(23).

One of Katy Grierson-Grayson's other lovers was an Alabama Afro-
American with whom she had two children, and this union, Grayson
believed, brought a "lasting cloud over his family's name" (qtd. in
Wright 78).[5] Grayson was not so proud of his family's tri-racial inheritance as he was of its bi-racial, white-Indian one. To have black
ancestors in Oklahoma in 1908 was not prestigious, and Grayson's
concern for family prestige was great – indeed, so great that many
people today might find him pompous and stuffy. Yet in an atmosphere where ancestry could be a source of shame as well as pride,
the best course may have been to express one's pride and hope to
cover up the shame. Moreover, Baird points out in an important
footnote to this section of the autobiography that Grayson benefitted
from his Creek maternal ancestors because of Creek matrilineal
practices (27n19). He did not benefit, evidently, from having black
relatives. A generation before, Okah Tubbee, author of *A Thrilling
Sketch of the Life of the Distinguished Chief Okah Tubbee* (first edition,
1848), had suppressed his African ancestry entirely.

About his immediate maternal ancestors Grayson writes little,
principally, he says, because "it is my misfortune to know scarcely
anything about [them]" (27). But his mother's family was also made
up of both whites and Creeks and was the source of his connection
to the Panther clan and the prominence he enjoyed in Creek society,
Baird says (27n19). Thus his mother, Jennie Wynne, supplied him
with a clan connection and his father and paternal relatives provided
him with many good stories, and the two together, clans and stories,
had provided Grayson with the first important parts of his identity:
a family inheritance and a way of using and interpreting it in the
present.[6]

Grayson's stories of his education are divided between ones of his
early schooling in country schools and the Asbury Manual Labor
School, run by the Methodist Episcopal Church, and his advanced
education at Arkansas College in Fayetteville. In the first he says he
stood out because he knew English better than most of his classmates

and because he looked white, even though he dressed in "buckskin leggings" and always tried to look Indian. "I was a rather slim boy with exceedingly red hair. As the Indians are never red haired or blondes, I was an exception, being also quite white in complexion, and always regretted being as I was – white and red headed" (45).

Conversely, he says that in Fayetteville he stood out because he was Indian and wore Indian clothes. He felt like a carnival attraction, "the only living 'Wild Man of Borneo' " (52). He had been selected to attend college by the Creek government, and his father was so pleased that he escorted G. W. all the way to Fayetteville. But his father wore "a turban" that emphasized "our uncouth appearance" (50), and for two months Grayson felt out of place. He tried to remain silent and unnoticed. Then one day he "went to the general merchandise establishment of Messrs. Stirman and Dixon where I laid in for myself a suit of ready made clothing . . ." (53). Although the suit was just durable and not handsome, buying it was a sign of reborn pride and a kind of rite of passage. He became a careful dresser for the rest of his life, having his clothing cut and sewn by the best tailors in the latest styles. Grayson had learned the importance of dress and started on his way to being a gentleman.

He had also learned the importance of language and of correct and elegant speech. Grayson did not just "buy a new suit." He "laid in for myself a suit of ready made clothing which I selected as I now recall with reference entirely to its adaptability to resistance of wear and tear, rather than its appeal to the requirements of the esthetic" (53). He had acquired a taste not only for stylish clothes but for fancy speech, and Arkansas College was where these tastes developed. Such tastes, of course, are not necessarily Indian or white, but it does seem significant that at Arkansas College Grayson also studied and did well in Latin. "I seemed to possess an aptitude for languages," he says, using the same long, ornate style, "and so marked was my proficiency in the Latin that some of my classmates expressed their firm belief that I studied the language when in school at home but was taking my place in a class of beginners where my former acquaintance with the study enabled me easily to lead the class" (54). Latin was the mark of an educated man, as was the ability to put together a long, correct English sentence, with every element carefully modified and elaborated. His diction thus polished and his clothes correct, Grayson gained "freely accorded entree to some of the best families" (54).

He left Fayetteville just a few days before the impending War closed the College in March, 1861, and took a job as a clerk in a general store back home. He was not quite eighteen, his father had died, and he was responsible for supporting his mother. So "I ignored my boyish inclinations and declined to join the army" (59). He seems to have had little interest in the political issues of the war. When he did enlist a year after it had begun, he did so mainly because people had begun to talk and to doubt his courage. Thus he looked upon the war less as an ideological conflict than as a personal test, and the stories he tells of it are rather unusual in Civil War memoirs for not being about great battles, sacrifice, and glory but about personal prowess. He also tells stories that emphasize the War's accidents and absurdities. As he clearly recognized later (whether or not he recognized it at the time), the Civil War divided Creeks deeply, though in the long run neither side really benefited. He may also downplay the ideological, patriotic side of the War because he had fought for the losing side. In any case, the result is an account which makes the War more a tribal rite of manhood than a great cause. The greatest suffering he himself experienced was in the winter and spring of 1865 when he nearly died of smallpox.

The stories of personal resourcefulness may also have made good ones to tell his children and his fellow Indian veterans. He once mistook a dead body for a log. One night he kept himself on guard against wolves by tying his horse to a tree, then sleeping near the tree so that the rope frequently awakened him. In telling these stories he also sometimes uses a much more colloquial diction. "I was in a fix. I was bothered, and in fact pretty well scared up," he writes at one point (74). But the most characteristic story may be a long one of becoming separated from his regiment and having to find his way back in the company of another soldier whom he did not like. "I had no excuses to urge against his becoming my traveling companion," Grayson says, "except that he was a blond – blond hair, eye lashes, moustache and gray eyes, in fact blond all over. I cannot explain why, but I am not partial toward, but on the contrary have to confess to having always as now rather a repugnance to blonds of all degrees" (66). They encounter two sleeping Union soldiers, and the blond wants to shoot them with his pistol. But Grayson notes that the man's pistol is corroded and might not fire, so they quietly move on. In the next few days Grayson's common sense, restraint, and good woodsmanship save their lives several more times. However, when they finally reach headquarters, "my blond friend, now somewhat bronzed by his exposure" takes all the credit for their survival (71). Grayson says that he said nothing at the time, yet in the autobiography, supposedly speaking only to his family, he confesses his annoyance. Finally, though, he forgives the man, whom he has never seen again, and says, "If dead, peace to his ashes; if alive still, abundant success to comrade Washington" (72).

What makes this incident so characteristic is, first, the elegant humor. He curses the man, yet with restraint. He also holds off naming him until the very end, aware of the irony that they share the name Washington. What else is characteristic is the suppressed dislike of white men, at least those most stereotypical ones, the "blonds." Adding to or justifying his hatred is the way the man has not only taken credit for their survival but owes his own survival to Grayson, the Indian. The incident is a wry turn on the mythic encounter in white–Indian relations where the wise, generous Indian native saves the white invader. The difference is that the overwhelming majority of such stories, from John Smith's Pocahontas story on, are told by the invaders to show how they have been loved, accepted, or adopted. Grayson has not loved or adopted this man, so he tells the story very sardonically.

The events after the Civil War, ending in the allotments and the dissolution of the Creek Nation, may have been largely responsible for Grayson's recalling and retelling this story in 1908, over forty years later. It was in those years that he grew wealthy, raised the family that sat around the dinner table and urged him to tell his stories, and gained his prominence in Creek affairs. Baird says in his introduction that Grayson Brothers, the business he shared with his brother Sam, owned "a retail outlet, rent properties, a cotton gin, cattle ranches, and agricultural activities" (7). They also owned the *Indian Journal,* the Creek newspaper which was published in Eufaula and for which G. W. Grayson sometimes wrote articles and editorials.[7] In her very readable and extensively researched Ph.D. dissertation, "George Washington Grayson and the Creek Nation, 1843–1920," Mary Jane Warde enumerates his many services to the Creek – serving in the House of Warriors (the national legislature), acting as National Treasurer, and making many long journeys to Washington, D.C., to act as an advocate to Congress, the Department of the Interior, the War Department, and other arms of the Federal Government. Frequently, he was an advisor and lobbyist for other tribes as well.

Comparatively little of all this is in his *Autobiography.* It appears that he intended to write a general history of the Creek Nation and planned to go into the political events there. In describing a conflict after the Civil War between the former Southern Creeks (Confederate) and Northern Creeks (Union), he says that this is only a hurriedly stated synopsis of the occurrence of those times, the details of which we cannot attempt to enter into for the reason that while they would doubtless be of interest to some, they would nevertheless not be strictly autobiographical. So what has been written is only intended to be prefatory to some things that shall hereafter be written more in line with the purposes of the work I have in hand. (125–6)

Or this somewhat ambiguous passage may only mean that he has here written just what is necessary as an introduction to later parts of the *Autobiography*. In any case, his concept of autobiography is brought in here to relieve him from describing painful tribal discord, and he may have done roughly the same with the rest of the events of the 1870s and after. By 1908 he was not just an elder statesman. By the late 1890s Grayson Bros. was in financial trouble (Warde, "George Washington Grayson" 226). When business recovered, he was not as rich as he had been. And by the early 1900s he and all his fellow Creek were literally dispossessed. There may have been little pleasure, therefore, in recollecting the business and political affairs that led to such a collapse. It seemed healthier and more rational to recall only a few pleasant or exciting stories such as would amuse children and grandchildren. And Grayson, it should be clear by now, usually tried to be a restrained, prudent, rational man.

Such a character also had a great cultural authority in the late nineteenth century, the great age of the Scottish-American businessmen. There is even a picture of Grayson that makes him look like Andrew Carnegie, and it is easy to imagine Grayson sitting in Pullman cars and fine hotels, talking to other bewhiskered lumbermen, merchants, bankers, and manufacturers from around the country. He has their solidity – and their prejudices. In describing the conflict between Northern and Southern Creeks, for instance, he writes this way:

> [The Northern Creeks] very naturally entertained a feeling that, as they were victors in war . . . , they should in the administration of government exercise superior privileges to those accorded the late adherents of the South. The intelligence and the little wealth that remained, however, was in the Southern Creeks, and this intelligence could not brook the idea of being dominated and governed by the ignorance of the northern Indians, supplemented by that of their late negro slaves. (124)

This is from Grayson's very condensed "synopsis" of the conflict. He is trying to be brief, balanced, and impartial. But the reader can easily sense where he stands – with "wealth" and "intelligence" against "ignorance" and the "late negro slaves." And offensive as these prejudices may be today, they were the prejudices of thousands of other successful American businessmen.

Yet Grayson also wants his readers to understand very clearly that he is a Creek and that his loyal, dedicated service to the Creek was never broken. Several of the longer, exciting stories in this part of the book are of the dangers he was in and the measures he took to protect tribal funds while he was Treasurer. He once had to carry over $70,000 in cash from the United States Agent for the Creeks to the National Council at a time when bands of outlaw Indians, whites, and blacks – many of them former soldiers – were roaming the countryside. He coolly hired a highly recommended member of the "Lighthorse-men," or Indian police, as his body guard and carried the money safely. He was not afraid, he says, because "there was still much of that old fashioned honesty and high respect for personal honor in those days that fully justified me in doing then with an ordinary unchristian Indian officer that which I would not now do with the ordinary christian sunday school superintendent of the white race." He adds, "Times and people certainly have changed" (136).

Times and people *have* changed, and with them not only the standards of virtue, as Grayson is saying, but the metaphors and examples by which we try to test and prove or illustrate virtue. That change, which is greater, possibly, than any changes in virtue itself, is what makes the discussion of Grayson's racial attitudes difficult. When he refers to "an ordinary unchristian Indian officer" is he being condescending or not? The unstated premise of such a description is that however honest the man is, the speaker is still markedly superior, and that is what disturbs us. But such a premise may lead us to something important, something more than a premise: Grayson's deep conviction that in certain ways he *was* a superior man. He was educated, bilingual, courageous, responsible, honest, and ambitious. This is what it meant, in his times, to be civilized. And he not only sought to personify these virtues in himself, he wished to extend them to others from a sense that others respected them, too. Thus he writes of his role and rank as secretary and translator at an international council of Indians that met in Okmulgee in the 1870s: "My complexion and person having so much the appearance of the white man[,] that I could speak the Indian as I did appeared decidedly striking to the wild Indians who attended these councils" (148). "Wild Indians" is another offensive term, perhaps. But Grayson uses it to denote the clear difference, recognized by both parties, between himself and them. Moreover, what is most important to Grayson is not the difference but the trust that came to exist between him and them. The proof of this is that later, "Whenever I met any of them either in Washington or elsewhere as I often did years afterwards, they would in perfect confidence state to me their business and ask my advice" (148). He still believes that there is immense difference between "them" and "me," but their trust in one another transcends such difference.

The foundation of this trust, to Grayson, was their all being Indians. Whether mixed blood or full blood, "educated" and "civilized" or "wild" and "blanket," to use Graysons' words, which were also the words of his time, they were all opposed to the people who wanted to take over their land. Those were the "white men," and to Grayson that meant essentially three different groups or forces. First, there were the "Boomers," the whites from Kansas and other surrounding states who tried repeatedly to move into Indian territory, hoping to squat or acquire land by one means or another and then have the United States government come to their aid. Second, there were the railroad interests, which not only wanted to build lines through Indian territory but to acquire the land grants which the U.S. gave out with railroad construction. During the 1870s and 1880s Grayson and his allies successfully fought both of these groups. But the third white force was the U.S. Government itself, which, as has already been said, finally imposed the allotment policy on the Creek in the early 1900s. Grayson, of course, fought the Government also, "begging Congress not to violate the terms of its treaties and agreements with our people" (162), but "the ruthless restless white man," as he calls his enemy (164), was ultimately too strong.

The reader might leave Grayson's autobiography with the suspicion that, patriotic Creek that he was, Grayson still had a financial motivation for his Creek nationalism that other Creeks did not necessarily have. As the owner of businesses and buildings, he could amass capital which other Indians did not have. With his cash he could also, he has intimated, rent grazing rights on tribal land. The allotting of tribal land would break up these large, communal tracts and make it more difficult for a man like Grayson to use them. The goal of the allotment policy was, ostensibly, to make small farmers and capitalists out of all Indians. But Grayson doubted that this was possible and also believed that this stated goal merely disguised underlying greed and cunning. He therefore found the Dawes Commission's proposal to abolish tribal government and sectionalize and individualize tribal land "bold effrontery" (163). It would take away self-government from people who had been self-governing for centuries. It would make these people poor, as poor as most white people.

Grayson therefore asks his readers to accept his analysis of the Dawes Commission and its proposals, phrasing the analysis in the form of a history and prophecy. It is the final paragraph of the book, with only three sentences, the second of which is one of Grayson's longest and most complex. But the paragraph is also one of his most eloquent and must be quoted in full. He says of the Dawes Commission:

> Here was a proposal which paralyzed the Indians for a time with its bold effrontery. Here we, a people who had been a self-governing people for hundreds and possibly a thousand years, who had a government and administered its affairs ages before such an entity as the United States was ever dreamed of, are asked and admonished that we must give up all idea of local government, change our system of land holdings to that which we confidently believed had pauperized thousands of white people – all for why; not because we had violated any treaties with the United States which guaranteed in solemn terms our undisturbed possession of these; not because of any change of conditions; not because of any non-enforcement of law prevailed to a greater extent in the Indian territory than elsewhere; but simply because regardless of the plain dictates of justice and christian conscience, the ruthless white man demanded it. Demanded it because in the general upheaval that would follow the change he, the white man, hoped and expected to obtain for a song, lands from ignorant Indians as others had done in other older states. (163–4)

Thus the ending of Grayson's autobiography, the end of the era of Creek national independence in which he had flourished, and the beginning, he predicted, of pauperism and dependence among the Creek people. Such enormous political and social changes seem to dwarf the changes in American Indian autobiography which I mentioned earlier. Grayson is also so unusual that the book does not fit into any of the genre's familiar categories. He was not a famous war chief, not a medicine man, and not a subject for an anthropologist's case study. He was an educated businessman, tribal treasurer, negotiator, and writer. But American Indian history and literature are notably richer for the fact that such a man was on hand in 1908 to describe his unusual life and tell the tragic story of the defeat of Creek nationalism.[8]

Notes

1. Howells's first column on autobiography appeared in the "Editor's Easy Chair" in February, 1904. Two more appeared in October, 1909, and April, 1911.
2. Warde says: "I can tell you that Grayson loved writing, reading, and history – all three being tools of his trade as a Creek delegate" (Letter). She also says that he had a large library. Daniel Littlefield's *Alex Posey: Creek Poet, Journalist, and Humorist* provides further general evidence of the literary accomplishments of Grayson's contemporaries.
3. The photograph of Grayson is Photo 1116, Smithsonian Anthropological Archives, Museum of Natural History, Washington, D.C.
4. I suggested later to Baird that this story may have derived from a trickster tale, and he answered that it was "probably . . . a trickster tale, although I wasn't thinking of this at the time [it was cut]" (Letter).
5. Wright is quoting from a Grayson manuscript in the University of Oklahoma Western Historical Collection. Wright adds that Robert Grierson also had a son who married a slave and that this disturbed Grayson even more. At the request of a relative, Baird cut the passages from the Autobiography which referred to Grayson's black ancestors (Letter).
6. It is also evident, from Warde's dissertation and Baird's footnotes, that some of this genealogical information was the product of Grayson's own exhaustive later research. It took work for him to dig it up. It was not just "given," but an inheritance he had to learn, in order to supply his later needs.
7. See Warde (163, passim) and Littlefield and Parins (*Biobibliography* 69, 244). Littlefield and Parins *Biobibliography . . . A Supplement* has additional Grayson titles (57–8).
8. I would like to thank W. David Baird for his answers to my questions about Grayson's manuscript and his editorial work on it and to thank Mary Jane Warde, his former student, for her generous answers to my questions about Grayson and her correction of a draft of this article.

Works Cited

Baird, W. David. Preface and Introduction. *Creek Warrior for the Confederacy: The Autobiography of Chief G.W. Grayson* by G. W. Grayson, ed. W. David Baird. Norman: University of Oklahoma Press, 1988.

Letter to the author, Feb. 22, 1993.

Brumble, H. David, III. *American Indian Autobiography*. Berkeley: University of California Press, 1988.

Grayson, G. W. *Creek Warrior for the Confederacy: The Autobiography of Chief G.*

W. *Grayson*, ed. W. David Baird. Norman University of Oklahoma Press, 1988.

Howells, William Dean. "Editor's Easy Chair." *Harper's Monthly Magazine* 108 (February 1904): 478–82; 119 (October 1909): 795–8; 122 (April 1911): 795–8.

Littlefield, Daniel F., Jr. *Alex Posey: Creek Poet, Journalist, and Humorist.* Lincoln: University of Nebraska Press, 1992.

Littlefield, Daniel F., Jr., and James W. Parins. *A Biobibliography of Native American Writers, 1772–1924.* Metuchen, NJ: Scarecrow, 1981.

A Biobibliography of Native American Writers, 1772–1924: A Supplement. Metuchen, NJ: Scarecrow, 1985.

Warde, Mary Jane. "George Washington Grayson and the Creek Nation, 1843–1920." Diss., Oklahoma State University, 1991.

Letter to the author. 19 Mar. 1993.

Wright, J. Leitch. *Creeks and Seminoles: The Destruction and Regeneration of the Muscogulge People.* Lincoln: University of Nebraska Press, 1966.

10

"AN INDIAN . . . AN AMERICAN"

ETHNICITY, ASSIMILATION, AND BALANCE IN CHARLES EASTMAN'S FROM THE DEEP WOODS TO CIVILIZATION

ERIK PETERSON

―――――

But after the white people came, elements in this world began to shift; and it became necessary to create new ceremonies. I have made changes in the rituals. The people mistrust this greatly, but only this growth keeps the ceremonies strong.

Leslie Marmon Silko, *Ceremony*

Four centuries after Columbus stumbled onto the "New World" and mistakenly named its inhabitants, over fifty representatives of the newly formed American Indian Association met on his birthday in Columbus, Ohio. Their purpose was to define their "common ground" as Indians and visibly demonstrate their ability to participate fully in American society (Hertzberg 59–78). At this conference, one of the delegates and founders of the new association, Doctor Charles A. Eastman, illustrated the contradictions that the conference and many of its delegates faced. On the one hand, Eastman sought to dispel the charge of racial inferiority pervasive in nineteenth-century anthropology by appealing to the assimilationist metaphor of the "melting pot" and the Spencerian logic of cultural evolution, both of which assumed the inevitable demise of Indian culture. On the other hand, however, he recognized who defined the "pot" – and its homogenizing effect – and challenged his listeners to preserve their Indian identity and redefine the pot. In this confrontation of Euro-American evolutionary progress and the traditions of his Santee Sioux culture, Eastman sought to bridge their divisions and discover their continuities.[1]

His negotiation between "two worlds," of course, is not unique; his autobiographies and other writings share with many ethnic and immigrant autobiographical narratives a preoccupation with cultural differences and a need to reconcile two (often conflicting) experiences. But, as Michael Fischer has recently suggested, it is precisely because they address these cultural tensions that ethnic autobiographies and fiction "can perhaps serve as key forms for explanations of pluralist, post-industrial, late twentieth century society" (195). I suggest that Eastman's intricate balancing act parallels our contemporary attempts to create narratives and critical postures that embrace a pluralistic world and recognize difference without reifying it.[2] His struggle to heal the divisions in his own life still urgently speaks to our desire to "delight in difference" while dissolving the boundaries that bind and divide us.

Nowhere do these divisions run more deeply than in his second autobiography, *From the Deep Woods to Civilization* (1916). When this autobiography came out, most reviewers gave it positive reviews. The reviewer for *The New York Times* wrote that Eastman "never failed to see the wise judgement that lay behind his old father's choice of civilized ways" (570), and in *The North American Review* the reviewer declared that Eastman's book was "a record of one who honestly sought to appropriate white man's civilization as the highest good" (949). This reviewer also celebrated Eastman's life as an example of an Indian who "in less than half a lifetime . . . [had] traversed the whole path from savagery to civilization" (949).

More recently, scholars have criticized, rather than praised, Eastman's intellectual debt to Social Darwinism and his embrace of civilization. H. David Brumble III devotes an entire chapter to Eastman in his study, *American Indian Autobiography,* but dismisses Eastman's first autobiography, *Indian Boyhood* (1902), as simply another example of Spencerian thinking. He gives only the faintest hint that Eastman's position might have become more problematic in *From the Deep Woods to Civilization.* Similarly, Marion Copeland argues that Eastman's "role as an apologist superseded his conviction that the Sioux had a viable perspective . . . [and] he fell into the role of functionary to one faction after another whose primary concern was to control and convert the Indian" (8). But both Eastman's early reviewers and his more recent critics assume his full assimilation and embrace of a dominant Euro-American sensibility even if they disagree on whether to praise or criticize it; in effect, they assume that after leaving his tribe, Eastman became somehow less "Indian."

Certainly, as Brumble has argued so convincingly, as a highly educated and Christianized Sioux, Eastman was deeply influenced by the evolutionary racialism of his day (149). But straight-line interpretations of Eastman's assimilation implicitly assume two mutually exclusive worlds – European-American or Indian – whose division, like the river Styx, can be crossed in only one direction.[3] They define borders but not borderlands. "Borders," Gloria Anzaldua writes, "are set up to define the places that are safe and unsafe, to distinguish us from them. . . . A borderland is a vague and undetermined place created by the emotional residue of an unnatural boundary. It is in a constant state of transition. The prohibited and forbidden are its inhabitants" (3). Eastman's autobiography represents one such cultural borderland and an interstitial position among other early American Indian autobiographies (Krupat *For Those* 30–1). As such, it can reveal other ways of understanding ethnicity, assimilation, and multiculturalism.

Ethnicity, as a critical category, emerged out of and in dialogic response to the intellectual and social movements of the 1950s and 1960s. It challenged the inherent racialism of the melting pot, which presumed the homogenized blending of diverse cultural ingredients into a unique American "stew" but which denied the institutional, economic, and political power exercised in coloring that stew a decidedly "Euro-American" beige. It also challenged a postwar, Cold War liberal consensus that had reproduced the homogenized stew under the banner of pluralistic tolerance.[4] Out of this scholarship, new descriptive and critical metaphors of assimilation and ethnic literature have also emerged; the most recent one has been that of the multicultural mosaic.

A mosaic is a beautiful metaphor, eliciting images of rich and dazzling pigments. But despite its aesthetic qualifications, as a social and literary metaphor it does raise some disturbing connotations; while acknowledging the brilliance of diversity, it also metaphorically separates and cements these differences as disparate cultural fragments. As a critical metaphor, it too often privileges the essentialisms of cultural authenticity or ignores differentials in power on a theoretically equal and level (literary) playing field. This does not mean that we should stop studying the differences that comprise our cultural diversity – as some recent conservative critics suggest – but rather that we must critically reexamine the borders we draw between different cultural experiences, borders that can delimit diversity rather than accommodate it. By taking another look at Eastman's life and autobiography, without either celebrating his assimilation or demanding of him some standard of authenticity, we can perhaps begin imagining borderlands rather than positioning borders.[5]

Eastman grew up in a cultural borderland. His father, Ite Wakanhdi Ota, descended from a long line of Wahpeton Sioux leaders. His mother was a mixed-blood: the daughter of Captain Seth Eastman, the noted painter of the West, and granddaughter of Chief

Cloud Man, one of the first Santee converts to Christianity. In 1862, at the age of four, Eastman fled from U.S. soldiers into Canada with his uncle and grandmother. There he heard that his father had been executed. This news sparked a hatred in him for all whites. For the next ten years, Eastman's uncle and grandmother raised him in the traditions of his tribe to become a successful warrior and avenge his father's death on the warpath. His father, however, had not been executed, and while in prison he had converted to Christianity.

Suddenly, when Eastman was fifteen, his father appeared in Canada to bring him back to Flandreau, South Dakota, to learn the ways of the white man. After his initial shock, Eastman stoically dedicated himself to succeeding along his new path. He converted to Christianity and began a very successful education, eventually graduating from Boston Medical School in 1890 as the first American Indian physician. But Eastman actively practiced medicine for fewer than six years. He left medical practice after his second job (and second controversy) as an agency physician, and for the rest of his life moved among a variety of jobs, as a YMCA field secretary, summer camp leader, Washington lobbyist for Sioux treaty rights, ethnographer, and, at various times, Indian Bureau agent.

Eastman, however, is perhaps best known as an author. As one of the most prolific writers and visible Indian leaders at the turn of the century, he dedicated his energies and education to making Euro-Americans aware of the significant contributions Indians had made to American society and to bettering the conditions of his people, although history has demonstrated that many of the programs and institutions he embraced often contributed more to his people's plight than their betterment.[6] For his efforts, Eastman was hailed by Commissioner of Indian Affairs T. J. Morgan as "one of the finest specimens of Indians . . . [and an] example of what can be done . . . by education" (quoted in Wilson 72). Nevertheless, Eastman himself steadfastly rejected the "assimilated" label, preferring instead to call himself an acculturated Sioux (Wilson 189).

Yet despite his reluctance to call himself assimilated, there is little doubt that Eastman saw the inevitable technological victory of "civilization" over traditional tribal ways. Many of his readers, convinced of evolutionary law and dedicated to "[k]ill[ing] the Indian and sav[ing] the man," understood this victory to mean that Indians must "shed" their identity as Indians in order to assimilate into white society.[7] Certainly Eastman's title, *From the Deep Woods to Civilization,* suggests this reading.[8] But Eastman also grew up being taught that the transition from the "old" to the "new" is not the same as the Western linear historical narrative.[9] In his autobiography we can see the complexities of these two understandings of history.

Like many nineteenth- and early-twentieth-century autobiographers, Eastman structures his account as a spiritual confession, with a predictable narrative that frames conversion in the "born again" language of a personal separation and spiritual growth away from the sins and failures of an old life.[10] Stylistically, Eastman shapes his struggle to become educated as a conventional confession, describing his growing awareness of God: his witness of the Wounded Knee massacre and troubles with government bureaucracy replace the confession's fall from grace, and his role as an emissary between the Indian and white worlds functions to bring them together in some form of reconciliation and recovery. But although he overtly structures his autobiography as a confessional jeremiad, his emphases, and hence his goals, are quite different.

Eastman notably departs from the climactic moments of divine inspiration and repentance usually expected in a conventional confessional narrative. The confession's central concern with Christian conversion completely disappears; Eastman does not even mention his baptism. His "conversion" to civilization is similarly understated. On his journey to Reverend Riggs's school, Eastman spends the night with an American family. After offering twice to pay and having his money refused, Eastman suddenly announces: "Then and there I loved civilization and renounced my wild life" (39). There is no intensification of the conflict building toward this "climactic" moment, as one would expect in a conventional confession. And when Eastman's "conversion" actually comes, his description seems so improbable and anticlimactic that it loses all of the moral authority and narrative force traditionally associated with conversion.

Eastman also subverts conventional narrative expectations in his account of the massacre at Wounded Knee. In November 1890, Eastman arrived at Pine Ridge as the agency's new physician. Less than two months later, on December 29, the Seventh Cavalry panicked and attacked an encampment of Sioux. Three days later, Eastman went with a party to search for survivors. For two pages in the center of his book he describes in detail the grim spectacle he found. Although Eastman's passage appears to be a prelude to an angry condemnation of white atrocities, his emotional tension does not lead to this expected resolution. Rather, he avoids condemnation altogether, reporting matter-of-factly: "I passed no hasty judgement, and was thankful that I might be of some service and relieve even a small part of the suffering" (114). Although his disillusionment at

Wounded Knee played a pivotal role in his life, in his autobiography Eastman quickly undercuts any expected climactic condemnation with his hesitancy to make hasty judgements.[11] Thus, Eastman's autobiography does not methodically build toward a climactic conversion in the conventional Western sense. In the one case, we saw a climactic resolution with no narrative tension; in the other, narrative tension with no climactic resolution.

Like many of his Progressive readers, Eastman stressed the inevitability of civilization's "victory," yet he does not simply rehearse the inevitable displacement of "inferior" cultures by "superior" ones. "Some people," he wrote, "imagine that we are still wild savages, living on the hunt or on rations; but as a matter of fact, we Sioux are now fully entrenched, for all practical purposes, in the warfare of civilized life" (165). The ironies in this passage work to subvert Eastman's optimism about the Sioux's transition to civilization. The metaphor of "trench warfare" is antithetical to the nomadic life Eastman experienced in his boyhood and contrary to a Sioux warrior's concept of bravery and battle. It becomes grimmer when read in the context of having being written twenty-five years after Eastman witnessed the literal entrenchment of the Sioux dead massacred at Wounded Knee – an act he clearly associated with civilization. While stressing the inevitability of civilization, this passage also implies that the Sioux will not simply be its victims or vanish in the face of its encroachment. Whether consciously ironic and subversive or not, Eastman suggests that within new cultural forms the Sioux will struggle and fight . . . as Sioux.

It is this suggestion of continuity that distinguishes Eastman's account from other spiritual confessions and early American Indian autobiographies. Paula Gunn Allen describes the nature of continuity to mean "bring[ing] those structures and symbols which retain their essential meaning forward into a changed context in such a way that the metaphysical point remains true, in spite of apparently changed circumstances" (573). In Eastman's changed circumstances he struggled to make sense of his new schooling and religion.

> I obeyed my father's wishes, and went regularly to the little day-school, but as yet my mind was in darkness. What has all of this talk of books to do with hunting or even with planting corn? I thought. The subject occupied my thoughts more and more, doubtless owing to my father's decided position on the matter; while on the other hand my grandmother's view of this new life was not encouraging.
>
> I took the situation seriously enough, and I remember I went

with it where all my people go when they want light – into the
thick woods. . . .

When I came back my heart was strong. I decided to follow
the new trail to the end. (25–6)

A few pages later, when he leaves for Santee to go to school, Eastman
instructs his neighbor Peter, "Tell my father . . . that I shall not return until I finish my warpath" (34). Eastman demonstrates his continuity with his past by depicting his journey in civilization as his first
warpath. He also resolves to "follow the new trail to the end," from
darkness into light, a metaphor that is easily accessible to his largely
Christian readership. Yet his irony in making the woods the source
of light just as he sets off to enter civilization and gain the knowledge
that will dispel his mind's darkness is striking. Even more striking is
the fact that Eastman does not try to resolve the contradictions between his two sympathies through the Western narrative of linear
progress available to him.

After relating the decision to follow his new trail with the "un-
daunted bravery and stoic resignation" he knew was proper for a
Sioux warrior, Eastman's narrative brings together the two conflicting forces in his life:

> It appears remarkable to me now that my father, thorough
> Indian as he was, should have had such deep and sound con-
> ceptions of true civilization. But there is the contrast – my fath-
> er's mother! whose faith in her people's philosophy and
> training could not be superseded by any other allegiance.
>
> To her such a life as we lead to-day would be no less than
> sacrilege. "It is not a true life," she often said. "It is a sham.
> I cannot bear to see my boy live a made-up life!"
>
> Ah, Grandmother! you had forgotten one of the first prin-
> ciples of your own teaching, namely: "When you see a new
> trail, or a footprint you do not know, follow it to the point of
> knowing."
>
> "All I want to say to you," the old grandmother seems to
> answer, "is this: Do not get lost on this new trail." (27–8)

Eastman begins the passage by juxtaposing his father's "sound
conceptions of true civilization" with his grandmother's emphatic
declaration, "It is a sham. I cannot bear to see my boy live a made-
up life." His grandmother's declaration takes on particular poign-
ancy for Eastman, who knows that she actually could not bear his
decision and died shortly after he had left to go to school. But mid-
way through the passage, Eastman turns from his readers and di-

rectly addresses his dead grandmother, reminding her that she had forgotten her own teaching. Eastman's switch in verb tense to past perfect is significant. In effect, it frames the action of his grandmother's "forgetting" before her condemnation of civilization as a "sham" and allows that at some earlier time she "knew" and taught him that a new path must be followed "to the point of knowing." Even more significant is Eastman's having his dead grandmother reply to him by giving a resigned blessing. Through this passage Eastman is able to demonstrate the continuity between his grandmother's and father's wishes while still retaining, at one level, the contradiction of their views.

Eastman's juxtaposition of two conflicting forces to demonstrate their inclusion, without resolving their contradiction, strikingly parallels a similar narrative pattern Elaine Jahner has analyzed in the creation stories written by the Oglala Sioux, George Sword ("Lakota Genesis" 45–6). A holy man who had converted to Christianity, Sword, like Eastman, wished to demonstrate the syncretisms of Lakota and Christian beliefs. Like Eastman's explanation of his new trail within his grandmother's teachings, Sword's tales attempt to demonstrate how the structure of one set of beliefs can be carried on within the other. A suggestive example of this narrative pattern is Sword's story "When the People Laughed at the Moon" (Walker 52–7).[12] Although this story is not directly cited in Eastman's autobiography or collections of Indian tales, it contains narrative tensions similar to those that Eastman created in the passage evoking his grandmother.

Sword begins his story by establishing the kinship relations between gods and humans, sun and moon, and children and their parents. Wazi, chief of the Buffalo People, is married to Kanka, the wise woman who can foretell future events. Their beautiful daughter, Ite, is married to the god Tate and has borne him four sons. By marrying Tate, Ite establishes a link between humans and the gods. Yet her human father, Wazi, desires the gods' powers and conspires with the trickster Iktomi to obtain them; then, with his wife, he conspires to trick Iktomi. But Iktomi overhears their plans and manipulates them into helping him convince Ite that she deserves to be honored as a god along with Wi, the sun. When Ite takes the moon Hanwi's seat next to Wi and shames her, Ite irrevocably disrupts the established order.

Jahner describes how Sword structures each character's punishment to demonstrate how oppositions can function together to help establish a new order and set of relationships ("Lakota Genesis" 48–50; Lakota Myth 44–6). Wi's forgetfulness of Hanwi results in their separation and the creation of a new temporal order; Ite's turning away from her family to become like the gods results in her becoming a wanderer in the world as Anog Ite, or the Double Woman; Kanka, who helped bring about what she foresaw, is also condemned to wander the world mediating between the present and the future; and Wazi, who worked inadvertently to bring about the Third Time, is ordered to help bring about the Fourth Time when the four sons of Tate and Ite will become the four directions at the edge of the world. Each character assumes a new mediatory role by acting out the opposite of his or her original action or intent.

Sword's tales are neither purely mythic (in the sense of traditional folklore) nor Western; rather, they draw on both Christian and Lakota beliefs in order to demonstrate the syncretisms of the two. Sword does this narratively by juxtaposing oppositions in order to show how they might function together. Jahner describes his tales as presenting "oppositions only to show how their development works to create a structure of inclusion," a combination that is not always simple or positive ("Lakota Genesis" 49). But it demonstrates how disruptions of the cosmic order require the establishment of new relationships to maintain a balance. The rules of reciprocity allow individuals to live within this dynamic and turn the opposing forces into fruitful relationships.

There is probably no way to know whether Sword and Eastman collaborated or even talked about their writings. We do know from Eastman's autobiography that they were friends during Eastman's stay at Pine Ridge. We may also never be able to determine the extent to which each author drew on oral stories and storytelling conventions. Nor, if we could, would it be easy to separate their narrative posture of being caught between two worlds from traditional oral narrative patterns. But without establishing (absolutely) the authentic roots of their stories, we can say that their stories represent a *different* narrative pattern. And there is at least strong circumstantial evidence to suggest that this narrative pattern, used by two Sioux storytellers who had different levels of education, who grew up in different geographical locations and who did not meet until well into adulthood, is initially Sioux. Elaine Jahner's work, which argues that Sword's tales contain the ethical and emotional forces that structure traditional Lakota oral narratives, further suggests this probability ("Lakota Genesis" 49; *Lakota Myth* 12–27, 46).[13]

Throughout his autobiography, Eastman repeats this narrative pattern of juxtaposing contradictions and opposing forces to demonstrate structures of inclusion. Like Sword, whose characters disrupted the established order and made necessary new roles and relationships to maintain the balance, Eastman demonstrates how his father's "true conceptions of civilization" might function within his grandmother's old teachings. In doing so, he appeals to the assimilationist argument that Indians were vanishing in the face of civilization and could be "saved" only if they forgot their past, yet then immediately undercuts this position by stressing his own continuity with that past.

Eastman's juxtaposition of progress and tradition is critical. It suggests that to maintain a balanced life, Eastman's traditional relationships and religious beliefs had to account for the shifting elements of his new world. It also establishes his position at the crossroads of two worlds, where the opposing forces of progress and tradition powerfully shape him in different and often contradictory ways: An Indian, in "civilization" Eastman assumed the role of Indian; a Christian, in the "deep woods" he assumed the role of Christian. Nowhere is this intricate intersection more present and hidden than in the autobiography's last chapter – "The Soul of the White Man."

In this closing chapter, Eastman does not recite, as might be expected, his final passage from the darkness of the "deep woods" into the light of "civilization." And, curiously, he spends very little time talking about the white man's soul. When he does, in the final two pages, his tone is critical:

> Why do we find so much evil and wickedness practised by the nations composed of professedly "Christian" individuals? The pages of history are full of licensed murder and the plundering of weaker and less developed peoples, and obviously the world to-day has not outgrown this system. Behind the material and intellectual splendour of our civilization, primitive savagery and cruelty and lust hold sway. (194)

Rather than showing civilization's progress over the deep woods, Eastman denounces its "savagery." Yet, he continues to employ Social Darwinist language and places himself within "our civilization" and against "primitive savagery." He invokes the moral outrage expected many pages earlier following the massacre at Wounded Knee, but this passage is no less puzzling than the earlier one.

Like his earlier conversion to civilization, his condemnation of it seems to lack any preparatory emotional intensification. With no apparent transition, Eastman shifts from describing his involvement in the Boy Scouts, whose "program appealed to [him] strongly," to condemning the "material and intellectual splendour" of civilization. And characteristically, he just as quickly subverts the climactic action with this statement: "Yet in the deep jungles God's own sun-light penetrates and I stand before my own people still as an advo-cate of civilization." Then he asks the obvious question: "Why?" (194). His answer lacks all of the emotional punch that his condem-nation contained: "First, because there is no chance for our former simple life any more; and second, because I realize that the white man's religion is not responsible for his mistakes" (195).

In distinguishing "true faith" from "practiced faith" while ap-pealing to the simplicity of a former time, Eastman aligns himself with a long Western apocalyptic tradition of "nostalgic innovation" that ties condemnation to communal revitalization.[14] His rhetorical jeremiad parallels what Sacvan Bercovitch has described as the "American jeremiad," the forward-looking rhetorical ritual that la-ments the distance between the community's ideals and its lived practice, only to prophesy that redemption is possible in the future if the community returns to its original ideals (3–30). Eastman lo-cates his promise of redemption in the "true" Christian and Indian ideals, which he sees as synchronous, then challenges his readers to remember the many civilizations that have "collapsed in physical and moral decadence," warning, "It is for us to avoid their fate if we can" (195).

But Eastman does not end his book apocalyptically or as a pro-gressive jeremiad. Rather, he ends it with a puzzling personal dec-laration that brings together, for the last time, the two conflicting forces in his life:

> I am an Indian; and while I have learned much from civiliza-tion, for which I am grateful, I have never lost my Indian sense of right and justice. I am for development and progress along social and spiritual lines, rather than those of commerce, na-tionalism, or material efficiency. Nevertheless, so long as I live, I am an American. (195)

Eastman's resolute statement that he is an Indian, and equally cer-tain pledge that he will always be an American, were contradictory statements in assimilationist and Social Darwinist thinking. In a world of borders, it is impossible to be on both sides at once. Either Eastman has assimilated or he has not. But "I am an Indian . . . I am an American" no longer contains the direction of "I was an Indian . . . I am now an American" implicit in his title. In his last chapter, the question shifts from "Who am I – American or Indian?" to "Which side am I most on now?"[15] Knowing who he is, Eastman derives power from this last paragraph in boldly bringing together the two public identities of what he has done. In doing so, he also suggests a successful warpath, a path that connects both deep woods and civilization.

Eastman's autobiography creates contexts for re-seeing meanings and possibilities obscured in a world of borders by challenging the lines that enclose and define the world in binary choices of either/ or. Like W. E. B. DuBois's "double consciousness" as "an American, a Negro,"[16] Eastman's contradictory roles as "an Indian, an American" challenge simplistic understandings of cultural assimilation and the moralistic charge of selling out often directed toward ethnic writers, particularly successful ones. Eastman tries to heal divisions not by "solving" them, or finding them to be unreal or false, but by bringing them together and acknowledging their contradictions. In his autobiography, he brings together "I am an Indian . . . I am an American" to find the balance, the borderlands, where he (and we) might be able to live well within and between their contradictions.

Notes

1. See Miller; Wilson; Stensland.
2. Paul Rabinow makes a similar appeal for what he calls "cosmopolitanism" (258).
3. For a discussion of the straight-line theory of assimilation, see Sandberg. For a perspective that suggests that assimilation is less a departure from some past than a negotiation with present conditions, see Yancy et al., Ericksen, and Juliani.
4. Many postwar liberal intellectuals embraced political and cultural diversity as long as it did not fundamentally challenge the political values of democratic liberalism, the economic values of corporate capitalism, and the aesthetic values of the classical works of Western civilization, values that were considered transcendent of the political, ideological, and economic struggles that comprise a multiethnic society. In literary studies, it was New Criticism, with its foregrounding of the isolate text apart from any historical or cultural context, that had achieved academic ascendancy by the 1940s and early 1950s.
5. Along similar lines, Werner Sollors has suggested that we must begin developing "a terminology that goes beyond the organicist imagery of roots and come[s] to the pervasiveness and inventiveness of syncretism" (*Beyond Ethnicity* 15). Hertha Dawn Wong, in her recent study of Native American autobiography, employs the term "literary boundary culture" to describe this type of complex negotiation between cultural positions, language, and self.

    Recently, many critics, including Sollors and Wong, have challenged the binary divisions often drawn in ethnic studies (us/them or inside/ outside) and inherent in most theories of assimilation. See, for example, Sollors, *The Invention of Ethnicity* and "Of Mules and Mares in a Land of

Difference"; Krupat, *New Voices in Native American Literary Criticism;* Hobsbaum; Steinberg; Gans; and Takaki.

6. For instance, Eastman supported the Dawes Severalty Act (1887) and the Lake Mohonk Conference of Friends of the Indians (1883), both of which worked to destroy tribal identity and sovereignty.

7. "Kill the Indian and save the man" was the infamous motto of General Pratt's Carlisle Indian School. It drew on the dominant anthropology of the day, which believed that Indians had to "lose" their archaic tribal identities if they were to evolve culturally and assimilate into American society. See Berkhofer (49–61, 134–175) and Bieder. For an overview of the importance of Social Darwinism in Anglo-American intellectual thought, see Bannister and Haller.

8. Eastman's title *From the Deep Woods to Civilization* parallels a number of "from . . . to" immigrant autobiographies published during the first decades of this century describing assimilation into American society: for example, Mary Antin, *From Plotzk to Boston* (1899); Edward Steiner, *From Alien to Citizen* (1914); Michael Pupin, *From Immigrant to Inventor* (1923); and Richard Bartholdt, *From Steerage to Congress* (1930) (Sollors, *Beyond Ethnicity* 31–2).

9. See Powers (159–208), Allen, and Martin. Wong also describes Eastman as drawing on both indigenous oral and Christian conversion narratives (9).

10. I am using the definition of the spiritual confession provided by Ruoff (191–201). Ruoff argues that William Apess, (*A Son of the Forest,* 1829) and George Copway (*Life, History, and Travels of Kah-ge-ga-gah-bowh,* 1847) both structure their autobiographies as spiritual confessions. Arnold Krupat parallels Ruoff's analysis of Apess, and extends it to *Black Hawk: An Autobiography* (1833) (*The Voice in the Margin* 141–55).

11. Brumble also points to the importance of this passage but argues that it is reflective of Eastman's "Romantic Racialism and Social Darwinist assumptions" (148). This is no doubt true, but Brumble does not elaborate on the role this passage plays in Eastman's total narrative, and subsequently he misses how it works to subvert precisely the ideological expectations Brumble suggests it represents.

12. James R. Walker arrived at Pine Ridge in 1896 as the agency physician. Over the next eighteen years he collected Sioux oral stories. George Sword was one of his primary informants. Jahner (Introduction, *Lakota Myth* 52–7).

13. To further complicate the problem of determining authenticity, Eastman's non-Indian wife, Elaine, was his chief editor, and it is probably impossible to distinguish in the final book his original manuscript from her corrections and additions. We know that they differed in their philosophical approaches to assimilation and that these differences may have contributed to their eventual separation. According to Raymond Wilson, Elaine "stressed total assimilation of Native Americans, while [Charles] favored a more selective process of acculturation" (164–5).

Perhaps there are parallels between Sword and Walker (as Sword's recorder) and between Charles and Elaine (as Charles' editor) as well. Jahner reports that Sword's original narratives stressed more "traditional" themes of kinship and the "controlling laws of the cosmos," whereas Walker's final revisions minimized these themes (*Lakota Myth* 15). Whether or not a similar muting of traditional themes occurred in Eastman's writings as a result of Elaine's editing we may never know, although Eastman's grandson recalls his grandfather's resentment because he believed that Elaine's revisions changed his intended meanings (Wilson 164).

14. "Nostalgic innovation" is the term Robert Crunden uses when describing the political/artistic projects of Progressive artists and writers. David Levin suggests that the narrative of progress, as a romantic narrative, must constantly be revitalized. Sacvan Bercovitch's work on the American jeremiad suggests a useful way of seeing how such narratives might be revitalized, as well as a way in which Eastman could prophesy that the corruptions of the present civilization could be overcome by returning to the "true faith" of his Sioux and Christian cultures. For an overview of the importance of this rhetorical convention for the Progressives, see Noble, Danbom, and Conn.

15. Eastman prepares for the interrogative switch from "Who am I?" to "What am I?" in the "silent" transitions and digressions of his final chapter. He begins the chapter by describing his last government job revising the Sioux allotment rolls. One of his main tasks was Anglicizing Sioux names and assigning surnames when necessary. The fact that he rearranged the chronology of his autobiography to begin his final chapter with this particular event suggests its importance for him, but it is significant for cultural reasons as well. Naming is an important and intimate event in Sioux culture, as is evident in Eastman's own extensive description of his becoming "Ohiyesa" in his earlier autobiography, *Indian Boyhood* (1902). By telling about his work "renaming" the Sioux, in effect, he affirms his identity and declares his "insight into the relationships and intimate history of 30,000 Sioux" (185).

After establishing this relationship, Eastman suddenly begins a lengthy account of his recognitions and honors in both "deep woods" and "civilization." But he ties his public accolades to healing the divisions between the Indian and white worlds. Eastman states that only after he had established that "the philosophy of the original American was demonstrably on a high plane" did he consent "to appear on stage in [the Sioux] ancestral garb of honor" (188). What is compelling in his last chapter is that only after he established himself as a Sioux did he "boast" of his different mediating roles. In effect, his boasting is similar to "coup stories," which were traditionally told by Sioux warriors following a successful warpath.

16. DuBois (45). James Weldon Johnson described the "dilemma of the Negro author" as the "problem of a double audience" (477). For an excellent discussion of "doubleness" in W. E. B. DuBois's work, see Holt.

Works Cited

Allen, Paula Gunn. "Bringing Home the Fact: Tradition and Continuity in the Imagination." *Recovering the Word: Essays on Native American Literature,* ed. Brian Swann and Arnold Krupat. Berkeley: University of California Press, 1987: 563–79.

Anzaldua, Gloria. *Borderlands La Frontera: The New Mestiza.* San Francisco: Spinsters/Aunt Lute, 1987.

Bannister, Robert C. *Social Darwinism: Science and Myth in Anglo-American Social Thought.* Philadelphia: Temple University Press, 1979.

Bercovitch, Sacvan. *The American Jeremiad.* Madison: University of Wisconsin Press, 1978.

Berkhofer, Robert F. *The White Man's Indian: Images of the American Indian from Colonialism to the Present.* New York: Knopf, 1978.

Bieder, Robert. *Science Encounters the Indian, 1820–1880: The Early Years of American Ethnology.* Norman: University of Oklahoma Press, 1986.

Brumble, H. David, III. *American Indian Autobiography.* Berkeley: University of California Press, 1988.

Conn, Peter. *The Divided Mind: Ideology and Imagination in America, 1898–1917.* Cambridge: Cambridge University Press, 1983.

Copeland, Marion W. *Charles Alexander Eastman (Ohiyesa).* Western Writers Series 33. Boise, ID: Boise State University, 1978.

Crunden, Robert. *Ministers of Reform: The Progressive Achievement in American Civilization, 1889–1920.* New York: Basic Books, 1982.

Danbom, David B. *The World of Hope: Progressives and the Struggle for an Ethical Public Life.* Philadelphia: Temple University Press, 1987.

DuBois, W. E. B. *The Souls of Black Folk.* New York: New American Library, 1969.

Eastman, Charles Alexander. *From the Deep Woods to Civilization: Chapters in the Autobiography of an Indian.* 1916. Introduction. by Raymond Wilson. Lincoln: University of Nebraska Press, 1977.

Indian Boyhood. 1902. Rpt. New York: Dover, 1971.

Fischer, Michael M. J. "Ethnicity and the Post-Modern Arts of Memory." *Writing Culture: The Poetics and Politics of Ethnography,* ed. James Clifford and George Marcus. Berkeley: University of California Press, 1986: 194–233.

Review of *From the Deep Woods to Civilization* by Charles A. Eastman. *The New York Times,* December 24, 1916, Sec. VI: 570.

Review of *From the Deep Woods to Civilization* by Charles A. Eastman. *The North American Review* 204 (December 1916): 948–9.

Gans, Herbert. "Symbolic Ethnicity: The Future of Ethnic Groups and Cultures in America." *On the Making of Americans: Essays in Honor of David Reisman,* ed. Herbert Gans et al. Philadelphia: University of Pennsylvania Press, 1979: 193–220.

Haller, John S. *Outcasts from Evolution: Scientific Attitudes of Racial Inferiority, 1859–1900.* Urbana: University of Illinois Press, 1971.

Hertzberg, Hazel. *The Search for an American Indian Identity: Modern Pan Indian Movements.* Syracuse, NY: Syracuse University Press, 1981.

Hobsbaum, Eric. "Introduction: Inventing Traditions." *The Invention of Tradition,* ed. Eric Hobsbaum and Terrence Ranger. Cambridge: Cambridge University Press, 1983: 1–14.

Holt, Thomas C. "The Political Uses of Alienation: W. E. B. Du Bois on Politics, Race, and Culture, 1903–1940." *American Quarterly* 42 (June 1990): 301–23.

Jahner, Elaine A. "Lakota Genesis: The Oral Tradition." *Sioux Indian Religion,* ed. Raymond DeMallie and Douglas R. Parks. Norman: University of Oklahoma Press, 1987: 45–56.

Introduction. *Lakota Myth* by James R. Walker, ed. Elaine A. Jahner. Lincoln: University of Nebraska Press, 1983: 1–52.

Johnson, James Weldon. "The Dilemma of the Negro Author." *American Mercury* (December 1928): 477–81.

Krupat, Arnold. *For Those Who Come After: A Study of Native American Autobiography.* Berkeley: University of California Press, 1985.

The Voice in the Margin: Native American Literature and the Canon. Berkeley: University of California Press, 1989.

Krupat, Arnold, ed. *New Voices in Native American Literary Criticism.* Washington, DC: Smithsonian Institution Press, 1993.

Levin, David. *History as Romantic Art.* New York: Harcourt, Brace, and World, 1959.

Martin, Calvin. *The American Indian and the Problem of History.* New York: Oxford University Press, 1987.

Miller, David R. "Charles A. Eastman: One Man's Journey in Two Worlds." MA thesis. University of North Dakota, 1976.

Noble, David W. *The Progressive Mind, 1890–1917.* Chicago: Rand McNally College Publishing House, 1970.

Powers, William K. *Oglala Religion.* Lincoln: University of Nebraska Press, 1975.

Rabinow, Paul. "Representations Are Social Facts: Modernity and Post-Modernity in Anthropology." *Writing Culture: The Poetics and Politics of Ethnography,* ed. James Clifford and George Marcus. Berkeley: University of California Press, 1986: 234–61.

Ruoff, A. Lavonne Brown. "American Indian Authors: 1774–1899." *Critical Essays on Native American Literature,* ed. Andrew Wiget. Boston: G. K. Hall, 1985: 191–201.

Sandberg, Neil. *Ethnic Identity and Assimilation: The Polish American Community.* New York: Praeger, 1974.

Sollors, Werner. *Beyond Ethnicity: Consent and Descent in American Culture.* New York: Oxford University Press, 1986.

"Of Mules and Mares in a Land of Difference: or, Quadrupeds All?" *American Quarterly* 42 (June 1990): 167–90.

Sollors, Werner, ed. *The Invention of Ethnicity.* New York: Oxford University Press, 1989.

Steinberg, Steven. *The Ethnic Myth: Race, Ethnicity, and Class in America.* New York: Atheneum, 1981.

Stensland, Anna Lee. "Charles Alexander Eastman: Sioux Storyteller and Historian." *American Indian Quarterly* 3 (1977): 199–208.

Takaki, Ronald, ed. *From Different Shores: Perspectives on Race and Culture in America.* Oxford: Oxford University Press, 1987.

Walker, James R. *Lakota Myth,* ed. Elaine A. Jahner. Lincoln: University of Nebraska Press 1983.

Wilson, Raymond. *Ohiyesa: Charles Eastman, Santee Sioux.* Urbana: University of Illinois Press, 1983.

Wong, Hertha Dawn. *Sending My Heart Back Across the Years: Tradition and Innovation in Native American Autobiography.* New York: Oxford University Press, 1992.

Yancy, W., E. Ericksen, and R. Juliani. "Emergent Ethnicity: A Review and Reformulation." *American Sociological Review* 41 (1976): 391–403.

11

"OVERCOMING ALL OBSTACLES"

THE ASSIMILATION DEBATE IN NATIVE AMERICAN WOMEN'S JOURNALISM OF THE DAWES ERA

CAROL BATKER

In an apparent contradiction, Native American women argued both for Pan-Indianism and for many of the assimilationist policies of the Dawes Era in their early journalism. The journalism examined here reproduces, at times, dominant assimilationist discourse. However, it does not predicate assimilation on a rejection of Native identity and culture. Native women refused to accept Dawes Era ideologies that defined white dominant culture and traditional Native American cultures simply as binary opposites. Their early journalism demonstrates, I argue, a complex negotiation between Native and non-Native practices that suggests cultural dynamism rather than cultural loss as a paradigm for assimilation.

Native women wrote political journalism in English for Native American periodicals and the journals of the off-reservation boarding schools in the early twentieth century.[1] Most of the women whose writing is examined here attended or were affiliated with off-reservation boarding schools and were influenced by assimilationists like General Richard Henry Pratt. Many also belonged to a Pan-Indian organization, the Society of American Indians.[2] I focus primarily on material from this society's journal, the *American Indian Magazine*, whose audience and contributors came from various tribes and white reform organizations.

The Dawes Era is generally represented as the period from the passage to the reversal of the General Allotment or Dawes Act (1887–1934). The act was named for its sponsor, Henry Dawes, who was an advocate of Indian assimilation and chair of the Senate Indian Affairs Committee. Assimilationist policy during the Dawes Era changed substantially from the 1880s to the 1920s. Frederick Hoxie demonstrates that early assimilationist policies advocated "total assimilation," or what might be called an integrationist program, which protected individual land ownership and citizenship rights in white society. By 1920, the policy had become colonialist. Its advocates used ideologies of racial difference to marginalize Native communities and to appropriate Native resources (Hoxie 147–238).

Both approaches insisted on the dissolution of tribal cultures. Integrationists demanded complete accommodation to white culture, and colonialists represented Native Americans as members of an inferior and inassimilable race on its way to extinction. The former position invited the collapse of differences through the erasure of traditional practices, beliefs, and organizations, whereas the latter reified differences between Native and white but positioned Native Americans at the margins of white society. Both policies opposed Native American cultures and identity to the dominant society either by eroding traditional cultures or by excluding/marginalizing them. According to James Clifton, later thinkers often assumed this same opposition, arguing that assimilation is the surrendering of traditions and that it represents a capitulation to the dominant culture (30).

Native women's early writing outlines a third position, presenting Native cultures as vital parts of American society. Native women journalists attempted both to legitimate a Native identity and to argue for inclusion as equals in the dominant culture.[3] Some Native women, including Lucy Hunter (Winnebago), Evelyn Pierce (Seneca), and Elvira Pike (Uintah Ute), argued for integrationist policies, but in doing so they established Native Americans as a constituency deserving equal rights. That is, they accepted integrationist policy and at the same time developed a rhetoric of Native rights that assumed a separate Native identity. They supported mainstream education, citizenship, and the dismantling of the reservation system in order to refute arguments about racial inferiority and to gain equal access to economic and government structures in the dominant society.

Women advocating these Dawes Era policies implicitly represented Native identity as a political matter. Other women, such as Angel DeCora (Winnebago), established a Native American identity more explicitly by trying to preserve Native cultures. Of course, retaining traditional cultures was also a political matter. These women tried to maintain traditional beliefs and practices by arguing that they were relevant to life in white society – holding, for example, that Native arts could make vocational training more marketable and that Native cultures produced loyal and skilled citizens. Like those who argued for "total assimilation" policies, these women also took seriously the position of Native Americans in the dominant culture.

Because all Dawes Era government policies worked so clearly for the elimination or marginalization of traditional cultures, contemporary thinkers tend both to accept the ideological oppositions on which those policies were based and to take sides. Scholars often devalue arguments advocating integration as inferior to those privileging the preservation of Native cultures. However, in Native women's early journalism, arguments for integration and cultural preservation work together to dismantle the opposition between Native and white societies. Native women attempt to keep in play a dialectic between sameness and difference, integration and separatism. Their political debates demonstrate the difficulty as well as the promise of attaining equality in white society while affirming a dynamic tribal or pan-Indian identity. Although many of the arguments reproduce dominant discourses on assimilation, when taken together they significantly alter that discourse. In various degrees, they represent dynamic Native cultures in complex political negotiation with white society.

Lucy Hunter, Evelyn Pierce, and Elvira Pike attended Hampton, Haskell, and the Phoenix Indian School, respectively, and published in the journal of the Society of American Indians. These women argued strategically for assimilation policies in order to gain civil rights. When advocating higher education, for example, they used theories of social evolution to claim an equal position for Native Americans in white society.[4] Hunter, Pierce, and Pike maintained that Native Americans could successfully assimilate if they had access to higher education. They challenged existing racist ideology on two grounds: They claimed that Native Americans were not by nature limited to vocational education and manual labor, as colonial educational policy asserted, and they argued that Native Americans could compete *on an equal basis* with whites and integrate fully into society, rather than occupy a marginalized position as inferiors. Paradoxically, by accepting the racist, social evolution premise that Native cultures were evolving from a "primitive" to a "civilized" state, these women tried to avoid racial determinism, which fixed Native Americans as "inferiors." They constructed a political Native identity for themselves by arguing for civil rights, but they also reproduced the dominant discourse by relegating Native American cultures to the "primitive" past.

Evelyn Pierce, for instance, advocated higher education for Indian students and at the same time used rhetoric based on the dominant ideology of progress and social evolution. She states, "at the time of the discovery of America by Columbus, our ancestors were at best but a semi-civilized race" (107). However, she uses the ideology of social evolution to criticize social inequity and to argue for integration and a greater investment in higher education for Native Americans:

Everywhere, we hear the cry for higher efficiency. Can the Indian take his place by the white man, and can he gain efficiency with a common school education that the government gives him? No, he cannot.

The white man today must be highly educated in order to keep his place among the thousands of his race. If he wishes to attain a place higher than that occupied by his fellow men, he must train and educate all parts of his nature to their highest possibilities.

If all this is necessary for the white man, how much more so is it for the Indian who is already handicapped by his ignorance of the English language and customs. (108)

Unlike proponents of industrial Indian education who argued for lower educational expectations and opportunity, Pierce believes that Indians deserve a better education than whites.[5] She relies on ethnocentric social evolution theory to make her point, but she argues against racial inferiority and for equal opportunity: "In almost every instance where the Indian has had higher academic training he has demonstrated his ability to compete with the whites in the activities of life" (109). Using early assimilationist ideology to organize as Native Americans proved a difficult task, often resulting in a rejection or a conflicted stance toward traditional culture. Although Pierce and others rejected ideologies of racial determinism and inferiority, they undermined their own arguments by depicting traditional Native cultures as primitive and the dominant culture as civilized. To a very real degree, however, they were able to construct a rhetoric of Native rights, establishing a political Native identity even as they advocated integration.

Rather than arguing primarily for Native equality or political rights in white society, Roberta Campbell Lawson (Delaware) and Angel DeCora focused on traditional Native cultural practices. Lawson collected Native American music artifacts and was elected president of the General Federation of Women's Clubs in 1935. DeCora attended Hampton Institute, was a member of the Society of American Indians, and taught at Carlisle. She illustrated the work of several prominent Native American writers, including Zitkala-Ša, Francis LaFlesche, and Charles Eastman, as well as at least two of her own stories published in *Harper's New Monthly Magazine*.[6]

In the face of assimilationist policies bent on the dissolution of tribal cultures, defending Native cultural practices seems far more straightforward than the political solutions discussed earlier. However, preserving traditional Native cultures without marginalizing them was not simple. Native arts had already found a place in dominant white society but only as curios and artifacts, evidence of dying cultures (Hoxie 122). Lawson did argue for the collection and preservation of Indian music, but her writing reproduced the discourses of ethnologists with whom she worked, relegating tribal music to the past. She argued that tribal songs "carry much of the manner and customs, religion and history of a fast disappearing race" (Lawson 447).[7] Lawson's political work certainly did help to preserve tribal culture. Ideologically, however, her belief in social evolution left those cultures without a future. She argued that, displaced by "civilization," "these songs, like their singers, come from we know not where or whence and while many of them are crude and often far from tuneful, they are the outward expression of the inward soul and feeling of a primitive people" (447). Ultimately, Lawson could only value tribal music and culture as antecedents to the dominant culture.

As the art instructor at Carlisle, Angel DeCora was more successful at legitimating tribal culture in a non-Native cultural context. DeCora also reiterated colonial government policy by questioning Native Americans' ability to assimilate:

> The method of educating the Indian in the past was an attempt to transform him into a brown Caucasian within the space of five years or a little more. . . . The Indian, bound up as he is in tribal laws and customs, knew not where to make a distinction, nor which of his natural instincts to discard, and the consequence was that he either became superficial and arrogant and denied his race, or he grew dispirited and silent. (527)

Furthermore, like those who supported later Dawes Era policy, DeCora emphasized racial difference: "Heretofore, the Indian pupil has been put through the same public school course as the white child, with no regard for his hereditary differences of mind and habits of life" (527). However, DeCora did not maintain, as the government did, that Native Americans were inferior and inassimilable. Her writing departs from colonialist policy because she represents Native art as relevant to contemporary society rather than as evidence of a distant past or of Native "savagery and degradation." DeCora did not relegate Native culture to the margins of white society by arguing for either its demise or its inferior status. Instead, she argued for the preservation of tribal cultures as well as their integration into the dominant society:

> We can perpetuate the use of Indian designs by applying them to modern articles of use and ornament that the Indian is

taught to make. . . . I believe that we shall be ready to adapt our Indian talents to the daily needs and uses of modern life. We want to find a place for our art even as the Japanese have found a place for theirs throughout the civilized world. The young Indian is now mastering all the industrial trades, and there is no reason why the Indian workman should not leave his own artistic mark on what he produces. (528)

DeCora created a use for Native arts within a non-Native cultural context, although her advocacy for decorative arts did not substantially challenge vocational education and the marginalization of tribal culture. By arguing that industrial arts inscribed with tribal designs could signify Native identity and culture, however, DeCora did depart significantly from the discourse of the dominant culture. She believed that Native arts could make Native Americans more competitive economically in white society. By seeing Native arts not as evidence of past achievement but as a tool of integration, DeCora helped deconstruct the opposition between Native and dominant cultures.

Zitkala-Ša (Yankton Sioux) and Laura Cornelius Kellogg (Oneida) worked to create a more explicit political Native identity and to validate traditional culture as well. They established pan-Indian or tribal political organizations; Zitkala-Ša established the National Council of American Indians, and Kellogg founded the Iroquois land claims movement.[8] Zitkala-Ša and Kellogg tried to argue for tribal treaty rights, control over Native resources, and the preservation of traditional culture without excluding Native Americans from white society.

Paradoxically, Zitkala-Ša advocated tribal rights by supporting Native American citizenship. Citizenship's legal emphasis on individualism was sometimes seen by Native Americans as a threat to tribal organization and to tribal status as separate nations.[9] Moreover, in an article on the Black Hills Council, Zitkala-Ša's critique of the reservation system seems to subordinate tribalism to Americanization and citizenship:

> In view of this situation it is quite apparent that the sooner the tribal corrals are thrown open, the sooner the Indian will become Americanized. There need be no fear that he may not measure up to the responsibilities of a citizen. Even after the blighting stagnation of the Indian reservations, the Indian will be equal to his opportunities. ("The Black Hills" 5)

However, Zitkala-Ša advocated citizenship not to oppose tribal organization, necessarily, but to protect tribal rights and treaties. She argued that civil rights would provide the legal mechanism to protest invasive government policy and to advocate for individual and tribal self-determination. She claimed that the reservation system marginalized Native Americans in white society and that the separatism of reservation life did not guarantee tribal self-determination. Without citizenship, she argued, tribes were unable to sue the government because "three-fourths of the Indian race being non-citizen, have no legal status" and "Indian tribes are by express statute excluded from the general jurisdiction of the Court of Claims; and in order to present their grievances, they must first obtain the consent of Congress, of which they are non-constituents" ("The Black Hills" 5). Zitkala-Să saw citizenship as a means to support legal petitions for tribal rights. She also advocated self-determination, arguing that tribes should retain their own councils rather than accept advice and counsel from the Indian Bureau, which consistently failed to represent tribal concerns.

Elsewhere, Zitkala-Să protested a Senate resolution to control the use of Ute pasture land, as well as the Indian Bureau's leasing policy. According to Zitkala-Să, "the Senate resolution states that the Ute Indians are not making an economic and adequate use of their grazing land; and will not in the future be able to make economic and adequate use of it" ("The Ute" 8). She pointed out the futility of the government's effort to have Utes farm allotted land with an inadequate water supply, and she argued for Ute control over grazing land, "with the hands of the Indian Bureau strictly off" ("The Ute" 9). Although Zitkala-Să did argue for tribal self-determination, protesting government control over the use of tribal land, her argument is somewhat problematic in that she failed to challenge Dawes Era notions of "progress" and development.[10] Although Zitkala-Să argued for early assimilationist policies like citizenship and tended not to challenge notions of progress, her politics are significant and transgressive in their aim to maintain a political tribal identity while at the same time creating a position of equality for Native Americans in white society.

The majority of Zitkala-Să's political discourse protested white abuses and constructed a pan-Indian political coalition; however, she did assert a cultural identity in a few pieces. In her article "A Protest Against the Abolition of the Indian Dance," for example, she defended Native American dance by praising the beauty of traditional culture and questioning dominant notions of "barbarism" and "civilization." In order to oppose reigning representations of tribal cultures as primitive, static, and thus doomed to extinction, she argued against the "abolition of the Indian Dance." She represented Native American culture as a partially frozen river waiting only for the spring to "rush forth from its icy bondage." White assimilationists chip away at the surface of the river, muttering "immodest" and "this dance of the Indian is a relic of barbarism." Not only were the white man's attempts to destroy traditional culture in vain, but he was also "unconscious . . . of the river's dream, which he may have disturbed; forgetful, too, of the murmuring water-songs he has not released through his tiny tapping." Zitkala-Să pictured traditional culture as a partially frozen river dreaming of the spring when "its rippling songs shall yet flood its rugged banks." Criticizing their marginalization, Zitkala-Să represented Native cultures as vital, about to be rejuvenated and unleashed, and much more powerful than non-Natives tapping at the frozen surface ("A Protest" 1).[11]

Zitkala-Să's river played on dominant notions of a doomed and static culture, decentering white society at the same time it asserted a strong Native presence. The metaphor can be read as a critique of white assimilationists, whose attempts to destroy traditional cultures are wrong-headed and ineffectual; their work will only unleash the river's vibrant forces. However, the figure of the river can also be read as ambivalent. If the partially frozen river represents traditional cultures at which whites are chipping away, then the spring thaw could also be read as the furthering of white ambitions: The thaw implies at least a transmutation of traditional cultures. Later in the article, Zitkala-Să is more ambivalent about traditional cultures, claiming that

> the old illiterate Indians, with a past irrevocably dead and no future, have but a few sunny hours between them and the grave. And this last amusement, their dance, surely is not begrudged them. The young Indian who has been taught to read English has his choice of amusements, and need not attend the old-time one. ("A Protest" 1)

In the figure of the thawing river, Zitkala-Să suggests Native cultural rejuvenation rather than extinction; however, she does not necessarily guarantee vital traditional tribal cultures.[12] In spite of her ambivalent stance toward traditionalism, Zitkala-Să consistently asserts Native "difference" while she critiques the marginalization of Native cultures. By interrogating notions of civilization, barbarism, and stasis, Zitkala-Să creates a legitimate space for Native American cultures in white society as surely as she does in her critique of disenfranchisement.

Like Zitkala-Să, Laura Cornelius Kellogg presented a conflicted politics, trying to sustain a tribal identity without excluding Native Americans from the mainstream. She condemned the reservation system in order to reject notions of racial inferiority, and she insisted on equality for Indians in white society. However, in so doing, she tended to reinforce white notions of progress as well. Nevertheless, her emphasis on political equality eventually led her to question social evolution and to argue for the legitimacy of tribal culture.

Initially, Kellogg critiques Native Americans' status as wards on the reservation:

> The Indian child's environment is the reservation, a world of deficits. The group has really custodian care. *There is no real personal liberty in wardship; there is no incentive in the community for any special effort; there is no reward for right doing; the social life is not organized.* A group of Indians may dance a whole week without impairing their personal estates. There are no markets of their own making and their own responsibility. There is no money continually in circulation. . . . There is nothing being learned by the adult population from necessity. ("Some Facts" 44)

However, she reinforces dominant notions of progress by rejecting traditional culture as unproductive in her statements about dance. Ultimately, she used her critique of the reservation system to expose the inequity between Native Americans and whites. She argued:

> We have allowed the country to discriminate against us in the segregation of the Indian from the rest of the population. We have allowed ourselves to be cooped up for thirty-five years away from the same advantages the rest of the country is getting. ("Some Facts" 39)

Indian education failed to measure up to education for whites. Kellogg argued that Indian school officials were poorly educated, criticized the inadequacy of health care in boarding schools, decried the graft in Indian education, and bemoaned the pervasive ethnocentrism that denied Native children pride in their heritage:

> Culture is but the fine flowering of real education, and it is the training of the feeling, the tastes and the manners that make it so. When we stop to think a little, old Indian training is not to be despised. The general tendency in the average Indian schools is to take away the child's set of Indian notions altogether, and to supplant them with the paleface's. There is no discrimination in that. Why should he not justly know his race's own heroes rather than through false teaching think them wrong? Have they not as much claim to valor as Hercules or Achilles? ("Some Facts" 37)

To some extent, Kellogg's critique of education as ethnocentric was fundamentally an extension of her earlier political commitment to social equality and her rejection of wardship and racial inferiority. For her, both the reservation and Native educational systems were corrupt, inequitable, and unpragmatic in a capitalist marketplace. In Kellogg's work, as in Zitkala-Šä's, a defense of traditional culture combined with a critique of the reservation system to establish a Native identity that undermined the exclusive policies of the dominant culture.[13]

To combine a political tribalism active in white society with an affirmation of cultural identity, Native women also created narratives of political Native American heroes. This narrative strategy allowed for cultural differences within a white context but maintained the political critique so necessary to avoid marginalization. Louise Johnson Bear (Winnebago), a member of the Society of American Indians, juxtaposes two such stories in "A Winnebago Question and a Tale of a Winnebago Hero." In her article, she discusses both the Winnebago removal and the political success of a young Winnebago youth in Washington, D.C. Initially, she exposes white incompetence, hypocrisy, and abuse and describes the ingenuity and fortitude of the Winnebagos: Government soldiers starve and rape the Winnebagos they had removed from Minnesota, but the tribe outwits them and escapes. Then she tells of a modern-day "Winnebago Hero" who walked to Washington, D.C., to petition "for allotments, for schools, policemen to keep order, implements to work with, for houses and cattle to start these Indians to be self-supporting" (153). A nephew of the Winnebago chief, this hero has come from the reservation and has worked politically to find a place for his people in white society. Although his negotiations with the government yield only the fruits of assimilation policy, Louise Johnson Bear's hero is significant because he is actively creating a Native American future. This is not the proud warrior hero who is doomed to extinction but a modern Indian, successful in politics and dedicated to his people. Louise Johnson Bear describes him as

> an uneducated Indian . . . [he] was the future of his people and worked faithfully for them, overcoming all obstacles, conquering poverty, distance, the terrors of an unknown East and he finally won an inheritance for the Winnebagos. His success came because he was not selfish but thought most of his people and his duty to them. (153)

Similarly, Zitkala-Šä used the figure of the Native American soldier in World War I not only to advocate for citizenship but to create

a modern, successful Native hero. She reversed the ideology positioning Native Americans as part of the national past, extinct and
proof of the triumph of "civilization," to create an *Indian* hero who
was successful in white society, although he does advocate for assimilation.

Supporting early Dawes Era ideology, Zitkala-Sǎ quoted a soldier
as rejecting the reservation system: "In my travels with the army I
have seen a great world. I did not know till then that I had been
living in a reservation wilderness." Later, she says: "the irksome va-
cuity of reservation exile may require as much heroism, if not more,
to live than it did to die in actual battle" ("Hope" 61–2). Her description of the reservation as "exile" is further reinforced by her
statements implying that Native Americans would gain from association with whites and from becoming citizens ("Indian Gifts" 116).

Zitkala-Sǎ used Indian participation in the war effort to argue for
citizenship: "America! Home of Democracy, when shall the Red Man
be emancipated? When shall the Red Man be deemed worthy of full
citizenship if not now?" ("America" 166). By demonstrating that Native Americans were successful patriots she refuted racist ideology,
which saw Native Americans as part of a disappearing past. Zitkala-Sǎ
argued that Native Americans were responsible not only for past contributions to society, such as the corn and potatoes that replace wheat
in a war economy, but also for contemporary contributions, giving
money, clothing, and men to the war effort ("Indian Gifts" 115).

At the same time that Native Americans embrace patriotism in
Zitkala-Sǎ's writing, they retain a distinctly Native identity. She describes Native soldiers stereotypically as "clothed with that divine
courage which some have called 'Indian stoicism'; and in their company we realize that each and every one of us possess the attributes
of heroism, as our divine heritage!" Native patriotism "reveals inherent in the Indian race a high and noble quality of mind" ("Hope"
62). However, Zitkala-Sǎ used stereotypes of "stoic" and "noble"
not to relegate Native Americans to the past but to show how these
qualities fit them to serve and participate in American culture.

Redefining the relationship between Native and white cultures was
a complex and difficult venture. The ethnic politics and strategies of
resistance that I have outlined here are often problematic; no one
strategy emerges as ideal, wholly successful, or even ultimately consistent. However, together, Native women's political writings constitute
an important transgression of oppressive assimilationist and colonial
policies and ideologies of the dominant society. Native women refused notions of racial biologism and inferiority, demanded positions
of equality in American society, and constructed a political Native
identity that could and did advocate for Native rights. Women like An-

gel DeCora, Louise Johnson Bear, and Zitkala-Sä also attempted to represent Native culture as adaptive and relevant to American society rather than static and doomed to extinction. What these strategies have in common is the desire to represent Native and white cultures in complex negotiation with one another. They argue implicitly that integration does not require the abandonment or marginalization of Native identity and culture. Instead, they figure Native culture as dynamic, adaptive, and central to the dominant society.

Notes

1. For a bibliography of early Native American magazine journalism, see Littlefield and Parins.
2. For information on the Society of American Indians and the *American Indian Magazine*, see Hertzberg (31–209).
3. That Native Americans educated in mainstream, boarding, or reservation schools were influenced by assimilationist ideology but also strove to maintain a tribal or pan-Indian identity during this period is discussed generally in Coleman (42–5); Hertzberg (22, 57–8); and Williams (3–4).
4. See, for example, Hunter; Pierce; Pike "Public Schools" and "The Right Spirit."
5. For more information on the debates over Native American vocational education, see Hoxie (189–210).
6. For biographical information on Lawson see Gridley (73–4). For biographical information on DeCora, see McAnulty.
7. Lawson's paper, "Indian Music Saved," had been presented at the Seventeenth Biennial Convention of the General Federation of Women's Clubs in Los Angeles on June 11, 1924.
8. For more information on Kellogg, see Hauptman and McLester. Kellogg is best known for her work on Iroquois land claims, but she occupies an uneasy position in Oneida history because she was accused of fraudulent dealings by tribal elders (Hauptman 161).
   Zitkala-Sä held office in the Society of American Indians and edited and wrote for their journal, the *American Indian Magazine*. The National Council of American Indians attempted to organize the Native American vote to influence government policy. For overviews of Zitkala-Sä's political activism, see Johnson and Wilson; Welch; and Willard ("Zitkala-Sä").
9. For an example of this argument, see Jane Zane Gordon (Wyandotte). For a summary of similar arguments by Native Americans on the issue of allotment, see Otis (42–3).
10. Although biographical accounts of Zitkala-Sä recognize that her life is characterized by a struggle to maintain tribal identity while participating in white society, they have often neglected the extent to which her politics embraced assimilationist policy as well as tribal institutions and culture. See, for example, Fisher and Welch.
    For information on the effects of assimilation policy on Native land holdings, see Deloria (108–9); Hoxie (44); and Prucha (305).

11. It is worth noting that Laura Cornelius Kellogg responded to "A Protest" by arguing that Indian dance was "debased" and could "only undo honorable labor" and consequently slow assimilation ("She Likes" 1).

12. I use Zitkala-Ša's defense of Native American dance rather than her better-known essay, "Why I Am a Pagan," as evidence of her legitimation of Native American culture because it is more characteristic of the ambivalence most of her political writing displays.

13. In spite of the controversy surrounding Kellogg's tribal activism, her work on land claims and her use of tribal language and folklore in oratory are evidence of her success in creating a dynamic tribal identity (Hauptman 161, 166, 172, 175).

Works Cited

Bear, Louise Johnson. "A Winnebago Question and a Tale of a Winnebago Hero." *American Indian Magazine* 4 (1916): 150–3.

Clifton, James A. "Alternate Identities and Cultural Frontiers." *Being and Becoming Indian: Biographical Studies of North American Frontiers,* ed. James A. Clifton. Chicago: Dorsey Press, 1989: 1–37.

Coleman, Michael C. "Motivations of Indian Children at Missionary and U.S. Government Schools." *Montana: The Magazine of Western History* 40 (Winter 1990): 30–45.

DeCora, Angel. "Native Indian Art." *Southern Workman* 36 (October 1907): 527–8.

Deloria, Vine, Jr. " 'Congress in Its Wisdom': The Course of Indian Legislation." *The Aggressions of Civilization,* ed. Sandra L. Cadwalader and Vine Deloria, Jr. Philadelphia: Temple University Press, 1984: 105–30.

Fisher, Dexter. "Zitkala-Ša: The Evolution of a Writer." *American Indian Quarterly* 5 (August 1979): 229–38.

Gordon, Jane Zane. "Will Indians Give Up Tribal Independence for Newly [sic] American Citizenship?" *Indian Tepee* (August 1924): 2–3.

Gridley, Marion E. *Indians of Today.* Chicago: Lakeside Press, 1936.

Hauptman, Laurence M. "Designing Woman: Minnie Kellogg, Iroquois Leader." *Indian Lives: Essays on Nineteenth and Twentieth Century Native American Leaders,* ed. L. G. Moses and Raymond Wilson. Albuquerque: University of New Mexico Press, 1985: 159–88.

Hertzberg, Hazel W. *The Search for an American Indian Identity: Modern Pan-Indian Movements.* Syracuse, NY: Syracuse University Press, 1971.

Hoxie, Frederick E. *A Final Promise: The Campaign to Assimilate the Indians, 1880–1920.* Lincoln: University of Nebraska Press, 1984.

Hunter, Lucy. "The Value and Necessity of Higher Academic Training for the Indian Student." *Quarterly Journal of the Society of American Indians* 3 (1915): 11–15.

Johnson, David L., and Raymond Wilson. "Gertrude Simmons Bonnin, 1876–1938: 'Americanize the First American.' " *American Indian Quarterly* 7 (Winter 1988): 27–40.

Kellogg, Laura Cornelius. "She Likes Indian Public Opinion." *Red Man and Helper* (October 1902): 1.

"Some Facts and Figures on Indian Education." *Quarterly Journal* 1 (1913): 36–46.

Lawson, Roberta Campbell. "Indian Music Saved." *General Federation of Women's Clubs Official Report*, ed. Mrs. James E. Hays. Washington, DC: General Federation of Women's Clubs, 1924: 447–9.

Littlefield, Daniel F., Jr., and James W. Parins. *A Biobibliography of Native American Writers 1772–1924*. Metuchen, NJ: Scarecrow Press, 1981.

McAnulty, Sarah. "Angel DeCora: American Indian Artist and Educator." *Nebraska History* 57 (1976): 143–99.

McLester, Thelma Cornelius. "Oneida Women Leaders." *The Oneida Indian Experience*, ed. Jack Campisi and Laurence M. Hauptman. Syracuse, NY: Syracuse University Press, 1988: 109–11.

Otis, D. S. *The Dawes Act and the Allotment of Indian Lands*, ed. Francis Paul Prucha. Norman: University of Oklahoma Press, 1973.

Pierce, Evelyn. "The Value of Higher Academic Training for the Indian Student." *Quarterly Journal* 3 (1915): 107–9.

Pike, Elvira. "Public Schools for Indians." *Quarterly Journal* 1 (1913): 59–60.

"The Right Spirit for the Indian Student and How to Get It." *Quarterly Journal* 1 (1913): 401–3.

Prucha, Francis Paul. *The Great Father: The United States Government and the American Indians*. Lincoln: University of Nebraska Press, 1984.

Welch, Deborah Sue. "Zitkala-ša: An American Indian Leader, 1876–1938." Ph.D. diss., University of Wyoming, 1985.

Willard, William. "The First Amendment, Anglo-Conformity and American Indian Religious Freedom." *Wicazo Sa Review* 7 (Spring 1991): 25–41.

"Zitkala-Ša: A Woman Who Would Be Heard." *Wicazo-Sa Review* 1 (Spring 1985): 11–16.

Williams, Walter L. "Twentieth Century Indian Leaders: Brokers and Providers." *Journal of the West* 23 (July 1984): 3–6.

Zitkala-Ša. "America, Home of the Red Man." *American Indian Magazine* 6 (July–September 1918): 165–7.

"The Black Hills Council." *American Indian Magazine* 7 (Spring 1919): 5–7.

"Hope in the Returned Indian Soldier." *American Indian Magazine* 7 (Summer, 1919): 61–2.

"Indian Gifts to Civilized Man." *American Indian Magazine* 6 (July–September, 1918): 115–16.

"A Protest Against the Abolition of the Indian Dance." *Red Man and Helper* 3 (August 22, 1902): 1, 4.

"The Ute Grazing Land." *American Indian Magazine* 7 (Spring 1919): 8–9.

"Why I Am a Pagan." *Atlantic* 90 (December 1902): 801–3.

12

"MY PEOPLE . . . MY KIND"

MOURNING DOVE'S COGEWEA, THE HALF-BLOOD AS A NARRATIVE OF MIXED DESCENT

MARTHA L. VIEHMANN

Gerald Vizenor, in his book *Earthdivers,* uses the term "mixed descent" as a symbolic category, moving beyond heredity to describe a strategy of discourse that promotes transformation. Bringing mixed descent to discourse undermines the modes of speech and thought that Vizenor calls "terminal creeds," that is, fixed, dogmatic beliefs or modes of expression that do not allow for ambiguity or change. The mixed-blood heroes of Vizenor's stories explode terminal creeds by their constantly shifting positions and discourses. Through figures that challenge boundaries, overturn expectations, and commit social offenses, and through narratives that break down genres and commit literary offenses, Vizenor opens a way for transformation. His concept allows for the expansion of mixed descent from a social and biological fact to a literary and cultural construct, thereby challenging readers to see mixed blood as a basis for a new literature rather than as a reason for questioning the "authenticity" of writings by Native Americans.

Vizenor's symbolic mixed descent is useful in understanding Mourning Dove, her novel, *Cogewea, the Half-blood: A Depiction of the Great Montana Cattle Range,* and her relationship to Lucullus Mc-Whorter, the white amateur historian who collaborated with her to produce that text. An expanded conceptualization of mixed descent helps one appreciate the complexity of a novel that at first glance appears to be a simple Western romance. Moreover, following Vizenor and using mixed descent as a metaphor enriches interpretation of *Cogewea* by creating a central place for the collaboration between Mourning Dove and McWhorter within the analysis. Mourning Dove herself seems to have played with the freedom that the open-endedness of mixed descent provides. She apparently created a new persona to go with her pen name. In the discussion that follows, I use her family name, Christine Quintasket, when writing of her personal history and her pen name, Mourning Dove, when writing of the author.

Christine Quintasket was probably biologically and certainly metaphorically a woman of mixed descent. She lived in a transitional era and grew up in a household that embraced Okanogan traditions and accommodation to white society. Her parents bridged both worlds: Her father worked in the wage economy and continued traditional food-gathering practices, and her mother urged her daughter to learn Native medicinal lore and took her to the local Catholic church. As an adult, Quintasket served her people as a leader of Native women's organizations and as an activist, arbitrating disputes, encouraging fulfillment of agreements, and acting as an advocate for girls in trouble with white authorities (Miller, "Mourning Dove" 174, 176; Introduction xxv). In her upbringing and as a mediator for her people, Quintasket experienced mixed descent as a cultural condition.

In creating her persona as Mourning Dove the writer, Quintasket claimed for herself a European grandfather on her father's side. In reviewing the tribal rolls, one scholar finds no substantiation for this claim, and another finds evidence that suggests that her biological *father* was white.[1] Whatever the facts, Mourning Dove's story resonates with the power of the ambiguities of cultural contact. By displacing the unfaithful white man one generation, she claims Joseph Quintasket as her only father, a role he in fact played. In addition, by claiming that Joseph was part white, Mourning Dove could rationalize the divergent sympathies in the Quintasket home. In her autobiographical writings, she emphasizes the role her mother played in promoting traditional education and the role of her father in encouraging formal schooling (*Mourning Dove* 27, 30–1, 43). By naming herself a mixed blood, she places herself in the position of her heroine, Cogewea, who creates contexts in which full bloods can rethink the divisions between the two cultures and between "pure" and "amalgamated" individuals. Through the persona of Mourning Dove, Quintasket creates for herself a transformative place in which she is a mixed blood yet has strong roots within the Okanogan community.

Within *Cogewea the Half-blood,* the themes of biological mixed descent and cultural contact add tension to the romance plot. Cogewea's two suitors, Alfred Densmore, who is white, and Jim LaGranger, who is a half blood, represent divergent choices not only for the heroine but for all mixed bloods and Indians. Paralleling the romance are legends from Okanogan folkloric tradition, related by Cogewea's grandmother, that dwell on interactions between whites

and Indians. Cultural contact produces the "issue," that is, the topic
and the offspring, of mixed descent. It is the ever-present background for biological and symbolic mixed descent and a major an-
alytical category in my approach to ethnic literature. Within the
novel, Cogewea's status as a half blood, whose education has brought
her additional contact with the white world, opens up both choices
and challenges that her full-blood grandmother never faced. Moreover, Mourning Dove employs her knowledge of Native American
and ranch life to rework a popular genre: She inserts Okanogan
folklore, western tall tales, and a transformed image of the maligned
"half breed" into the western romance, thereby altering its formula.
Her incorporation of stories told directly by the grandmother is an
example of Bakhtin's concept of the dialogic, as outlined in *The
Dialogic Imagination,* which is, in turn, closely allied to Vizenor's idea
of mixed descent. Both Vizenor and Bakhtin are interested in the
breakdown of formulaic genres, the blurring of boundaries, and the
power of humor and transformation as literary strategies. Mourning
Dove transforms the western romance formula, creates a heroine
based on a humorous figure from Okanogan folklore, and plays with
the boundaries between Native and European American, between
mixed bloods and full bloods to create a powerful novel that, in spite
of its flaws, challenges conceptions of the half blood and of Native
American literature.

Moreover, her editor, Lucullus Virgil McWhorter, further shaped
Cogewea by adding sections in his distinctive literary style.[2] The result
of the collaboration of a white man sympathetic to his Native American neighbors and an Indian woman operating between the two
cultures is a multivoiced text reflecting different approaches to the
material and to the audience. A notable difference between Mourning Dove and McWhorter is that she has strong faith in the power
of stories (or fiction) to sway readers to her point of view, whereas
he places his faith in the power of historical facts. Where Mourning
Dove included dramatic vignettes of western life and incorporated
Okanogan folktales into the novel, McWhorter added footnotes and
arguments against the Indian Bureau. His additions of notes, epi-
graphs, a photograph of the author, and an introduction describing
her alter the reader's experience of the book. McWhorter's front
and back matter also create a sort of "genetic map" that we may
use to trace his additions to the main body of the text. In the novel
proper, his inserted arguments can jolt the reader. The different
voices, visions, and emphases that result from the collaboration reveal differences in the way the two chose to represent Native Amer-

ican culture as they demonstrate how mixed descent permeates every aspect of the text.

A Novel of Mixed Descent: Romance and Folklore in Cogewea

Cogewea passes an afternoon reading a western romance. Reading marks her as a heroine. She has leisure time during which she indulges in an activity that is emblematic of middle-class heroines; her comfortable location on the "veranda" (88) also attests to the leisure and spaciousness of her life. By contrast, Cogewea's Salish grandmother, having spent the morning weaving a basket, rests in her tipi, which lies in sight of the porch. Mourning Dove's juxtaposition implies that while Cogewea has adopted many aspects of the white world, the traditional ways of her Indian ancestry are literally still in view. The enduring presence of the grandmother, or *stemteemä*, in Cogewea's life provides an image that contrasts with and points up the failures of the romance Cogewea reads.

Mourning Dove's fictional character reads an actual book, Therese Broderick's *The Brand: A Tale of the Flathead Reservation (1909)*. *The Brand*, like *Cogewea, the Half-blood*, is set in the Flathead region of Montana. Both books feature a protagonist of part Indian parentage and a romantic interest who is white. *The Brand* portrays Henry West, a young mixed blood, as a model hero; he possesses superhuman strength and outstanding moral character. He passes all the tests that demonstrate his worthiness of the affection of the refined eastern heroine, who is, of course, white.[3] However, throughout the novel, Henry believes himself unworthy of Bess's affection because of his Indian blood. When first published, Broderick's novel was read as sympathetic to Native Americans because it shows that a man of mixed blood is capable of education and refinement (Rev. of *The Brand*). Broderick contrasts Henry's good character with occasional portraits of pathetic, impoverished full bloods, showing us just how far his half-blood mother's choice of a white rancher for a husband and of a Harvard education for her son can bring a descendant of Indians. At the end of the novel, Bess pledges her love to Henry West, vowing that she will forget that he is part Indian. Broderick asserts forgetting as the solution to the so-called Indian problem. However, events in the novel make it clear that "savagery," a word Broderick uses, still haunts the Wests. Furthermore, Bess ultimately gives in to her love for Henry only because she has fallen in love with the west itself; it is her love of the land that brings her back to Henry. The power of the landscape overcomes the repulsion

she felt when she witnessed West's violent attack on Dave Davis, the
white suitor who proved unworthy. West's name links him to the
landscape's power, as if to cement his association with the individualism embodied in the myth of the American frontier. It is the force
of the land and the force of individuals' characters that prevail over
race. *The Brand* implies that the west is the true home of vigorous,
wholesome individualists like Bess and Henry. The Indians as a people will give way before them; the best of that race will merge with
the white population, and the few full-blood hangers-on provide an
outlet for Christian charity until they finally disappear for good. Although *The Brand* treats the themes of cultural contact and mixed
descent, Broderick recoils from the implications of intermarriage by
whitewashing her hero.

Mourning Dove uses Broderick's book to highlight the significance of mixed descent and its multifaceted repercussions. Cogewea's summary of *The Brand* distorts the book but gets to the heart of
the problem in Broderick's portrayal of a mixed-blood hero. According to Cogewea, West "curses his own mother" for "branding"
him with Native blood, marries the white heroine, and then "slaves
for her the rest of his life" (91). Although Henry West neither curses
his mother nor slaves for Bess, Cogewea's description underscores
the assumption of white superiority that runs throughout the text. I
begin my reading of *Cogewea* with the heroine's response to *The
Brand* because Mourning Dove's novel is in part a response to popular images of Indians, images that she counters with her own, producing figures that arise from both popular romance and the
experiences of an Okanogan woman. Mourning Dove creates her
heroine in contrast to Henry West. In response to the struggle to
negotiate a way of life between divergent worlds, Cogewea is cheerful
and mischievous, like her namesake, the chipmunk,[4] whereas West
is consistently serious, even stoic, like the stereotyped noble Indian.
Moreover, throughout *The Brand,* Henry remains consistently aware
of the biological "fact" of his mixed blood. Even the closing call to
forget race is a self-conscious turning away from biology. Broderick's
emphasis on biology amounts to a form of determinism. Because of
their Indian ancestry, Henry and Mrs. West are susceptible to "savage" reactions; their drive for vengeance consistently horrifies Bess,
whom I take to represent the "civilized" norm in *The Brand.* Broderick draws scenes that suggest that in extreme situations, instinctual
racial reactions break through the veneer of an acquired way of life.
Race is apparently such a persistent influence on behavior that only
denial, sheer force of will, and the love of the right woman serve to
overcome its power.

Cogewea, on the other hand, can ignore race. For instance, at a basket social, she is flirtatious, as any young woman might be: She plays one suitor off the other, teasing Jim like the mischievous chipmunk of folklore. When Cogewea focuses on problems of race, her attention is on Native Americans as a group – the history of European-American injustice against them or the uncertainty of their future as a people. This is not the same as Henry West's concern for himself; drawn as an individualist, Henry mourns only his fate, not the fate of his people. Mourning Dove's attention to Indian *people* changes the terms of discourse from blood and biology to culture. She replaces the "facts" of biology with characters based on her own experience of mixed descent, thereby treating race as a story arising from a social context. Her full-blood Indians are dignified and forceful, not the inarticulate and helpless figures in Broderick's novel (figures that I suspect upset Mourning Dove at least as much as the morose Henry). Cogewea's grandmother is a living embodiment of the old ways, whose strength represents the continuing power of Native ways and beliefs. In contrast to her is Alfred Densmore, the self-serving and morally suspect white suitor, who represents the worst characteristics of American individualism. In between stands the heroine, negotiating a way between two apparently incompatible worlds.

Christine Quintasket's anger about the portrayal of Indians in books such as *The Brand* surely inspired her to write a novel of her own that attempts to bring to life the experience of an Indian woman in the early twentieth century. As she expressed it in an interview with the Spokane *Spokesman Review*, Quintasket was frustrated by the popular image of the stoic Indian, so she was determined to use her ability to write to describe the "true Indian character" (April 19, 1916, quoted in *Mourning Dove* xxi). In her writing, Mourning Dove draws on her education in both cultures. The yellowback novels, from which she learned to read, provide a model in the form of the popular romance, and the stories told by Long Theresa and other elders from the Colville reserve give her models for reshaping the melodramatic characters and plot. From the brief descriptions of reading in her autobiographical work and from accounts of collecting folklore in her letters, I infer that Quintasket found both methods of storytelling absorbing and so readily claimed both as "ancestors" for her own novel. Trusting in the power of stories to both reach and sway an audience, Mourning Dove revised the familiar western romance to show readers that Indians " 'felt as deeply as whites' " (*Mourning Dove* xxi). Following the general plot lines of Broderick's novel, Mourning Dove drew on her own experience of life on the Flathead reserve and its ranches, thereby creating Indian characters and portraits of ranching that were more true to life than Broderick's.

In her writing, Mourning Dove also aimed to present and preserve some of the tribal folklore that influenced her and that, at the urging of McWhorter, she collected.[5] *Cogewea* is perhaps the earliest work by an American Indian author that successfully combines fiction and folklore by using the folklore as a model for the protagonist's story. The romance plot overlaps with the stories recounted by the *stemteemä*, which warn of the dangers of intermarriage between Native women and white men. The reader early on knows that Alfred Densmore is false and the *stemteemä* correct in her suspicion that he will prove unfaithful. But Mourning Dove holds true to melodramatic form by bringing her heroine to the brink of disaster, thereby extending the parallel between legend and plot as long as possible. The stories related within the context of the novel reflect the main plot of the false love of the white man, or *shoyahpee*, for the Native woman, and they occupy a central place – literally and figuratively – in the novel. Through them, the reader gains insight into the true nature of the *shoyahpee* (meaning both Densmore and whites in general) and into the wisdom of the grandmother.

Mourning Dove also selects folkloric figures as models for her characters. In two stories that Mourning Dove collected but did not include in her novel, we see the chipmunk, called Cogewea, as a mischievous creature who is unable to keep out of trouble. Little Chipmunk, who lives with her grandmother, is sent to the lodge of Fisher and Skunk. She is to show herself to Fisher so that this good hunter will take her as a wife. But Chipmunk laughs at Skunk's bad smell, giving herself away to this undesirable mate. Fisher rescues her, but Chipmunk is again careless, putting them in danger. Mourning Dove makes her heroine a practical joker who herself brings Densmore to the ranch to tease her brother-in-law. Like the chipmunk of legend, Cogewea faces serious consequences because of her foolishness. The novel reaches its climax as Densmore and Cogewea run away to be married. When he discovers that the wealth attributed to her is only a cowboy's tall tale, he ties her up, leaving her helpless as he runs for the east-bound train. Only then does the heroine realize that she, too, has been led astray by lies. Like the Chipmunk, Cogewea gets into trouble because of her propensity for laughter and her disregard of her grandmother's advice.

In another story, the monster Owl Woman lures Little Chipmunk with lies, only to take out her heart. Densmore similarly steals Cogewea's heart with lies of love. Only time and the workings of spirit power restore the hearts of Cogewea and Little Chipmunk. Densmore's actions mimic those of the Owl Woman, but his true model is Coyote. Coyote, an important figure in Salish folklore, is the trickster responsible for shaping the world to suit humans, but he is also an antihero, consumed by insatiable desires and constantly in trouble. Alfred Densmore inherits the negative characteristics of Coyote. He is self-centered, greedy, and mendacious. Like Coyote, he conceals his true identity. But the lies are always uncovered, so Densmore and Coyote typically lose the prizes they seek. Like Fisher, Jim LaGranger is favored by the grandmother, and he rescues Cogewea. Finally recognizing that the spirit power urges her to do so, Cogewea gives her heart to Jim. When she is sure of his love, she reveals the small fortune left by the father who deserted her and her sisters. Densmore, in a cheap eastern boarding house, reads of his rival's success and so, like Coyote, recognizes the extent of his loss.[6]

Mourning Dove and McWhorter

On completing a draft of her book, Quintasket, discouraged by the results, stowed the pages in the bottom of a trunk. At about this time, she enrolled in a business school, hoping to improve her English, perhaps with the aim of returning to her writing. She also must have spoken to friends about her desire to write. On September 30, 1914, J. W. Langdon wrote to her recommending that she contact Lucullus McWhorter to assist her in preparing her book for publication (quoted by Fisher, Introduction v). Quintasket eventually met McWhorter, and he provided a great deal of assistance with *Cogewea* and with the only other work she published in her lifetime, *Coyote Stories* (1933). McWhorter invited Quintasket to stay in his home, where she revised the draft that he subsequently edited (Brown, "Mourning Dove's Voice" 2). By 1919 the book was ready for publication, but the paper shortage of World War I interfered. Hopeful of increasing the appeal of the book, McWhorter made more changes to the text, which the author did not see until it was published. Eventually he found a press, and together Quintasket and McWhorter raised the necessary funds (Brown, "Mourning Dove's Voice" 2; "Legacy Profile" 53–4). Because of his efforts, the novel finally was published in 1927. As Quintasket wrote in 1933: "My book of Cogeawea [*sic*] would never have been anything but the cheap foolscap paper that it was written on if you had not helped me get it in shape" (quoted by Fisher, Introduction xiii). But McWhorter's work with the manuscript went beyond editorial corrections and suggestions. By adding sections to *Cogewea*, McWhorter left his mark on the text, making it noticeably the product of two collaborators.

McWhorter's various additions to the text reveal substantial differences between his and Mourning Dove's appeal to white readers on behalf of American Indians. Where Mourning Dove works with the power of stories, McWhorter asserts the power of facts. Where she draws on romance and folklore, he draws on European-American conventions of biographical and historical writing. The photograph of Mourning Dove, McWhorter's prefatory remarks, and the footnotes all perform verifying functions. They assert that Mourning Dove is a real person, that she writes from actual experience of Native life, that some of the events are drawn from history, and that the descriptions of customs and events are accurate. McWhorter foresaw that doubt about the literary ability of an Indian woman would detract from *Cogewea's* impact. His doubts proved true when an agency employee accused Mourning Dove of contributing only her name and photograph to the novel (*Mourning Dove* xi). In this instance, McWhorter's faith in the factual shows sensitivity to Mourning Dove's vulnerability as an author, even if all the verifying material was not enough to convince the most skeptical readers.

Some of McWhorter's additions reveal his apparent anxiety about readers' acceptance of the negative portrayal of Alfred Densmore and other white men. He includes factual items to show that whites have been unjust in their dealings with American Indians. Moreover, he seems to have viewed the book as a vehicle for the exposure of this injustice, for he described the book in a letter to J. P. McLean, saying that it " 'is NOT fiction in the full sense of the word' " (quoted in Fisher, "Transformation" 119 n. 4). For McWhorter, the facts were essential. His own writings about Native Americans are historical and are concerned with expressing the Native point of view – a point of view essential for revealing the "truth" of historic events.[7] Lucullus McWhorter's addition of attacks on the Bureau of Indian Affairs, of footnotes reiterating the tendency of white men on the frontier to abandon Native women, and of further examples of social injustices suffered by Native Americans as a group subtly change the stress of *Cogewea, the Half-blood*. The story becomes not simply the struggle of a young Okanogan woman to recognize her desire to live in affirmation of her tribal heritage. Under Mc-Whorter's hand, the novel directly takes on the defense of all mixed-blood and full-blood Native Americans and urges the reform of the reader's feelings and of the social and governmental machinery that oppresses Native people.

Mourning Dove was concerned with this social struggle, yet she was content to leave the larger tale of oppression implicit in the story of an individual. Mourning Dove focuses on the wily Densmore's attempt to seduce Cogewea and steal her supposed wealth, a small-scale reenactment of the history of white–Indian relations. Using legends, Mourning Dove links the contemporary story to the tribal past, making the plot archetypal and the figures symbolic. Mc-Whorter and Quintasket clearly agree on bringing to light the Native American view of race relations. They both see the importance of defending Indians and reforming social attitudes and structures. Her approval of his alterations attest to that. But McWhorter has less faith in the persuasive power of metaphor. Not content with the social implications of the novel, McWhorter, an amateur historian, inserts facts and verifying material into the romance.

Some of the polemical passages that stylistically appear to be McWhorter's have the unfortunate effect of weakening the portrayal of the villainous Densmore; they make him party to conversations that are inconsistent with his actions. To pave the way for Cogewea's critique of the Indian Bureau in chapter XVI, Densmore must feign interest in the future of the Indian tribes. The conversation is stilted, and the words ring false when spoken by this self-absorbed character. Despite this awkwardness, McWhorter's additions bring into high relief issues already implicit in the text.

As Dexter Fisher notes, the difference between McWhorter's stiff, rhetorical style and Mourning Dove's simplicity of expression highlights the importance of language in Cogewea's struggle to make a place for herself ("Transformation" 102–3). She is a mixed blood and an educated Indian, versed in the ways of two societies yet rejected by both. Cogewea's command of Salish, range slang, and proper English brings to life her indeterminate status. Her tendency to switch rapidly from one form of speech to another shows the moody character with which Mourning Dove endows her and her inability to choose between two different ways of life. Likewise, the passages in which Cogewea speaks up for her race – meaning the Indian people – contrast with Densmore's invocation of the individual. The novel sets up an opposition between the Native virtue of taking responsibility for the group and the Anglo-American virtue of individualism (which shades into the vice of greed). Polemics that I attribute to McWhorter keep the question of duty to one's people – indeed, of the Indian people's need for advocates – active in the text and underscore the opposition between white and Indian values.

The conclusion of the book sits squarely in the popular literary tradition of neat and happy endings: Cogewea and her sisters inherit fortunes, Cogewea marries Jim, and Mary, her younger sister, marries Frenchy, the sympathetic greenhorn who acts as a positive double for Densmore. McWhorter's additions qualify the romantic optimism of this ending, which should be qualified by the historical reality that Quintasket knew all too well. At her best, Mourning Dove transcends the limitations of the popular romance genre by adding sketches of cowboy and range life and by including the *stemteemä's* legends. With these, Mourning Dove adds the voices of range slang, tall tales, and an implicit Native American language that complicate the fixed form and enrich her work.

Folktale and Fact: The Story of Green-blanket Feet

Lucullus McWhorter also appended notes to the novel that explain Native words, verify historical references, and expand on injustice as a theme. The information establishes the authentic grounding of the book in Native American experience. The emphasis on authenticity gives us a context for the book, but it does not help readers grasp the literary workings of it. McWhorter's notes to the *stemteemä's* story of Green-blanket Feet provide a good example. This is one of three tales that the grandmother relates; all of them are central to the novel, for they deal with European–Native contact and provide a mythic model for the fictional plot. By including the legend, Mourning Dove reworks the popular romance through the addition of folklore, and her use of the *stemteemä's* voice contributes to the dialogism of the text. McWhorter's treatment of the legend in his footnotes represents the collaborative aspect of mixed descent and demonstrates his own tendency toward a historical point of view.

In this chapter, Mourning Dove adopts the grandmother's voice and skillfully relates a pathetic story of a woman's losses. Green-blanket Feet marries a white man, bearing him two children. When the younger one is two years old, the man informs his wife that he is returning east with the children. She may come with him, never to see her people again, or she may remain. She chooses to go. As they travel, her husband treats her cruelly. Green-blanket Feet realizes that he wants his son and daughter but not her. She vows to escape with the younger, and, with the help of a loyal wolf-dog, she does. But on her return journey, she is captured by the Blackfeet, her people's enemy. The woman is enslaved and mistreated. In relating her tale, she reflects: " 'Much of this hardship, I think, was because I had chosen a Shoyahpee husband instead of one of my own kind; that my child was half white. The Great Spirit must have been displeased with me' " (172–3).

Her words sum up the grandmother's intent in telling the story. To the *stemteemä*, white men are dangerous and bring suffering, so she hopes to dissuade Cogewea from accepting Densmore's attentions. Like Green-blanket Feet, Cogewea believes the lies of the *shoyahpee;* to him she loses her small savings (acquired through the lease of her allotment). Green-blanket Feet gains children and Cogewea money through contact with whites, and, in turn, they lose them. Green-blanket Feet eventually returns alone to her people with her feet wrapped in the last strips of the blanket her husband had given her. She finds comfort and gains a new name (Green-blanket Feet) that acknowledges her sufferings and her stamina. Likewise, Cogewea ends her suffering and her sense of failure for having been duped by Densmore when she heeds the "voice from the buffalo skull" (280).

Heeding this spirit power marks her reawakened respect for tribal traditions, a metaphoric return to her people. The green blanket is the legendary woman's last refuge and gives her a new identity. Cogewea finds refuge and begins a new stage in her life by accepting Jim. As a half blood, the son of a white man who abandoned his Native wife, Jim, like the blanket, is a legacy of the false *shoyahpee.* Jim and Cogewea are the inheritors and the issue of a history of suffering, yet their union is a positive event, covering the sad history with romantic happiness and promising a better future as it hints at the positive power of mixed descent.

The chapter in which the tale of Green-blanket Feet is related rates more notes than any other. Most of them define Okanogan words or describe Native customs and clarify events in the story. Note four is particularly helpful, for it describes the significance of Green-blanket Feet's acts when she escapes from the Blackfeet. McWhorter tells us that by touching the chief's sacred objects and mimicking their ritual use, she desecrates them, destroying their magic and humiliating the chief (293–4). McWhorter's remarks help give meaning to an otherwise mysterious action. Notes such as this show the benefits of the collaboration and the strength arising from the "mixed heritage" of the book.

However, the first note to the story of Green-blanket Feet is especially curious. Mourning Dove describes a suspenseful scene in which Green-blanket Feet plunges into a large badger hole to escape from her armed husband. McWhorter appends a note asserting that such large holes "are often met with in the loose desert soil" (293). Here and throughout the book, McWhorter reveals his anxiety that Mourning Dove's words be taken as true and shows his lack of faith in the power of stories. The note interrupts the scene, distracting the reader with facts. Instead of seeing Green-blanket Feet cowering in a hole, we see McWhorter hovering about the text like a nervous hen, trying to assure us that the words are true.

McWhorter's concern for veracity and detail also comes across in the last, lengthy footnote to the chapter. He begins by saying that "in the Stemteemä's narrative of *Green-blanket Feet,* the author has purposely incorporated incidents connected with two or three different occurrences" (295). McWhorter then repeats the story as passed down through Green-blanket Feet's children. His tale can be as compelling as Mourning Dove's version, but his main concern seems to be factual accuracy, with names, places, and dates listed. He concludes with a few paragraphs about the fickleness of the Indian Bureau in dealing with children of mixed parentage. This information is not pertinent to the story of Green-blanket Feet or to Mourning Dove's reasons for relating it. Instead, it contributes to the arguments against the Indian Bureau and to the development of the broader theme of institutionally based injustice meted out to Native Americans, primary concerns of McWhorter. When McWhorter tells us that the author purposely connects several distinct occurrences, it is not clear whether he simply wants to set the story straight or if he truly appreciates Mourning Dove's artistry. By blending several tales of woe, Mourning Dove intensifies the pathos, building up to Green-blanket Feet's declaration of the Great Spirit's displeasure and her final warning to all Okanogan women to "shun the Shoyahpee. His words are poison! his touch is death." If the protagonist of the inserted tale has not made the point clear, the *stemteemä* repeats it, telling Cogewea that "the fate of Green-blanket Feet is for you; my grandchild unless you turn from him" (176). Where Mourning Dove relies on a character and narrator from a story within the story to express her theme, McWhorter adds an accumulation of facts to sway the readers.

Racing Race: The Social Context of Mixed Descent

In contrast to popular portrayals of half bloods as despicable and consumed by self-hatred, such as we find in *The Brand,* Mourning Dove goes to great lengths to show that mixed bloods exist mainly because white men took Indian wives and abandoned them and their children. These children are part of a Native community in contact with whites. Cogewea and her sisters are raised by their Okanogan grandmother and learn to speak English. Moreover, Cogewea appears both as a mixed blood and as an Indian. She refers to Native Americans as "my people" and to half bloods as "my kind." When she asserts her European-American heritage, she is clearly calling on the social rights she deems to be hers, challenging others to put democracy into practice. Cogewea's changing self-identification demonstrates that identity is contextual: Among whites, she is Indian; among Indians she is a "lowly breed"; among friends and family, she is a lively young woman. What at first glance appear to be inconsistencies resolve into a compelling portrayal of contextual identity.

The events of the Fourth of July celebration best illustrate Cogewea's shifting social identity. On this holiday, all gather together to celebrate. Cowboys join in the rodeo, Kootenais hold a powwow, and everyone races. Cogewea plans to compete with whites in the "Ladies" race. As Jim says, she hopes to "put it over them there high toned white gals who think they can beat the Injun gals a ridin'." Trying to choose between two good horses, Cogewea decides to ride both: one in the "Ladies" race, the other in the "Squaw" race, saying, "If there's any difference between a *squaw* and a *lady,* I want to know it. I am going to pose as both for this day" (58–9). The conversation between Jim and Cogewea sets up chapter VII, "The 'Ladies' and the 'Squaw' Races," as a racial contest in which the "half-breed" heroine challenges the social distinctions between whites, Natives, and mixed bloods.

For the Fourth, Cogewea wears a blue riding habit and red, white, and blue ribbons in her hair. She is appropriately patriotic for the occasion, yet her long hair "streaming to the racer's back, lent a picturesque wildness to her figure" (62). The long, loose black hair attests to her Native ancestry even as it asserts her "wildness" and symbolizes the daring of her participation in a "whites-only" race. Cogewea's nerve earns her the jeers of the best non-Indian rider, Verona Webster, who loudly complains, "Why is this *squaw* permitted to ride? This is a *ladies* race!" The insult reiterates the linguistic and social distinctions that provide the moral undertone of this chapter. Cogewea and Verona, expert riders on well-matched mounts, run a close race. Near the end, Cogewea's bay pulls ahead of Verona's black. "Verona, maddened at the thought of being beaten by a presumptuous 'squaw,'" raises her quirt to strike Cogewea (63). Heroically, Cogewea dodges the blow and wrests the whip from her opponent. She strikes back, missing Verona but hitting the black. The bay pulls further ahead; Cogewea wins, and the men from Carter's ranch wildly cheer.

Quickly, Cogewea exchanges horses and goes to the Kootenai camp to "rent" Native dress (64). The costume is convincing; the judge takes her for a full blood and makes a lascivious remark in

English, thereby clarifying the social distinction between "squaw" and "lady." Indian women receive none of the respect usually granted to white women. Once again, Cogewea's entrance in the race sparks the displeasure of the other contestants. One rider says, "You have no right to be here! You are half-white! This race is for Indians and not for *breeds!*" (66). The second race mirrors the first, ending in a close finish between Cogewea and the other favorite. Here, though, there is no violence, no resentment. The Indians take "winnings and losses alike . . . with stoic indifference" (67). The decorum at the end of the second race foreshadows the reconciliation between Cogewea and the full-blood Natives. Later, during the pow-wow, the Pend d'Oreille chief takes Cogewea as his partner for the friendship dance, and he gives her the pinto that his wife rode in the race. Her standing among Native peoples, shot down by the insulting remark about "breeds," is now restored.

In contrast, the "caucasians" maintain the insults and exclusion. After Cogewea wins the race with the Native women, she approaches the judge. He is "anxious" to see her until he realizes that she speaks English and thus understood his lascivious remarks. The judge covers his embarrassment with strictly businesslike behavior, giving Cogewea the prize money for the second race. She then politely requests the prize for the first race. But she is told that to ride in both races is "irregular and will not be allowed" (67). "Because . . . she is a *squaw* [she has] no right to ride in the *ladies'* race" (68). Jim presses the point with the judge, to the official's discomfort and for the reader's edification: "I take it that the little gal bein' a *squaw*, she can't be a *lady!* Is that it? She's a waitin' to hear you say that. Tell these here people your 'cisin regardin' the character of the little gal" (69). The judge makes no response – it is unthinkable to state explicitly society's racist principles. Cogewea ends the dispute by tossing back the "tainted money" so that the "*racial* prizes" may go to full-blooded Natives and whites (70). The judge's ruling prevails but at the cost of his dignity.

Throughout the chapter, Mourning Dove uses quotation marks and italics to bracket the words "breed," "squaw," and "lady."[8] She distances herself, Jim, and Cogewea from these terms to show that they are the words, in Bakhtin's phrase, of "public opinion." Bracketing the words, Mourning Dove makes clear that the social distinctions implied by the terms are the product of a white society that defines itself against an Other, in this case those of Native American descent. It is the interracial context that makes the word "breed" possible and that gives meaning to "squaw" and "lady." Through Jim we come to realize this, for he congratulates Cogewea on her riding while calling her a "squaw" without causing insult: "Her eyes sparkled at the compliment, for 'squaw' had not been intended as epithetical" (65). Between two friends of the same racial makeup, the social distinctions implied in the language do not obtain.

Throughout "The 'Ladies' and the 'Squaw' Races," Cogewea's identity shifts according to her social context. Mourning Dove's portrayal of contextual identity shows the isolation of those who are always in between. But this chapter also acknowledges the power of mixed descent. Because Cogewea is neither strictly "squaw" nor "lady," she is free to challenge these artificial distinctions. Although the white officials do not alter their dealings with Natives and mixed bloods, the confident white judge is left speechless, unable to assert his social power. The true hope for the transformative power of discourses of mixed descent is that readers will be affected. Such seems to be the goal of Mourning Dove, especially in this chapter that tells a simple, clear, and powerful story.

I have argued that Mourning Dove favors the use of story to sway readers, whereas Lucullus McWhorter favors history (in the form of verifying and verifiable elements). His frequent recourse to footnotes and the occasional polemical passages that appear to be in his hand show the editor's preference for the factual. McWhorter's preference for history adds a somber note to a text that is frequently light in tone. He reminds us that, for all the power of Mourning Dove's optimism, cultural contact between Europeans and Native Americans has deadly serious repercussions. The grandmother's historically based legends also place this grim view before the reader. The emphasis that both author and editor give to the story of Green-blanket Feet shows how the impulses of each can converge even though one values the story as an effective tale, whereas the other concerns himself with showing its relation to actual events and people.

The carefully constructed horse race chapter tells a compelling story simply and clearly. It is detailed enough to paint a picture but contains no unnecessary description. McWhorter finds no references worthy of a footnote. The chapter contains no allusions to Salish traditions or history, no Salish words, no apparent Native elements. Yet it is most assuredly about ethnicity and social identity. The chapter confirms Mourning Dove's faith in the power of story to address social issues as it raises questions about the necessary elements in authentic Native American literature.

The horse race scene poses a challenge to popular conceptions of ethnicity and social status, and the novel as a whole poses a challenge to popular literature. Mourning Dove maintains the stereo-

types of the moral purity of the heroine, the false and base
pretensions of the villain, and the undying loyalty of the hero, but
she reshapes the racial and regional identity of the figures. *Cogewea,
the Half-blood* thus moves the western romance into new realms that
allow for the expression of a Native point of view and that alter the
conventional alignment of the heroine with the forces of "civilization." The central place that Mourning Dove gives to folklore alters
the romance framework even more significantly. The legends provide an element of dialogism, introducing a new voice and a new
implied language (Salish) that push at the boundaries of the formulaic genre. The folklore provides more than a revision; it marks
Cogewea as a narrative of mixed descent.[9]

Notes

1. Mourning Dove provided McWhorter with a biographical statement,
   which he used for his note to the reader in *Cogewea*. He writes that Mourning Dove "bears a remote strain" or a "tinge of Caucasian blood" (9,
   12). Fisher, in her 1981 introduction to the text, traces that "remote
   strain" to Quintasket's paternal grandfather, identified as a Hudson Bay
   employee who abandoned her grandmother. Fisher's source is the preface to the only other book Mourning Dove published during her life,
   Coyote Stories. However, ethnographer Jay Miller, who edited Mourning
   Dove's last manuscripts, could not find corroboration of a white grandfather in the census records or among the living Quintasket relatives that
   he consulted (Introduction xvi, 196 n. 4). Alanna Kathleen Brown finds
   evidence in Mourning Dove's papers for yet another version of the biography. She concludes that it was Christine's *mother* who was abandoned
   by an unfaithful white lover, so Christine (rather than Joseph) was a half
   blood who took the name of her stepfather ("Canadian Recovery Years"
   113). In a letter of September 4, 1916, to McWhorter, Quintasket refers
   to herself as a mixed blood (Brown, "Mourning Dove's Voice" 6).
2. For information on the collaboration between Mourning Dove and
   McWhorter, see Fisher, "Transformation" and "Introduction"; and
   Brown, "Mourning Dove's Voice."
3. Henry Nash Smith's analysis of Cooper describes the complex negotiations of social status between heroine, hero, and Westerner and their
   relationship to "civilization," for which the heroine serves as a figure. See
   chapters VI, "Leatherstocking and the Problem of Social Order," and X,
   "The Dime Novel Heroine." Cooper's concern with the heroine's gentility and her effect on the west and the westerner were, according to
   Smith, lost in the dime novel tradition as it turned to sensationalism.
   However, the heroine's influence appears in twentieth-century western
   romance/adventure novels such as Owen Wister's *The Virginian* (1902)
   and the works of Zane Grey. Here, however, western mores and manli-

ness, in Wister, and the landscape, in Grey and Broderick, alter the heroines, loosening the strict bonds of gentility while preserving something of civilization's and woman's power. Few mixed blood female characters in American fiction function as romantic heroines and survive to reach the happy ending. A notable exception is Ramona, yet her Indian characteristics are never strongly developed and are completely submerged in her Spanish identity at the novel's end. Mourning Dove's creation of Cogewea as a vital, Indian-identified heroine was a unique achievement. For an analysis of half-blood female characters, see Scheick.

4. "Cogewea" is a simplification of the Okanogan word for chipmunk, an important figure in Salish folklore.
5. Lucullus McWhorter wrote to Mourning Dove, describing his vision of her as a preserver of the traditions of her people. The letter must have been especially compelling for Mourning Dove, who grew up with the belief in visions. See Fisher, Introduction (viii–ix) and "Transformation," Appendix B, 173–7.
6. Mourning Dove collected the story of "Skunk and Fisher" but omitted it from *Coyote Stories*. It can be found in the expanded volume *Tales of the Okanogans*, Donald M. Hines, ed. "Chipmunk and Owl Woman" is in *Coyote Stories* (49–59). Chipmunk's character is revealed in these stories. Miller and Mourning Dove describe Coyote in *Coyote Stories* (x–xii and 7).
7. See, for example, Lucullus Virgil McWhorter, *Yellow Wolf: His Own Story* (Caldwell, ID: Caxton Printers, 1940).
8. The use of quotation marks and italics shows a degree of literary skill that Quintasket may not have possessed. Nonetheless, she could have communicated the implied change of tone to McWhorter orally or with underlining or capital letters. The chapter clearly expresses skepticism about the social distinction conveyed in these words. Yet if we assume that McWhorter is wholly responsible for setting these words apart, we have an example of how the collaboration could intensify Mourning Dove's message.
9. I am grateful to Alan Trachtenberg, Michael Denning, and Laura Wexler for their comments and encouragement and to Richard Boyce for his support.

Works Cited

Bakhtin, Mikhail Mikhailovich. *The Dialogic Imagination: Four Essays,* trans. Caryl Emerson and Michael Holquist; ed. Michael Holquist. Austin: University of Texas Press, 1981.
Review of *The Brand* by Therese Broderick. *New York Times,* January 29, 1910: 54.
Broderick, Therese. *The Brand: A Tale of the Flathead Reservation.* Seattle: Alice Harriman Co., 1909.
Brown, Alanna Kathleen. "Legacy Profile: Mourning Dove (Humishuma) (1888–1936)." *Legacy* 6.1 (1989): 51–8.

"Mourning Dove's Canadian Recovery Years, 1917–1919." *Canadian Literature* 124–125 (1990): 113–22.

"Mourning Dove's Voice in *Cogewea*." *Wicazo Sa Review* 4.2 (1988): 2–15.

Fisher, Alice Poindexter. "The Transformation of Tradition: A Study of Zitkala Sa and Mourning Dove, Two Transitional American Indian Writers." Ph.D. diss., City University of New York, 1979.

Introduction. *Cogewea the Half-blood: A Depiction of the Great Montana Cattle Range*. By Mourning Dove. Lincoln: University of Nebraska Press, 1981: v–xxix.

Miller, Jay. Introduction. *Mourning Dove: A Salishan Autobiography* by Mourning Dove, ed. Jay Miller. Lincoln: University of Nebraska Press, 1990: xi–xxxix.

"Mourning Dove: The Author as Mediator." *Being and Becoming Indian: Biographical Studies of North American Frontiers*, ed. James A. Clifton. Chicago: Dorsey Press, 1989: 171–80.

Mourning Dove. *Cogewea, the Half-blood: A Depiction of the Great Montana Cattle Range*. 1927. Lincoln: University of Nebraska Press, 1981.

Coyote Stories, ed. Heister Dean Guie. 1933. Lincoln: University of Nebraska Press, 1990.

Mourning Dove: A Salishan Autobiography, ed. Jay Miller. Lincoln: University of Nebraska Press, 1990.

Tales of the Okanogans, ed. Donald M. Hines. Fairfield, WA: Ye Galleon Press, 1976.

Scheick, William J. *The Half-blood: A Cultural Symbol in Nineteenth Century American Fiction*. Lexington: University Press of Kentucky, 1979.

Smith, Henry Nash. *The Virgin Land: The American West as Symbol and Myth*. Cambridge, MA: Harvard University Press, 1950.

Vizenor, Gerald. *Earthdivers: Tribal Narratives on Mixed Descent*. Minneapolis: University of Minnesota Press, 1981.

13

"BECAUSE I UNDERSTAND THE STORYTELLING ART"

THE EVOLUTION OF D'ARCY MCNICKLE'S
THE SURROUNDED

BIRGIT HANS

> Has Morgan the right to take my child from me when I want to raise
> him as white man, and fit him for a better lot in Life, than the com-
> mon indian?
>
> Philomene McNickle

D'Arcy McNickle, who was born on the Flathead Reservation in
1904, was ten years old when his mother wrote this letter to the
Commissioner of Indian Affairs in a futile attempt to regain custody
of her three children, especially of her son, after her divorce from
her white husband, William McNickle. Even though she was unsuc-
cessful and D'Arcy McNickle had to remain in Chemawa, the Indian
boarding school, for four years, her wish to "raise him as white man"
determined his life until 1934, when financial necessity and a growing sense of himself as Indian led McNickle to apply for a position
in the Bureau of Indian affairs, headed by John Collier.

As a student in the English Department at the University of Montana (1921–5), McNickle began his career as a writer. He published
several short stories and poems in the university's literary journal,
Frontier. When he left Montana in 1925 to attend Oxford University
in England for a year, he took with him a letter of recommendation
in which Prof. H. G. Merriam expressed his hopes for his student:
"He wrote prose of quiet energy and subtlety of expression. I can
therefore recommend him to Oxford University as a student of sincere purpose, of considerable promise, and of devotion to literature" (Merriam, letter). McNickle had hoped to finish his degree at
Oxford, but his funds, acquired by the sale of his allotment on the
Flathead Reservation, gave out, and he settled in New York City in
1926 on his return from Europe. The journal entries of those New

York years from 1926 to 1935 show that McNickle was well aware of the difficulties of establishing himself as a professional writer; however, he never doubted his ultimate success and even managed to publish at least two short stories during those years. To support himself, his wife, and, later, his daughter, he did research, editorial work, manuscript reading, and freelance writing.

McNickle's secure, comfortable city life lasted until the Great Depression really took hold in 1934. Then the financial situation of the McNickle family grew desperate at times. McNickle could no longer afford the luxury of waiting for success. He accepted work with the Federal Writers Project in Washington, D.C., in 1935. Shortly after his move to the capital, he was offered the position in the Bureau of Indian Affairs that he had first applied for in 1934 and that he would hold until 1952. At this point, his literary career was put on hold; after the publication of *The Surrounded* in 1936, McNickle applied his powers of writing to nonfiction, and his second novel, *Wind from an Enemy Sky,* was only published posthumously in 1978.

Those years in New York City represent a crucial period in McNickle's personal development that found reflection in his writing. His earliest years in the city were marked by a reluctance to acknowledge his mixed-blood heritage. McNickle immersed himself completely in the life of the city, hoping that it would help him attain the goal that his mother had set for him at an early age: to become an American and to participate in what has been called the "American dream."

The final break with this ambition occurred when he applied to the Bureau of Indian Affairs in 1934, but a journal entry of August 1932 shows that McNickle's disenchantment with mainstream American life and its stifling materialism had begun earlier:

> Naturally the first years were confusion. Scorning, instinctively the ways of the prudent and worldly-wise, I had no substitute for worldly wisdom. The instinct which led me away from one path, was not competent to stumble upon another. I knew that I wanted to write and that I did not want to return to the scenes from which I had fled. . . .
>
> In my first job, selling automobiles, I went through a seven months' daily betrayal of my birthright in opposition. Everything I was called upon to do was a violation of instinct and desire. I continued the effort under the impression that my instincts and desires were untutored and therefore probably in error. . . . I should have learned this: instincts, right or wrong,

cannot be abandoned without seriously impairing integrity, out of which rise self-possession, confidence, the very ability to act and think. (McNickle, Journal)

McNickle's confidence in his ability as a writer, hinted at here and stated clearly in other journal entries of the New York years, was not shaken by publishers or their rejections of *The Surrounded*. Manuscript versions were making the rounds of publishers by 1929, and a list among his papers at the Newberry Library in Chicago indicates that the manuscript must have passed through almost every publishing house in New York City until it was published by Dodd, Mead in 1936. Despite the rejections, the manuscript versions often received positive reviews, and readers encouraged McNickle to revise the manuscript – which he did. Yet despite revisions and revisions of revisions, publishers kept rejecting the manuscript. In his discussion of the last versions of *The Surrounded* in *Word Ways*, Purdy asserts that the rejections were largely due to the readers' inability to recognize that two plots were juxtaposed in the novel, "one Salish and one Anglo. The publishers saw only one" (38). By 1934 McNickle himself had reached the conclusion that publishing was merely a business for the publishers. It was not his writing they objected to; in his opinion, they were afraid of the financial failure of a novel dealing in a new way with the theme of the American Indian.

McNickle probably returned from Europe with the first version of *The Surrounded* in his suitcase. However, the actual number of revisions the novel subsequently went through is unknown. The manuscript seems to have undergone three major structural stages, each marked by a different working title: *The Hungry Generations, Dead Grass*, and, finally, *The Surrounded*. Today one earlier version of *The Surrounded* is still in existence among the McNickle papers at the Newberry Library. It is a longhand version, unfortunately undated and untitled, but a reader's review and McNickle's journals suggest that it is one of the versions called *The Hungry Generations*.

The manuscript seems to be part of McNickle's earlier years of complete assimilation, and in the text Archilde's journey of self-discovery reflects McNickle's own unquestioning acceptance of mainstream American values of the time, though it is not, as Parker claims in *Singing an Indian Song*, an autobiography. If McNickle had managed to get this early manuscript version published, it might have become the hoped-for popular success, since it was in accordance with the zeitgeist, helping the reader to escape the increasingly pressing industrial problems in the East by turning to the West, which had always been associated with the promise of an agricultural paradise in the American mind. At the same time, McNickle's plot focuses on the half-breed Archilde and the issues associated with mixed bloodedness, rather than "Indians," who are merely minor characters in the manuscript version. To write a successful and popular contemporary Native American novel, McNickle would have had to romanticize the Native peoples and their reservation lives, as Oliver La Farge had done in *Laughing Boy*, something his personal experiences would not permit him to do.

In 1934 McNickle began his most thorough revision of *The Surrounded*. As the plot summary indicates, this revision affected not only the plot structure but also the entire focus of the novel: The thoroughly Americanized Archilde of the manuscript version became the Archilde who reluctantly rediscovers his mother's Indian heritage in *The Surrounded*. The deletion of the Paris episode from the manuscript version eliminates one of the major themes of the book, the confrontation of East and West, and thereby makes the plot more cohesive and unified in *The Surrounded*. At the same time, the rearrangement of scenes allowed McNickle to add material to the other major theme, the Flatheads' reservation life. A look at the plot summary makes it immediately apparent that McNickle places more emphasis on the "Indianness" of his characters in the published version; he has added the story of Big Paul, elements of Flathead oral tradition, and stories of the missionaries' arrival and work on the Flathead Reservation.

Although the relationship of Archilde, the main character, with his white father, Max, remains basically the same in the manuscript version and *The Surrounded*, Archilde's relationship with his Flathead mother changes drastically from one version to the other. Unable to forgive his mother for her "Indianness" and her killing of the game warden, which forces him to lie to the white authorities, the Archilde of the manuscript version exiles himself from Montana to acquire the necessary knowledge to leave behind forever the Indian part of his character. Only his mother's death makes it possible for him to return to his father's land and to struggle for the agrarian paradise that is his father's heritage. Claudia's imminent arrival at the end of the manuscript version indicates that Archilde will find the happiness that Max claims was denied to him because of his marriage to an Indian woman. In *The Surrounded*, on the other hand, Archilde's initial resentment of his mother's retribution for her son Louis's death changes to understanding and a protective attitude. Because of Archilde's reorientation toward the Indian part of his heritage in the published version, he, too, is "surrounded" at the end of the novel; McNickle holds out no hope to the reader that the Archilde

Plot summary of *The Surrounded*: manuscript version and published version

MONTANA (Flathead Reservation)
Archilde's return to his father's ranch
• Harvest
• Hunting trip with his mother; death of Louis and the game warden
• Father Grepilloux's death
• Archilde's arrest and release
• Reconciliation with and death of father

Manuscript version	Published version
PARIS	MONTANA
• Archilde practicing on his violin, interest in history, the city	• Recollections of missionaries' arrival by Archilde's mother
• "Friendship" with several young American musicians and Claudia Burness	• Return of his nephews from school
	• Dance and "covering the fault with the whip"
• Memories of Chemawa	• Relationship with Elise
• Confrontation with Mrs. Burness about her sons, who are among his new friends	• "Badlands" episode
	• Death of Archilde's mother
• Death of Archilde's mother	
• Departure for Montana	
MONTANA	
• Archilde's unsuccessful attempts to make his nephews into white farmers after their return from Chemawa	
• Trouble with the storekeeper Moser	
• Archilde's arrest for murder of the game warden	• Flight to the mountains to escape arrest for game warden's murder
• Kangaroo court and weeks in jail	• Arrest in mountains after Elise has killed the sheriff
• Trial with lengthy speeches of the prosecuting and defense attorneys	
• Archilde's acquittal and return to the ranch	
• Announcement of Claudia's arrival	

of the published version will be acquitted as the Archilde of the manuscript version was. The Big Paul story and the new priest show that, once "surrounded," there is no escape for either full-blood or half-blood.

The manuscript story makes for heavy reading. Archilde, whose point of view is the only one given, is inarticulate to the very end, and his attempts to explain his feelings and thoughts, especially in the Paris part, come to nothing. There is too much interior monologue. Occasionally, McNickle spends too much time on descriptions of place and the customs of Montana people. One instance is the kangaroo court that tries Archilde in jail. The descriptions of inmates and their sentencing are excellent but they serve no purpose, since Archilde refuses from the first to have anything to do with the other prisoners and prefers isolation. Interesting though these examples of western realism are, they hold up the development of the plot, especially since McNickle has not achieved the degree of mastery of English prose that is so prominent in the published novel.

The plot summary shows that McNickle treated a variety of issues in the manuscript version, especially in the Paris episode (e.g., ambition and formal education), later explored in the short stories "In the Alien Corn" and "Six Beautiful in Paris." This essay deals only with the central theme of the manuscript version: miscegenation and the destruction of the ideal of the Noble Savage to prove the need for assimilation.

The theme of miscegenation runs like a red thread through the manuscript version, since the protagonist Archilde himself is a half blood, born to a Flathead mother and a white father. Despite his wish to become part of white Montana society, Archilde finds it most difficult to talk to his white father due to Max's preconceptions about mixed bloods. At the very beginning of the novel's earlier version, Archilde acknowledges that physically he is part of both of his parents. There is nothing in his outward appearance, however, to remind Max (whose older sons have become criminals despite the same educational advantages offered to them) of his mixed-blood status. "Distinct from his brothers, he had few of the features of the Indian; most people who were accustomed to seeing breeds were genuinely surprised when they learned that he was a half-breed. . . . It almost seemed that he was his father's sole inheritor" (Manuscript 265). Initially, Max cannot see that difference, even though his youngest son's outward appearance sets him physically apart from his brothers; Max simply generalizes his experiences with his mixed-blood older sons and decides that all mixed bloods will return to their Indian heritage. Even though Indians are to be pitied for what the white man has done to them, they are lost beyond hope to alcohol, disease, and lethargy. The future of both communities, the Indian as well as the white, is a dark one.

> He could not think of that yardful of energetic youngsters without a shudder. In his mind's eyes he saw them as they would

be in ten or fifteen years. He saw the misery they would bring
to themselves and such of their relatives as had any sense. . . .
He was responsible for some part of the condition. In the
enthusiasm of conquest he had turned squaw-man and now he
could walk along the road and reflect on its consequences.
Never had he seen a white man who was happy with his Indian
wife and family. (Manuscript 57)

Despite his resentment toward his family, Max feels an individual
responsibility for what is happening in the Flathead Valley, but he
is sure that nothing can be done to reclaim these children of mixed-
blood marriages who are doomed to a criminal or at least unproductive life from birth. After Father Grepilloux's death, he
summarizes his feelings when talking to George Moser, the storekeeper:

> Wives were makeshift too. A white man married a squaw in the
> same way that he put dirt on the roof of his cabin in place of
> shingles. . . .
> A squaw was all right until she gave you a child. There he
> lay in front of you, ugly and black. What could you do? Give
> him the best Christian name you could think of and let it go
> at that. . . . For his squaw, he had no hard words. She worked,
> not hard and what she did was of little account, but she minded
> her own business and never asked for anything. . . .
> "I tell you we've been fools. Did we think we could build a
> paradise here? Did we think the Indians were lambs, free of sin
> and ready to be made into Christians? Look at them! They're
> all diseased, many are born blind and crippled. The rest are
> drinking themselves to death and gambling away every penny,
> every shred of property that they get their hands on." (Man-
> uscript 86–8)

Max stereotypes the roles of the white man and the Indian here.
The white man is seen as an idealist who believed in the natural
purity of the Indian; the Indian would have had the ability to acquire
civilization, that is, to become a Christian and farmer, if he had
chosen to do so. On their arrival in the Flathead Valley, Max, the
first-generation American of European descent, and Father Grepilloux originally shared the idealistic views of Indians that had been
developed by the French philosophers Baron de Lahontan and Jean
Jacques Rousseau. Of course, their idealized image of the Noble Savage and the sense of their own loss that the members of the Euro-

pean immigrant community experienced could not survive the
reality of the settlers' daily encounters with the American Indian.
Max's ideas about the agrarian paradise that the white settlers and
the Noble Savage share remain nebulous in the manuscript version,
just as his feeling of responsibility does not go beyond a generalized
pity. There is no basic doubt in the manuscript version that the
settlers could have created an agrarian paradise in the Flathead
Valley if there had been no mixing of blood.

McNickle comments much more critically on the agrarian paradise in the published version of *The Surrounded*. Max refers to Rousseau's Noble Savage very early in the novel: "It was not laziness, and
it was not romanticism. He never thought the Indians were 'noble'
or children of a lost paradise. While it was true that the old life was
much cleaner than the present existence, it was still hard for a white
man to stomach" (*The Surrounded* 42). And Father Grepilloux shows
Max in *The Surrounded* what the white pursuit of the agrarian paradise has done to the Flathead. "You have least to complain of. You
lose your sons, but these people have lost a way of life, and with it
their pride, their dignity, their strength" (*The Surrounded* 59). Here
there is a doubt regarding the validity of the French philosophers'
ideals that is entirely lacking in the manuscript version. There, Max
and Father Grepilloux, and later Archilde, pursue their dream of an
agrarian paradise without ever critically examining its premise. Their
failure to change the Noble Savages to contented farmers becomes,
in their minds, the Flatheads' inability to be taught. There is no
response from the full-blood or mixed-blood community; Archilde's
brother Pete, for instance, has all the right tools, but they decay in
the rich soil of the wheat fields because he does not know what to
do with them. The General Allotment Act (1887) gave Pete individual ownership of land and the Indian agent provided the tools, but
neither can force him to become, by white standards, a productive
member of the mainstream culture.

In the manuscript version the case is even more desperate, in
Max's eyes, than mere failure of government policy or of his idealistic preconceptions about Indians: Even the Christian names of his
sons cannot save the "ugly" and "black" babies of the mixed-blood
marriages. The good cannot overcome the evil, and his sons must
be regarded as servants of the Devil. Max's final statement that he
will never return to the Mission after Father Grepilloux's death indicates that the forces of evil, the children of these two worlds, have
destroyed all possibilities of a Christian paradise in the valley as well.
God, in Max's view, is the God of the Old Testament who has marked

these children of the Devil with disease and deformity. Nothing honorable can be attributed to them, not even gratitude to their greatest benefactor, Father Grepilloux. "In the back of his brain he [Max] still heard the Indians wailing in that dismal tone and he wondered if, after all, they did have human feelings and if their weeping was genuine" (Manuscript 89). In their possible ingratitude to Father Grepilloux, Max finds his justification for rejection of his sons.

In contrast to Max, Father Grepilloux attempts – in the manuscript version – to discredit the long perpetuated stereotype that Indians are children of the Devil. Max thinks, however, that even saintly Father Grepilloux has lost faith in the idealistic beliefs of the beginning, since he did not commit the "mistake" of leaving his order to marry a Native woman. "Possibly Grepilloux had even thought of putting aside the robe and living what he thought was more powerful than the word. His wisdom was that he kept to the robe" (Manuscript 87). The dream that the mixed-blood children would inherit the best qualities of their parents has given way to reality; these children combine the worst qualities of both, and civilization has embarked on a course of self-destruction. Max summarily dismisses all dreams. "I came from Spain when I was a small boy and I don't remember the town in which I was born. If I hadn't married a squaw no doubt I should have been happy" (Manuscript 30).

McNickle's early view of the Indians' place in Christianity is neither new nor original but is based on such colonial writings as William Bradford's *Of Plymouth Plantation*. The underlying belief was that Christianity would naturally lead to assimilation. The same idea is expressed in *The Surrounded;* however, McNickle chooses to contrast the old missionary with the new priest, Father Jerome, in the published novel. Father Grepilloux realizes that even the Christian faith does not make the Flatheads into partners of the white farmers. He withdraws from reality and writes the mission's history in isolation, thereby living in a past where dreams of a Christian community seemed based on fact. Father Jerome is the opposite of Father Grepilloux. He represents a church that is no longer interested in the spiritual welfare of the Indian community. "Father Jerome was not really prejudiced; it could hardly be said that he looked down upon the Indians. . . . He was dull; he neither scolded nor exhorted; he dogmatized" (*The Surrounded* 263). In the published version of the novel, this demand for blind adherence to the Catholic faith closes the door to all change; the church will not be able to help the Indian community adjust to its new life, and the Indians can no longer find

help in the mission, as they did in Father Grepilloux's time. Mc-
Nickle uses the new rigidity of the church in *The Surrounded* to close
the circle; the Flatheads are surrounded by whites who have set physical and spiritual boundaries.

Father Grepilloux is one of the forceful characters who appear in
both the manuscript and published versions of the novel, and despite the numerous revisions of the novel his character remains the
same. However, his role in the two versions differs. Being the only
representative of the church in the manuscript version, Father Grepilloux serves to emphasize the hopelessness of the struggle to civi-
lize the Flatheads. The juxtaposition of the old priest and the young
priest in *The Surrounded* permits Father Grepilloux to assume some
of the burden for the failure of the church to make assimilation
work to make the Flatheads full members of white Montana society.
It is one of the major achievements of the manuscript revisions, then,
that McNickle manages to reverse the well-worn stereotypes of Christianity and civilization in *The Surrounded* without damaging the integrity of Father Grepilloux.

Other white characters in the manuscript version share Max's negative view of Indians and mixed bloods. One of them is George
Moser, the white storekeeper, who is only interested in financial
gain. His exploitation extends to Flatheads and whites alike. Mc-
Nickle's negative characterization throughout the manuscript version is explained by Moser's outsider position in Montana society;
he is a Yankee. He remains a negative force to the end: He corrupts
Archilde's nephews, provides drink for Archilde's brothers, accuses
Archilde of murder, and gives a damning character reference for
Archilde during the trial. His desire for revenge, caused by Archilde's refusal to be taken advantage of, moves the plot of the manuscript version sluggishly along. His outsider position defeats him in
the end, since the defense attorney uses his Yankee origin and its
negative connotations to turn the court against him. Since he is not
needed as a foil to Archilde's character in *The Surrounded,* Moser
basically disappears from the published version after the chapter relating Max's death. In the manuscript, his negative perception of
Archilde is taken up by the prosecuting attorney. Representing law
and government, the prosecuting attorney rejects the Indians' right
to self-determination and advocates forced assimilation. He is trying
not only Archilde but the entire Indian and half-blood community
in his indictment.

> We have labored under the theory that we are under debt to
> the Indians and we have permitted them privileges which we

deny to ourselves. I think it is high time we questioned the wisdom of such a course of action. If the Indian is to form a part of our state he must learn the duties and qualities of a citizen. How is he to get this knowledge? By granting him special privileges and dealing leniently with him when he defies our laws? Is that the way we treat our own children when they disobey our wishes and wander from the straight path? . . . We come from a race of sturdy Pilgrim fathers who knew the virtues of discipline. They built for us a great nation on that very principle. Let us not give over their work into the hands of a race undisciplined in either spirit or mind. Let us be stern in our justice – but rightous, always. (Manuscript 315–16)

In the early manuscript version even Claudia, the young American girl Archilde had met in Paris, subscribes to stereotypes. Having met Archilde in France, the country of Lahontan and Rousseau, she regards Archilde in the light of their doctrine of the Noble Savage, despite the fact that she has come to know him first on a more personal basis through their day-to-day encounters. "Is it true that you are – Indian? . . . Do you know, I think that's too marvelous for words! It gives me the queerest thrill. Now I understand many things that puzzled me before – your reticence, directness, honesty, your genuine wonder – all that is so unusual and – admirable" (Manuscript 199–200). The reality of her mother's illness forces her, however, to rethink her own past and future; in the end, she sees Archilde as an individual rather than the representative of a noble but disappearing race and joins him in Montana.

Two or three instances at the end of the manuscript version give a glimpse of the character Archilde was to become in *The Surrounded*. A chance encounter with Blind Michael after he is acquitted of murdering the game warden provides a more sympathetic picture of the disappearing full bloods. Archilde's earlier evaluation of the full bloods he encounters in the Indian agent's office after his first arrest is thoroughly negative. "He felt as if he were being vivisected, analysed and judged by the lowest stratum of society in the world" (Manuscript 90). During his time in jail, where he must confront "feelings of inexcusable guilt and shame," Archilde also feels kinship to his Salish mother for the first time:

He stood arm in arm with his mother those days, breathing the unhealthy mist of a hundred generations before his day. Inhabitants of a bleak world into which the sunlight had not yet penetrated, these were his people. They gazed into the sky and scanned the earth, picking their food from under the rocks and in the meadows. They feared the passing shadow of a bird overhead, they stood in awe before a blasted tree, they worshipped the wind that howled at night. They murdered their enemies, who were no more than their brothers, casually. They wrought hideous distortions on their own bodies in deference to savage pride. On all these faces, not a laugh or smile. They walked grim faced through life and passed out amidst a burst of wailing. When opposition and adversity overtook them and threatened death and starvation on the snowy flats of winter, they sat in a huddle before a [sick] fire and with blank eyes, awaiting the hand to fall. . . . Dull, naked, savage, the breath of their nostrils was fatalism – these were the hundred generations who stood behind Archilde. (Manuscript 301–2)

Archilde admires his ancestors' fortitude, their ability to sustain themselves in a basically hostile environment with which they nevertheless lived in harmony. Archilde's viewpoint is that of an educated white man, though; he understands his ancestors intellectually, but as his choice of words already indicates, does not share their "primitive" laws. His guilt feelings and his commitment to the white community do not permit him to go beyond a basic understanding, do not allow him to abandon the stereotypes and ethnocentrisms learned from them. Significantly, it is a letter from Claudia that shakes him out of his state of suspension and renews his faith in the white man's world and his membership in it.

Archilde's mother is one of the handful of full bloods to appear in the manuscript version. Whereas Catherine is a vital force in *The Surrounded,* she remains flat and undeveloped in the manuscript version. For Archilde his mother, who remains nameless throughout the manuscript version, is merely a symbol for that negative side in himself that he intends to eradicate. Also, in contrast to *The Surrounded,* Archilde's mother is not seen in a tribal context and seems to be a self-contained individual, like her husband, Max. Archilde's rather indifferent memories of happy childhood days in her company turn to hatred when she kills the game warden.

And at this moment he felt utterly detached from his mother. He felt no love, no hatred, no friendliness, nothing in particular at the thought of her. . . . But he couldn't even feel affection on principle. She was totally foreign and unappealing. . . . I wasn't ashamed of my blood to begin with because I never even thought about it. . . . It is only now that I have grown ashamed of it, now I have seen things, as it were, for the first time. (Manuscript 118–19)

There is no recognition on Archilde's part that she is motivated by a mother's grief. Louis was her son, and she instinctively reacts to his death by killing his murderer. However, neither Archilde nor the prosecuting attorney recognizes the balance of death; the murder of the white man is regarded as the only true murder, and the game warden and his family are represented as the victims of an irrational violence. Indeed, Louis is barely mentioned in both the prosecuting and defense attorney's speeches. Leaving Montana, Archilde simply puts his mother out of his mind; her death while he is in Paris causes him no grief but relieves him of his self-imposed exile. There is no reconciliation with his mother beyond that momentary feeling of kinship in jail. The treatment of the deaths could have been a powerful statement on miscegenation and racism if Archilde did not so clearly share the views of the attorneys, who, in turn, represent the community he struggles to join. The death of an Indian is simply of no account.

At the end of the manuscript version, Archilde is more than a supplicant for membership in the white community. Despite his increased sympathy for the Indians and mixed bloods, Archilde is prepared to accept Max's preconceptions about mixed bloods with only slight modifications. In contrast to his father, Archilde does not believe that every mixed blood is predestined to lead an unproductive life from birth, but he believes that assimilation is a must. The effort rests with the individual mixed blood, though. After his reconciliation with his nephews after the trial, Archilde expects them to make the effort to leave the negative Indian part of their characters behind, just as he did: "One thing he knew, he'd waste no more words on them here after. They could make their own choices and his shoe would be ready to boot them through the door the first time they strayed too far. He was standing now in the footprints his father had left twenty-five years ago. Already he had said in his mind: 'If they will not live on my terms – then they will get out and stay out!'" (Manuscript 337)

Throughout the manuscript version Archilde has striven for a voice, and he finally attains the voice of his father. At the end of the trial his unconditional acceptance by white Montana society is formalized by the judge: "Nor could he [Archilde] forget that the judge had shook his hand after the trial and commended his [stolid] qualities that would, no doubt, make him a splendid citizen. 'I commend you!' were the judge's words and as Archilde passed through the corridors packed with people, everyone paused to let him pass and smiles and pleasant words met him on every hand" (Manuscript 335–6). His taking of his father's place in white Montana society makes it possible for Archilde to await Claudia's arrival with confidence. They are equals. The Archilde of the manuscript version is not "surrounded," that is, "set upon and destroyed" (*The Surrounded*, epigraph).

The novel that grew out of the manuscript version was unusual for its time. Other American Indian novelists, for instance John Joseph Mathews, whose novel *Sundown* preceded D'Arcy McNickle's *The Surrounded* by two years, and Mourning Dove, who published *Co-ge-we-a, the Half-Blood* in 1927, were still advocating assimilation in their work, as McNickle had also done in his earlier manuscript version. White writers dealing with Indian themes, on the other hand, were focusing "their interest on the most picturesque, least complex situations of the 'blanket Indian' in the Southwest, or turning their faces towards the past," as Oliver La Farge pointed out in his review of McNickle's novel ("Half-Breed Hero"). That is what La Farge himself had done in his Pulitzer Prize-winning novel *Laughing Boy*. *The Surrounded*, however, fit into neither of the accepted two categories, the assimilated Indian of the present or the idealized Indian of the past.

Reviews of D'Arcy McNickle's *The Surrounded* were complimentary; La Farge, for instance, says of McNickle that he "adds 'The Surrounded' to the small list of creditable modern novels using the first American as theme" ("Half-Breed Hero"). A number of reviews stress the novel's epic quality, as for example Mary Heaton Vorse's: "But the book is graver and deeper than the story of Archilde. It is also the account of the destruction of the Indian people" ("End of the Trail"). Despite the positive reception by critics, however, *The Surrounded* was not a financial success, since neither the American Indian theme nor its realistic treatment catered to the taste of white American readers during the Great Depression. Public taste ran to sentimental fiction or realistic fiction set in cities and towns located primarily in the industrial areas of the United States. A novel of the West, as Long explained in *American Literature*, was read not as "a novel of character but a yarn of adventure" (482). Throughout both editions of his literary history (1913; rev. ed. 1923), Long maintains that America lacks "ancient folklore, . . . settled traditions, . . . native population" for "the great American novel" (476–7). The rich oral traditions of the various Indian tribes are ignored, and the American continent is considered to have been a vast, spiritually empty place at the time of the European settlers' advent.

Long is one of the literary critics and historians who attempt objectively to evaluate the negative image of American Indians in American fiction in the first decades of the twentieth century. He blames the "fighting stories" of colonial literature for "hatred of the Indians . . . deeply ingrained into the popular mind. Even at the present day it is difficult to make the average American understand that the Indians were often actuated by noble motives and possessed some admirable native virtues" (42). Pattee, a literary critic whose primary concern was not objectivity, mentions the American Indian theme only as an afterthought in his list of future American themes and claims that only the destruction of the tribes can lead to a mythologizing of their past. And of Whittier's poetry he says: "Whittier began his literary career under the impression that there was a rich mine of poetry and romance in the history and traditions of the Indians – a delusion that was widespread during the early years of the century" (335). This was not a receptive climate in which to publish *The Surrounded,* and McNickle, whose journals show that he was an avid reader, was aware of this fact.

McNickle spent at least nine years writing and revising *The Surrounded* as well as writing some short fiction. Despite his problems with various publishers, he was certain of his craftsmanship, as is evident in his application letter to the Bureau of Indian Affairs, and he was not prepared to compromise this artistic integrity to indulge the literary taste of his time.

> I have chosen the medium of fiction, first of all because I understand the storytelling art, and in the second place I know by rationalization that fiction reaches a wider audience than any other form of writing; and, if it is good fiction it should tell a man as much about himself as a text combining something of philosophy and psychology, a little physiology, and some history, and should send him off with the will to make use of his best quality, which is his understanding. (Letter to John Collier)

Fiction, as McNickle understood it, combined most other fields within it and exerted more power than other disciplines. Surprisingly, he did not publish any more fiction, apart from a juvenile novel that does not deal with contemporary problems, until forty years later. It must be said, though, that his second novel, *Wind from an Enemy Sky,* published posthumously in 1978, shows fine literary craftsmanship, but it lacks the "descriptive power of *The Surrounded*" (Ruoff) and the personal involvement of the author. The later novel had a point to make, and its fictional tribe becomes the symbol of all other tribes. McNickle also published several books of nonfiction and numerous articles on subjects related to Indian policy in those forty years. It is possible that McNickle considered *The Surrounded* his literary masterpiece and had condensed the personal and artistic development of a lifetime into those nine years of continuous revision of *The Surrounded*. That would also explain how McNickle, no longer interested in popular taste despite increasing economic pressures, came to write a novel that anticipated the novels of the American Indian Renaissance thirty years later.

Works Cited

La Farge, Oliver. "Half-Breed Hero." Rev. of *The Surrounded* by D'Arcy McNickle. *The Saturday Review*, March 14, 1936: 10.

Long, William J. *American Literature.* 1913. Rev. ed. Boston: Ginn and Co., 1923.

McNickle, D'Arcy. Letter to John Collier. Exhibit C, May 25, 1934 (?). Chicago: D'Arcy McNickle Collection, Newberry Library.

 The Surrounded. 1936. Rpt. Albuquerque: University of New Mexico Press, 1978.

 Manuscript of *The Surrounded.* Chicago: D'Arcy McNickle Collection, the Newberry Library.

 Journal. 1932. Chicago: D'Arcy McNickle Collection, Newberry Library.

McNickle, Philomene Parenteau. Letter to Commissioner of Indian Affairs, October 27, 1914. Chicago: D'Arcy McNickle Collection, Newberry Library.

Merriam, H. G. Letter to Oxford University. 1925. Chicago: D'Arcy McNickle Collection, Newberry Library.

Parker, Dorothy R. *Singing an Indian Song: A Biography of D'Arcy McNickle.* Lincoln: University of Nebraska Press, 1992.

Pattee, Fred Lewis. *A History of American Literature.* New York: Silver, Burdett, 1897.

Purdy, John Lloyd. *Word Ways: The Novels of D'Arcy McNickle.* Tucson: University of Arizona Press, 1990.

Ruoff, A. LaVonne. Rev. of *Wind from an Enemy Sky* by D'Arcy McNickle. *American Indian Quarterly* 5.2 (1979): 167–9.

Vorse, Mary Heaton. "End of the Trail." Rev. of *The Surrounded* by D'Arcy McNickle. *The New Republic,* April 15, 1936: 295–6.